Prophets and Protons

THE NEW AND ALTERNATIVE RELIGIONS SERIES

GENERAL EDITORS: Timothy Miller and Susan J. Palmer

Hare Krishna Transformed
Burke Rochford, Jr.

*Transcendent in America: Hindu-Inspired
Meditation Movements as New Religion*
Lola Williamson

*Prophets and Protons: New Religious Movements
and Science in Late Twentieth-Century America*
Benjamin E. Zeller

Prophets and Protons

*New Religious Movements and Science
in Late Twentieth-Century America*

Benjamin E. Zeller

NEW YORK UNIVERSITY PRESS

New York and London

NEW YORK UNIVERSITY PRESS
New York and London
www.nyupress.org

Library of Congress Cataloging-in-Publication Data
Zeller, Benjamin E.
Prophets and protons : new religious movements and science
in late twentieth-century America / Benjamin E. Zeller.
p. cm. — (The new and alternative religions series)
Includes bibliographical references and index.
ISBN–13: 978–0–8147–9720–4 (cl : alk. paper)
ISBN–10: 0–8147–9720–2 (cl : alk. paper)
ISBN–13: 978–0–8147–9721–1 (pbk. : alk. paper)
ISBN–10: 0–8147–9721–0 (pbk. : alk. paper)
1. United States—Religion—20th century.   2. United States—
Religion—21st century.   3. Religion and science—United States—
20th century.   4. Religion and science—United States—21st
century.   I. Title.
BL2525.Z46   2010
201'.65097309045—dc22   2009038449

New York University Press books are printed on acid-free paper,
and their binding materials are chosen for strength and durability.
We strive to use environmentally responsible suppliers and materials
to the greatest extent possible in publishing our books.

Manufactured in the United States of America

C 10 9 8 7 6 5 4 3 2 1

P 10 9 8 7 6 5 4 3 2 1

To my parents, who have always represented
the best of science and religion

Over the entrance to the gates of the temple of science are written the words: Ye must have faith.
—Max Planck, Where Is Science Going?

Contents

Acknowledgments

This book did not begin with an epiphany but grew from years of reading primary sources produced by new religious movements. I recognized slowly that my marginalia proliferated whenever sources involved science and so began an exploration of how the leaders and members of new religions wrote and spoke about science. My past experience with science—I studied computer science as an undergraduate—no doubt contributed to my interest in the subject. Yet it was in conversations with friends, mentors, and colleagues that the germ of this book really took form, and to them that I owe a debt of gratitude. Yaakov Ariel read the entire manuscript and offered helpful criticisms and suggestions, and my work is much stronger because of his help. Thomas A. Tweed, Grant Wacker, Laurie Maffly-Kipp, and Seymour Mauskopf have each read the entire manuscript and offered valuable critiques, as has Ronald L. Numbers. Emily Mace has also carefully read and evaluated the text, and has helped me to better articulate my thesis. Jennifer Hammer of NYU Press, New and Alternative Religions Series editors Timothy Miller and Susan J. Palmer, and the manuscript referees all offered valuable critiques as I continued to craft the book. I would have liked the chance to share this book with the late William Hutchison, under whom I first explored the historiography of religion and science, and even a decade later I recall his suggestion that my interests in new religions and in science need not remain separate.

My friends and colleagues at the University of North Carolina, Duke University, Temple University, Princeton University, and Brevard College have been wonderful friends and conversation partners, especially Brantley Gasaway, Reid Neilson, and Jeffrey Wilson. Others have also traveled alongside me as I researched and wrote, though I cannot name them all. Conversations with several of my colleagues at Temple University assisted me in articulating my project, namely Rebecca Alpert, Lucy Bregman, Marie Dallam, Aron Dunlap, Laura Levitt, Randall Prebish, and Terry Rey. At Princeton University, Eduard Iricinschi has answered my questions on early Christian theology, and Laura Bennett made me feel welcome as a fellow American religious historian. Emily Mace has helped more than anyone else: in addition to reading drafts, she has given me perspective and encouragement. I couldn't have written this book without her. I am grateful to these many people who have read drafts, offered critiques, and commented on the book throughout its development; I did not always take their advice, and whatever errors and omissions remain are my own.

Librarians of every stripe have made this book possible. Archivists at the special collections departments of the Graduate Theological Union and the University of California, Santa Barbara, provided invaluable aid during my visits to those institutions. Michael Mickler of the Unification Theological Seminary kindly opened the seminary's archives to me as well as shared his own experiences. Reference, microfiche, and interlibrary loan librarians at least a half dozen universities also provided aid, especially those of the University of North Carolina, Temple University, Princeton University, and Brevard College. I especially thank Fred Rowland of Temple University and Brenda Spillman of Brevard College, librarians at my two academic homes as I wrote this book.

Chapters 5 and 6 include some material drawn from my previously published article, "Scaling Heaven's Gate: Individualism and Salvation in a New Religious Movement," *Nova Religio: The Journal of Alternative and Emergent Religions*, vol. 10, no. 2, November 2006. (© The University of California Press) I am grateful to the University of California Press for permission to republish that material here.

Introduction

The year 1972 was a good one for the American scientific community. That year several groups of biologists across the nation created the first recombinant DNA molecules, artificial genetic chains that opened the door for research into human genetics and new medical treatments. In Batavia, Illinois, physicists activated the main accelerator ring of the Fermi National Accelerator Laboratory, inaugurating what would become one of the world's most productive subatomic particle research centers. At Bell Laboratories in New Jersey, computer scientists invented a new programming language called "C" that allowed them to write more complex programs, reshaping the field of computer science and computer technology more broadly. Such scientific progress contrasted with the harsh realities of politics and international affairs: the Watergate break-ins, the Munich massacre of eleven Israeli athletes, and the Bloody Sunday riots in Northern Ireland all occurred that year as well.[1]

The year 1972 also witnessed developments among new religions in America. The International Society for Krishna Consciousness, better known as the Hare Krishna movement, released under its publishing wing a new American edition of its founder's seminal text on religion and science. This short book, *Easy Journeys to Other Planets*, outlined their leader's vision of how a science rooted in Indian religiosity could supplant or replace Western materialistic science, not to mention religion. That spring, two spiritual seekers named Marshall Herff Applewhite and Bonnie Lu Nettles met in a Houston hospital, bonded over their shared interest in astrology, and founded the movement eventually named Heaven's Gate. The two would seek to incorporate or absorb science and scientific thinking into the religion that they founded. In the autumn, the Holy Spirit Association for the Unification of World Christianity, more widely called the Unification Church, sponsored the first of what would become a series of symposia called the International Conferences on the Unity of the Sciences (ICUS). The conferences brought together scientists, ethicists, philosophers, and scholars of religion, and demonstrated how the Unification Church and its leaders hoped that religion could shepherd or guide scientific research and development.

This book considers how three new religious movements—the Hare Krishnas, Unification Church, and Heaven's Gate—treated the idea of science and the relation of science to religion and wider American society during the latter half of the twentieth century. Though these religions were small, their study reveals an important fact about religions in America during the late twentieth century. Science had become so big, powerful, and important that all religions had to respond to it. New religions reacted to science with a clarity and alacrity that more established religions could not. During the period considered in this book, each of these new religions possessed a living founder who shaped the movement's theology and philosophy, responding to science directly. Understanding these religions' treatments of science sheds light on the power and prestige that science had come to take hold in American society during the latter half of the twentieth century. The manner in which these new religious movements reacted to the scientific endeavor and to individual crises and debates within the scientific world acted as bellwethers for how older, more established religions would come to contend with—and sometimes be shaken by—such issues. As the sociologist of religion William Sims Bainbridge has written of new religious movements, "[b]y being small and fast-changing, and possessing distinctive characteristics, they give scientists clear vision into the processes that create and sustain new culture."[2] This book considers such new cultures, and what they reveal about the older religious cultures of America. The manner in which new religions responded to science generally reflected broader religious responses to science, though taken to greater extremes. I have found that the ideological and theological positions of new religions are not so different from old religions after all. In addition, they offer a useful typology of how religious movements—old or new—respond to science.

Each of the three religions offered a distinct position on the nature of science and how religion and science ought to interact. Yet all of the three new religions understood their views of science as crucial to their wider theological views and social stances. For each of these new religious movements, the nature and meaning of science served a central role in the group's self-understanding and conceptualization. Because the roles and boundaries of science so concerned each of the groups, their founders, leaders, and ordinary members offered both implicit and explicit re-envisionings of science. These views developed out of each group's historical circumstances and theological positions, but also evolved in concert with concurrent social develop-

ments and cultural influences. Such varying factors resulted in three different perspectives on science. The Unification Church aimed to *guide* science
and the American scientific establishment. It positioned science as a sphere
separate from religion, yet at the same time attempted to direct science's ethical boundaries, methods, and even research goals. The Hare Krishnas sought
to *replace* Western science with an alternative scientific-religious system
rooted in their own Hindu religious tradition. The science of ancient Indian
religious texts, they insisted, offered a more accurate and socially healthy
paradigm than that of the contemporary American scientific establishment.
Heaven's Gate attempted to *absorb* or incorporate science and scientific elements into their religious system. It looked to methodological materialism
and naturalism as the ideal epistemology, and declared itself the truest form
of both science and religion.

The Construction and Meaning of Science

Thomas Kuhn, in *The Structure of Scientific Revolutions*, reminds scholars
that scientific paradigms develop historically and change periodically as new
scientific models replace earlier ones. Such shifts entail that the science of
one era, community, or region might look very different than alternative
scientific paradigms.[3] Other scholars, such as Michel Foucault and Bruno
Latour, extend the Kuhnian conceptualization of paradigm shifts within science by arguing that human social groups construct the meaning of science
itself. In *Birth of the Clinic*, for example, Foucault argues that the modern
understanding of medical science grew out of a specific European social
location and defeated alternative conceptualizations of disease, healing, and
the body.[4] Latour's *Laboratory Life: The Social Construction of Scientific Facts*,
coauthored with Steve Woolgar, indicates that production of knowledge
in the physical sciences depend as much on social networks as it does on
empiricism or the scientific method.[5] Though some scholars have criticized
the particular arguments of Kuhn, Foucault, and Latour, most accept that the
meaning of science is not static.[6]

The meaning of science also varied among the new religious movements
considered here. Even within single movements or even single individuals
within a movement, science meant something different in different contexts.
For members of the Hare Krishna movement, for example, science sometimes represented an empiricist epistemology with which they differed, a
modern technological worldview that they rejected, or the collective corpus
of legitimate knowledge that they claimed to possess. This book untangles

these multiple meanings of science and how they related to religion, showing how three religious groups constructed alternative definitions of science and illuminating, as appropriate, parallels to wider religious engagements with science, both inside and outside new religions.

One must be wary of any attempt to codify any single definition of science, since individuals and groups use the word in so many different ways. Yet because I argue that members of leaders of new religions responded to science, I want to explain how I understand the term. When I use the word "science" in this book, I use it to signify both an epistemology and a worldview dependent on that epistemology. I make no claims as to the universality of this approach to the concept of science, and indeed philosophers of science continue to debate the definition and limits of science. Yet this understanding provides traction for the study of how religious groups responded to, and engaged with, science. It also reflects a wider cultural view of science. In the way that the American pubic commonly employs the term, "science" represents several distinct phenomena. It is both a way of knowing (an epistemology) as well as a manner of understanding predicated on that epistemology (a worldview). Science—meaning scientific research—might prove one chemical dangerous and another benign, for example, but one also relies on science—meaning something much broader—to cure the sick, fix (or destroy!) the ozone layer, or improve crop production.

Historically, Western science has depended on empiricism and the naturalistic assumption that observable origins cause observable effects. The professional practitioners of American science, those calling themselves scientists, depend on such a definition to police the boundaries of their field. In 1986/87 the United States Supreme Court considered a case that raised the issue of whether Creationism counted as science. A group of seventy-two Nobel laureate scientists and twenty-four scientific organizations filed an amicus curiae brief that offered an explicit formulation of science as an empirical and naturalistic epistemology. They declared that "[s]cience is devoted to formulating and testing naturalistic explanations for natural phenomena. It is a process for systematically collecting and recording data about the physical world, then categorizing and studying the collected data in an effort to infer the principles of nature that best explain the observed phenomena."[7] Here, science operates as a process of gathering information through observation and producing new knowledge based on those observations. It is both empirical and naturalistic, meaning it considers only the observable world. Importantly, the brief's authors composed the statement in order to distinguish what they considered real science from the nonscientific alternative of Creationism, something they considered neither empirical nor naturalistic. Though its authors intended it as a polemic, the amicus curiae brief correctly notes that science operates as an epistemology. However, not everyone agrees on the boundaries or nature of that epistemology. Just as Creationists did, the religious groups considered here each challenged scientists' assumptions about what such an epistemology should entail.

Yet the scientists' brief indicates a second view of science as well, one that reflects the way in which many Americans employ the term. In the abstract of their statement, the amicus curiae scientists employed the term "science" to represent something far broader than merely an epistemology. They used the word to mean a system of thought and way of understanding the world, what one might call a worldview. They wrote that "[t]eaching religious ideas mislabeled as science is detrimental to scientific education: It sets up a false conflict between science and religion, misleads our youth about the nature of scientific inquiry, and thereby compromises our ability to respond to the problems of an increasingly technological world."[8] That there might exist a conflict between science and religion hints at the possibility that the former may also function as an entity more akin to religion than to alternative epistemologies such as Kantian rationalism or social constructivism. The scientists implied in their brief that science entails a manner of not only knowing the world, but understanding that knowledge and relating to it. That is, science is more than an epistemology. It is also a worldview. The new religious movements considered here also understood science in that way, in addition to its epistemological nature. As I use the term "science" in this book, I mean both science as an epistemology as well as science as the worldview that grows out of such an epistemology.

Yet the new religions of late twentieth-century America understood science in another manner as well, one in keeping with a wide cultural view. In the United States of the 1950s through 1990s, "science" also stood for an industrial-technological-scientific establishment, what some scholars have called American "big science."[9] Big science was (and is) the massive government- and corporate-sponsored scientific apparatus that led to the growth of the prestige, power, and place of science and technology in American culture during the late twentieth century. Many people merely called it "American science." Big science galvanized economic growth, increased standards of living, and maintained a defense against the Cold War enemy of the Soviet Union. It brought televisions, antibiotics, microwave ovens, and plastic to American households. It also enabled Agent Orange, Three Mile Island, and Love Canal. Throughout the latter half of the twentieth century, Americans both inside and outside new religions attempted to come to grips with the potential of big science to improve as well as destroy life.

Americans responded to big science in multiple ways. Paul Boyer has documented the immediate boost of interest in science and respect for scientists after the war, tendencies that coexisted with anxieties about the nuclear bomb and the possibilities of atomic annihilation.[10] The atomic physicist Heinz Haber gave voice to the perspective emphasizing the almost utopian possibilities of science in his 1956 book, *Our Friend the Atom*. Haber regaled the reader with promises of endless cheap atomic energy, supersonic atomic-powered planes, and stout nuclear-powered naval ships to defend American borders. In the broadest sense, science offered universal beneficence, he insisted. "The magic power of atomic energy will soon begin to work for mankind throughout the world. It will grant the gifts of modern technology to even the remotest of areas. It will give more food, better health—the many benefits of science—to everyone."[11] Haber represented a wider assumption that science and technology held solutions to the nation's problems, an approach so popular that his book received corporate sponsorship. The Walt Disney corporation subsidized its publication as well as produced a filmstrip and amusement park exhibit of the same name. Even when the allure with nuclear science faded, Americans' dependence on technology and continuing scientific development increased. The Cold War itself led to a reliance on science and technology and encouraged increased spending on defense research, much of which occurred in the new centers of government-sponsored science.[12] Yet not everyone shared Heinz Haber and Walt Disney's enthusiasm.

Some commentators in America offered a less affirmative view of the growth of American science. The 1960s witnessed an increase in the criticism of the growing place and power of science in the United States, alongside criticisms of America's other establishments, such as educational institutions, corporations, the nuclear family, and the churches.[13] Such opponents of mainstream culture, eventually called the counterculture, linked the critique of modern science and technology to a variety of concerns. One popular criticism of science during this period complained that science failed to live up to the expectations of its postwar proponents, that rather than usher in a brave new world of utopian life, science had fostered a Huxleyan *Brave New World* of dystopic social control and devaluation of human individuality. Others made the opposite accusation, that science had devastated community and the social fabric of life. Those with more Marxist leanings charged science and technology with contributing to an unjust capitalist culture, while still others focused on environmental damage or risks to human health. Popular culture often combined these sentiments. Kurt Vonnegut's *Cat's Cradle* (1963) described worldwide environmental devastation and the destruction of the human race at the hands of an irresponsible scientific community, as well as that community's tendency to enable dictatorial social control.[14] Ernst Schumacher's *Small is Beautiful*, published a decade later in 1973, accused science of "mutilating" humanity's self-worth and fostering a harmful economic system.[15] Among the countercultural readers of Vonnegut and Schumacher, the new religious movements played an important role, serving as theological nuclei that presented new options to the religious mainstream. Each offered alternative religious visions of the ideal individual and society, and several of them—the Unification Church, the Hare Krishnas, and Heaven's Gate—offered alternative imaginings of science as central components of those visions.

Creative Tension

The Unification Church, the Hare Krishnas, and Heaven's Gate adopted three different perspectives on the meaning, nature, and role of science, and its relation to religion. The first of these movements to arrive in the United States, known formally as the Holy Spirit Association for the Unification of World Christianity, looked to science as an analog of religion. Though they sometimes disagreed on details, generally its members viewed science as a separate sphere that considered the material nature of the cosmos, just as religion explained the spiritual levels. In their proselytizing and training of seminarians, Unificationists stressed the compatibility of their own religious perspective with that of Western science. Eventually the Unification Church assumed a generally supportive perspective toward the American scientific establishment, as demonstrated through the International Conferences on the Unity of the Sciences that they sponsored. As a whole, Unificationism looked to *guide* science, to set boundaries and goals for its research, and to help scientists focus on improving both human knowledge and human living conditions. They took a particularly positive position—albeit sometimes paternalistic—toward America's science establishments. The Unificationist position evolved from its founder's hopes to merge what he considered Oriental religiosity and Occidental science, a position that emerged from the colonial Korean experience.

The International Society for Krishna Consciousness (ISKCON, or Hare Krishnas) took a much dimmer view of the science of the Western world. Whereas Unification's founder Sun Myung Moon had accepted the Western science introduced to Korea through Japanese colonialism, ISKCON's originator Swami A. C. Bhaktivedanta rejected the bulk of the Western modern worldview that he encountered during his life in British-colonized India. The majority of the intellectual leaders of the Hare Krishna movement considered Western science, like Western society more broadly, a bankrupt system. They singled out government- and corporate-sponsored science as particularly unlikely to either alleviate human suffering or increase quality of life. Yet the adherents of the group did not reject the concept of science. Instead, they looked to the Hindu tradition for a replacement to that of the West. ISKCON offered a scientific approach to understanding God, they declared, but members of the group rooted this science in ancient Indian texts rather than the norms and establishments of American science. The Hare Krishnas sought to *replace* the form of science most prevalent in the United States with an alternative scientific approach. This position developed not only from Bhaktivedanta's experience in India but from the countercultural perspective of the Hare Krishna converts and leaders.

Heaven's Gate, the final of these three new religions to emerge, took yet another approach to science. Led by two Americans who rejected their Protestant heritage as well as many of America's social mores, this movement nevertheless looked to science as a legitimate form of knowledge. Ambivalent about scientists and the institutions of science, they nonetheless borrowed from science its methodological underpinning—materialistic naturalism—and applied that approach to religion. In their engagement with the outside world, Heaven's Gate's founders and members used naturalistic explanations of religious terms and the scientific language of biology and chemistry in order to present themselves as a scientific religion. At the heart of their message they offered an explicitly naturalistic explanation of what most would regard as a religious concept: heavenly salvation. Heaven's Gate attempted to *absorb* from science its foundation of naturalism and build upon it a religious edifice. This movement fundamentally embraced American technology and science, transforming it into a religious ideology.

These three approaches—guiding, replacing, or absorbing—offer a typology of how religious movements, both new and old, responded to the tremendous growth of the presence, power, and prestige of science in late twentieth-century America. These perspectives represent three ways of answering the same questions: What is science, How does science relate to religion, and What can religions do in response to science? Americans far removed from new religions asked similar questions and came to similar conclusions. As Robert Booth Fowler has documented, during the 1970s and 1980s American Protestants increasingly turned their attention to environmental issues. Protestants as diverse as mainline liberals, evangelicals, fundamentalists, and ecofeminists each sought to guide environmental science and policy. Their approaches varied, but like Unificationists, these American Protestants hoped to set limits and goals for the American scientific establishment.[16] Though it would not achieve prominence until the twenty-first century, an alliance of conservative Protestants, Catholics, and Jews calling itself the Intelligent Design (ID) movement meanwhile worked toward replacing the Darwinian scientific paradigm with a new theologically oriented one. Like the Hare Krishnas, the ID movement rejected the naturalistic assumptions and approaches of Western science, preferring a methodology more in keeping with their particular religious sensibilities.[17] While mainstream examples of the absorption of science into religion may seem less likely, the naturalizing or demythologizing movements within mainline and liberal churches during the late twentieth-century belie that assumption. During the era of *TIME* magazine's "Is God Dead?" cover story and Harvey Cox's *The Secular City*, liberal religious leaders increasingly adopted the naturalistic and empiricist epistemologies more often associated with science than religion. When such liberal theologians are considered synoptically with the ID movement and Protestant engagement with ecology, the history of American religion during this time frame clearly reveals an engagement with science. Though few Americans joined new religious movements (NRMs), their positions on science serve as a useful barometer of the social forces facing the wider religious world. The rapidly emerging and transforming NRMs often prefaced how more established religious groups responded to those social forces.

Tension, Not Warfare

Despite their many differences, the three new religions considered here share a commonality: none took the position that religion innately conflicted with science. They complicate the popularly held belief that science and religion are at war, the "warfare thesis" (sometimes "conflict thesis") as historiographers call it. Though each of these movements contested specific positions and establishments of science, they did not call for holy war against it. Creative tension, not outright conflict, characterized the three new religions on science, as it does other new religions and "old religions."

The nineteenth-century chemist John William Draper and the Cornell historian Andrew Dickson White offered the most concise distillations of the warfare thesis. Both Draper's *History of the Conflict Between Religion* and *Science* and White's *History of the Warfare of Science with Theology in Christendom* positioned science as involved in a continual war with religion, particularly conservative or hierarchal religion.[18] The Draper-White perspective gained wide parlance among scholars and other readers, and their books enjoyed frequent reprintings for decades. Later historians stressed the warfare thesis and used it to explain late nineteenth- and early twentieth-century debates over evolution, geology, critical historical study of the Bible, and scientific approaches to social reform. Edward White's *Science and Religion in American Thought* and Norman F. Furniss's *The Fundamentalist Controversy, 1918–1931* repeated and amplified the Draper-White warfare model.[19] The historian Richard Hofstadter incorporated it as a central motif in his *Anti-Intellectualism in American Life*, viewing the warfare between science as religion as part of a wider gulf between intellectual and practical culture.[20]

Nevertheless, recent historians have pointed to the failings of the warfare thesis. Two recent edited collections focus particularly on the history of Christianity and science.[21] The twenty-seven essays included in these two collections correctly note that Christians, and particularly Christians in America, have responded to science in a multitude of ways, ranging from constructive engagement to complete acceptance to strong disagreement. David Livingstone's "Situating Evangelical Responses to Evolution," included in the anthology that he also edited, represents the consensus of all the contributors to both compilations. Religious people encountered science in different historical, social, and cultural circumstances, and careful study of each of those circumstances must precede assessments of how they responded to science.[22] The warfare thesis simply does not fit the evidence.

The intellectual positions of the three new religious movements add to the growing mound of evidence covering the pitfall of the warfare thesis. None of the new religions rejected science or fled from it. Even the Hare Krishna position calling for the replacement of Western science with an Indian alternative represented not a war with science, but creative tension with it. ISKCON critiqued the American scientific establishment and the methodologies of Western science, but it also offered an alternative science embedded within an alternative religion. Individuals within the movement lived out this approach. One of the movement's leading proponents of Indian science, Svarupa Damodara, obtained a PhD in chemistry from a secular American university and later sought out fellow scientists to participate in the alternative scientific institute that he founded. ISKCON did not go to war with science, though in a Kuhnian move, it did wish to replace the major paradigms of Western science.

The other two new religious movements, Unificationism and Heaven's Gate, explicitly valued science, and both rejected any notion of conflict between their own religious positions and science. The Unification Church upheld science and religion as deeply compatible. Whereas science examined the material world, religion considered the spiritual world and thus provided moral and ethical guidance to science. The two could not go to war, because they occupied separate territories. Heaven's Gate took an even more positive view of science, embracing the concept and absorbing its methodological foundations. While the leaders and members of the movement admitted that they sometimes disagreed with particular scientists, for example on the need for faith in their religious leaders, they believed that science and religion could not conflict because a true religion followed the same approaches as did science.

Three New Religions

This book considers three new religious movements so as to triangulate the different ways that the adherents of new religions, alongside religious people more broadly, talked about science. By examining three groups synoptically one finds that new religions responded to similar historical circumstances and ideological questions in very different manners. Though I recognize that my work makes an implicit comparison between the three groups, I have chosen to structure the book around three separate treatments of the new religions. This allows them to stand on their own as three different traditions that developed apart from one another.

Nevertheless, the three new religions considered here shared several commonalities. First, they each grew and thrived during the American counterculture of the 1960s and 1970s, though all three movements continued to exist well past those decades, and each has origins in their founders' experiences before that time. They continued to relate and react to the same wider cultural events, ranging from the political to the social to the scientific. In addition to reservations about big science, they responded to the assassination of John F. Kennedy, the Summer of Love, Woodstock, and the rise and fall of Richard Nixon. The era witnessed the widespread availability of the birth control pill, the moon landings, the birth of ecology, and rapid developments in computer technology. Second, each of the movements offered a comprehensive vision of the world, which included everything from explanations of the meaning of life and death to instructions on how a person should date and marry, what to eat, and predictions of the future shape of global society. Therefore the movements offered wide-ranging pronouncements on science that fit within broader imaginings of how the groups and their members ought to relate to American culture. Third, while each group had centralized leadership, the membership of the movement took active roles in formulating and explicating the religious groups' ideological positions. This participation resulted in a chorus of voices that, although sometimes contradicting one another, indicated the boundaries of the movements' positions.

The three groups had major cultural and intellectual differences as well. Two of the groups, the Hare Krishnas and Unificationism, formed abroad but experienced their greatest numerical growth and intellectual development in the United States during the countercultural period. The third, Heaven's Gate, emerged and grew within the United States. The Unification Church imported Korean cultural and social norms as well as religious ideas, and the Hare Krishnas did the same with Indian perspectives. Heaven's Gate, however, responded to the American social mores of its founders by both assuming and rejecting those norms. Both Heaven's Gate and the Unification Church developed out of Christian backgrounds and incorporated many elements of Christian theology in their approaches, though one (Heaven's Gate) combined such Christian presuppositions with influences from the New Age, whereas the other (Unification Church) synergized Korean spiritualism and Daoism. In contrast, the Hare Krishna movement grew out of a preexisting sectarian movement within Hinduism and, in America, drew from the countercultural positions of its many new members. These specificities combined with the shared cultural location and era to yield three district approaches to science and religion.

Three parts comprise the core of the text, each of which treats one of the NRMs in two chapters. I move chronologically within each, and the parts themselves follow the order in which the new religions appeared in the United States: the Unification Church in the late 1950s, the International Society for Krishna Consciousness in the mid-1960s, and Heaven's Gate in the 1970s. The founders' births represent the beginning points for each of the parts. In the case of the International Society for Krishna Consciousness and Heaven's Gate, the death of their founders mark a natural end point for this study (1977 and 1997, respectively). Since the Reverend Sun Myung Moon, founder and leader of Unificationism, is still alive as of the time of this writing, I examined only what I consider the movement's most formative era, its first three decades of existence. In each case, I cover the periods during which the movements achieved their greatest success and made the most concerted effort to define themselves intellectually.

The first part explores the Unification Church, sometimes also called "the Moonies." Many Americans remember the Unification Church because of its mass wedding celebrations wherein Moon solemnized the marriages of hundreds or even thousands of couples in arenas and stadiums. Such weddings represented part of Unificationism's millennial attempt to construct the new kingdom of God on Earth, which also hints at how the movement treated science. Unificationism attempted to *guide* science, envisioning it as a helpful tool with which humanity could build a better future, alleviate suffering, and glimpse the divine mysteries of the universe. Unificationists believed that they could guide science by helping it prioritize its research agenda as well as bring scientists together to consider central problems that cut across all fields.

The first chapter, "Science and the Foundation of Unificationism," traces the emergence of the Unification movement from the nucleus of Rev. Sun Myung Moon to its burgeoning in the United States of America in the form of three distinct Unificationist movements. I begin with the early life and mission of Reverend Sun Myung Moon. Biographical details provide evidence of the importance of science in his formative years, as well as how such influences emerged in the church he founded. Next, I look at the movement's transition from Korea to the United States at the cusp of the 1960s, and the sacred text that solidified its North American arm, *Divine Principle* (1973). This text, the central sacred text for English-speaking Unificationists, directly commented on science, scientific thinking, and the relation of science to religion, which forcefully shaped the resultant movement.

The second chapter, "Science in the American Unification Church," focuses on the institutions and organizations during this period, beginning with the Collegiate Association for the Research of Principles (CARP), the Unification Church's public face on college campuses. The church also embraced a more systematic approach to studying and teachings its theological tradition, creating its own divinity school in 1975. Students and faculty at the new school, the Unification Theological Seminary, hoped to bridge the gap between science and religion and demonstrate that their Unificationist tradition embraced the modern scientific world. Finally, I turn to the topic that opens part I, the International Conferences on the Unity of the Sciences (ICUS) and the manner in which Unificationism sought to bring its approach to science and religion to a wider audience. I conclude by analyzing the underlying logic of science and religion in Unificationist thought, with reference to wider American cultural currents and views.

The second part of the book turns to the International Society for Krishna Consciousness, known informally as the Hare Krishna movement and more formally as ISKCON. This new religion emerged when its founder, the Swami (religious leader) A. C. Bhaktivedanta transplanted an existent form of Hinduism into America and introduced it to members of the American counterculture. Unlike Unificationism, which adopted a positive view of Western science, ISKCON rejected the scientific paradigm and establishment of the West and, instead, insisted that it offered an alterative. The Hare Krishnas sought to *replace* American science with an alternative model predicated on Indian religious texts, which their founder and converts found both more accurate and better attuned to social needs than the empiricism and naturalism of Western science.

I begin chapter 3 by examining the life circumstances of Swami Bhaktivedanta, considering his exposure to Western-style education in British colonial schools. Bhaktivedanta would come to reject the English educational foundation that he encountered, instead embracing a traditional sect of devotional Hinduism known as Gaudiya Vaishnavism. This Hindu sect itself formed in response to cultural encounters, first with Muslims in the sixteenth century and then with the British three centuries later. Having considered Bhaktivedanta's background in Gaudiya Vaishnavism, the chapter treats his earliest published writings, the English-language *Back to Godhead* magazine, which the swami published in India. Bhaktivedanta focused on science in many of that journal's articles, and I examine his underlying approach through a close reading of several of his most detailed contributions on the topic. I find that Swami Bhaktivedanta attempted to both claim the mantle and prestige of science as well as contest the value of the Western naturalistic science that the British had imported to India. The chapter concludes by considering Bhaktivedanta's early work in the United States, to which he came as a missionary in 1965.

Chapter 4, "Science and the Expansion of ISKCON," considers how the International Society for Krishna Consciousness expanded and institutionalized its founder's views on science and religion, covering the group's most productive and successful era, which ended with the death of its leader Swami Bhaktivedanta in November 1977. The chapter begins with the movement's new American-born converts, who added their own countercultural opposition to America's scientific establishments to their guru's suspicions of science. I also consider a series of conversations that these new leaders of the movement had with their elder swami. In these dialogues, originally meant for internal use as a guide the members of ISKCON on matters of science, Bhaktivedanta assumed a stridently dismissive view of science and particularly biology. The conversations showed how the group's founder and the new cadre of leaders rejected the major paradigms of American science, particularly its empirical and naturalistic foundations. The new intellectual leaders of ISKCON took differing views on science within the Hare Krishna movement, ranging from envisioning science as irrelevant to rejecting it outright to accepting science as a possible support for the movement's own positions. In particular I explore the work of Svarupa Damodara (Thoudam Damodar Singh), a Hare Krishna devotee, holder of a PhD in chemistry, and administrator of the Bhaktivedanta Institute. The chapter concludes by considering ISKCON's attempt to convey its positions on science to an outside audience as well as the disintegration of consensus following the guru's death.

Part III, on Heaven's Gate, notes a third way that new religions could respond to science, by *absorbing* science into religion. While many people had not heard of Heaven's Gate until the 1997 suicides that ended its existence, the movement had twenty-five years of history and represented the intellectual development of two Americans, born and raised as Protestants in Texas, who developed an alternative religion rejecting much of what Americans consider normative. Heaven's Gate upheld a monastic vision of life, rejecting sexuality, consumption, and self-orientation. However, Heaven's Gate extolled American science, in particular the epistemological foundation of science. Heaven's Gate looked to absorb materialistic naturalism—the approach that looks to only the physical world and physical laws as sources of knowledge—into religion.

Chapter 5, "Science and the Foundation of Heaven's Gate," treats the period during which the group's founders Marshall Herff Applewhite and Bonnie Lu Nettles led the group together, from the mid-1970s until Nettles's death in 1985. The chapter first considers Nettles and Applewhite's cultural and religious backgrounds. Though both had been raised as Christians, Nettles had left her Baptist heritage behind and become involved in the New Age movement, whereas Applewhite had followed his father's vocation and trained at a Presbyterian seminary before dropping out to study music. I focus on the two's transformation into "the Two," as they came to call themselves, and their successful spread of a religious movement that questioned the very category of religion. Fundamentally, the Two attempted to absorb the methodological naturalism and materialism of science, and recast religion in that ethos, an act that they accomplished through a rereading of both Christian and New

Age concepts. The chapter concludes with a close examination of a meditative prayer that the Two and their followers used during the early 1980s. The prayer combined a fiercely naturalistic approach using the language of chemistry and biology with the overtly religious form of prayer.

Chapter 6, "Science and the End of Heaven's Gate," treats the era between the death of Bonnie Lu Nettles and the mass suicide that ended the group's existence. I analyze the shifts in the group's naturalistic approach engendered by the loss of Nettles, whose death resulted in a moment of cognitive dissonance for the group. The group had hitherto insisted that its members would enter the heavens in their current living bodies, something that failed to occur for Nettles. Applewhite and the other members of the group therefore shifted toward a more supernatural or nonmaterial interpretation of bodily salvation predicated on the transmigration of the souls, a clear break from Heaven's Gate's earlier position. Overall, however, the movement continued to attempt during this time to recast religious concepts in the languages of materialistic naturalism. Several sources from the 1980s and 1990s revealed the continuing emphasis on the incorporation of scientific language and the methodological foundations of science into the movement. This chapter also considers sources from this latter period of Heaven's Gate that began to assume a vocally anti-religious perspective. These sources indicate how the group attempted to situate itself as more scientific than religious, despite making claims about salvation, God, and the nature of human life that most observers would consider religious by nature. Finally I consider the material produced in the final years of the group's history by the adherents of Heaven's Gate, especially the three longtime members of the group calling themselves Jnnody, Chkody, and Jwnody. These three individuals, and others within the movement, wrote a number of statements that revealed their movement's position as highly critical of both scientific and religious institutions. The chapter ends with an analysis of how the group's view of science and the absorption of scientific approaches into religion led to the 1997 mass suicides that ended Heaven's Gate.

Methodological Considerations

The approach I have used throughout this text fuses intellectual and cultural history methodologies. Intellectual history concerns itself with the development of ideas and ideologies and those who embody them. As an intellectual history, this study asks how ideas about science developed within each of the three movements and how these ideas resonated with wider culture. I consider the historical forces that led to the development of these ideas, and how these ideologies of science and religion emerged from intellectual and cultural changes such as colonialism or new social movements. Here, the impact of these ideas emerges most forcefully in how ideologies of science proliferated through publications, institutions, and religious practices within each of the new religious movements, spreading from the mind of one founder to the words of an entire generation of new leaders. Although interesting, I leave questions of a more sociological nature—how these ideas might have impacted recruitment, social cohesion, or attrition—for other scholars. I find that one must understand new religions' views of science as embedded within their historical and intellectual development. Particularly I look to the history of colonialism, modernization, and wider religious changes sweeping through culture. When considered alongside those forces, we see that new religions possessed remarkably well-developed assessments of modern science that in many cases paralleled wider intellectual currents.

This study also employs the tools of cultural history, which consider meanings, symbols, and socially embedded human identities. The historian Peter Burke has written that "[t]he common ground of cultural historians might be described as a concern with the symbolic and its interpretation. Symbols, conscious or unconscious, can be found everywhere, from art to everyday life, but an approach to the past in terms of symbolism is just one approach among others."[23] In this study, I consider how science operated as a powerful symbol within the religious rhetoric of three new religions, and where those operations intersect wider culture. For students of religion, the analysis of symbols through cultural history offers particular worth. Cultural history allows the historian of religion to analyze the subject while avoiding the perils of reductionism. Reductionism posits that religion is really something else—politics, psychology, social forces, etc.—other than the symbolic expressions of belief and practice. As a cultural history, this study takes religion seriously on its own ground, without claiming that the religions considered are really representative of something else. For this reason I consider resonances and parallels with wider culture without implying causation. For example, the first chapter of this book argues that Unificationist leader Sun Myung Moon's ideas about science resonated with particular subcultures in both Korea and the United States, but it makes no claims about the origins of those ideas, or the Unificationist belief that Moon received divine revelation. Rather, I argue that Unificationism reflected the society out of which it emerged, without commenting on the nature of what its members consider divine revelation.

With intellectual and cultural history to guide me, this book asks what the study of science in three new religious movements can show us about wider cultural and intellectual changes. I find that science operates as a powerful symbol in how new religions understand themselves and their relationship to wider culture, including other religions. Ideas about science encapsulate perspectives on a much broader set of issues—among them colonialism, millennialism, and modernity. The consideration of how these three new religious movements have constructed alternative understandings of science and its relation to religion reveals multiple currents in the modern world. Together, they also illuminate a threefold paradigm of how new religious can respond to the place of science: guide, replace, absorb.

Part I

Science and the Unification Church

Religion and science have been the methods of searching for the two aspects of truth, in order to overcome the two aspects of ignorance and restore the two aspects of knowledge.
—Sun Myung Moon, *Divine Principle* (1973)

Introduction

Boston, Massachusetts, Thanksgiving Day, 1978. Eugene Wigner, emeritus professor of physics at Princeton, Manhattan Project veteran, and Nobel laureate, placed his notes on the podium and began his address. His brief speech opened a conference dedicated, in his words, to fostering unity between the natural sciences and the sciences of life—that is, the social sciences—and the discussion of "the effects of religion on human needs, on happiness."[1] Wigner added that he hoped to stimulate a conversation on the psychology of animals, which would benefit the scientific study of human psychology as well. A long table of VIPs dominated the front of the banquet hall, with Wigner's podium in the center. At the physicist's left sat the neuroscientist Sir John Eccles, another Nobel laureate; Fredrick Seitz, former president of the National Academy of Sciences and Rockefeller University; Kenneth Mellanby, the ecologist who founded and directed the British science establishment of Monks Wood Experimental Station; and the MIT sociologist Daniel Lerner. R. V. Jones, the wartime scientific adviser to Winston Churchill, Richard Rubenstein, a leading American Jewish theologian, and Michael Warder, journalist and conference director, sat to Wigner's right. In the audience, four hundred and fifty scientists from more than fifty countries listened to the opening addresses of the Seventh International Conference on the Unity of the Sciences (ICUS VII, 1978). In the coming four days, they would speak on such subjects as Burkitt's Lymphoma in Paraequatorial Africa, the supernationality of science, species selfishness, and theories of religious consciousness.

One small detail, however, distinguished the ICUS from the many other academic conferences that occurred in 1978. Also at the dais sat the Reverend Sun Myung Moon, founder and leader of the Unification Church, the controversial new religious movement known to Americans as "the Moonies." The International Cultural Foundation (ICF), a Unification-funded organization, provided the half million dollars that sponsored the Seventh International Conference on the Unity of the Sciences, as it had done for the six preceding and fifteen following meetings of ICUS.[2] In the ICF's words, "the purpose of ICUS [was] to provide an opportunity for scholars and scientists to reflect on the nature of knowledge and to discuss the relationship of science to the standard of value."[3] At the conferences scientists delivered papers on topics ranging from the technical and obscure to the nearly universal. Many extolled the conference as one of the few that encouraged true interdisciplinary conversation. Professor Max Jammer, president of the Association for the Advancement of Science in Israel, offered a representative comment, calling ICUS "a uniquely stimulating event by providing the rare possibilities of an interdisciplinary exchange on problems of profound significance for the intellectual situation of our time."[4] Previous conferences featured addresses and papers by sociologists, historians, theologians, and Nobel-winning scientists. For example, the fourth ICUS included presentations by the inventor of holographs, Dennis Gabor, as well as the chemist who first isolated vitamin C, Albert Szent-Gyorgi, both past winners of Nobel Prizes.[5] In addition to the physical scientists, J. B. Rhine, the famous ESP researcher from Duke University, Theodore Roszak, academic spokesman for the counterculture, and the historian Oscar Handlin, the Pulitzer Prize–winning scholar of immigration, had all attended preceding ICUS meetings. But outside the Sheraton Boston Hotel demonstrators protested against the Unification Church as a dangerous cult and the conference as a publicity stunt and scientific sham. "These cultists must be destroyed, imprisoned—anything to STOP their mind control of society," read the protestors' leaflet.[6] Responding to the ICUS conference, a former member of the Unification Church now affiliated with the anti-cult movement released a statement comparing the Unificationists to Nazis. The scientists, he warned, were "legitimating a demagogue and are lending credence to a movement whose goals and methods find their parallel in the National Socialist Movement in Germany under Hitler."[7] One possible explanation of the demonstrators' fiery rhetoric: less than two weeks earlier, almost one thousand people had committed mass suicide at Jonestown, a commune in Guyana, South America, run by another new religion, Jim Jones' Peoples Temple.[8] "Dangerous cults," as media sources referred to them, occupied Americans' minds.[9] Ironically, one ICUS panel featured the well-respected scholar of religion Ninian Smart discussing "Death and Suicide in Contemporary Thought," which conference organizers hastened to explain had been organized long before the Guyana tragedy.

What would bring the Unification Church to sponsor a science conference, one at which, its attendees insisted, in the words of Sir John Eccles, "the conferences have been notable for complete freedom to all participants"?[10] Scientists themselves determined the topics and subjects of their papers, sessions, and panels, and a committee of academics oversaw the process. Critics suggested that Moon and his church sought the publicity and legitimization that hobnobbing with savants brought. This does provide part of the answer. Certainly Moon enjoyed and benefited from the exposure, but the sources indicate that the Unificationists sponsored ICUS because the conferences forwarded the movement's program of reconciliation between science and religion, and unity within science itself. Although the church set no limits on the participants or their papers, it provided the overall theme, always one that stressed the need for moral or religious guidance of science. The Boston conference considered "the re-evaluation of existing values and the search for absolute values," or, as the conference's organizer and Unification member Michael Young Warder explained to the press, ICUS "provide[d] an opportunity for scholars and scientists to discuss questions of values," and considered "concerns about the crisis of values in the modern world."[11] Other meetings of the international conferences considered such subjects as "modern science and moral values" (ICUS I, 1972), "harmony among the sciences" (ICUS V, 1976), "the responsibility of the academic community" (ICUS VIII, 1979), "absolute values and the new reassessment of the contemporary world" (ICUS XVI, 1987), and "absolute values and the unity of the sciences: the origin of human responsibility" (ICUS XX, 1995). Through such topical guidance, the Unification Church and its International Cultural Foundation sought to shepherd science toward working within a moral paradigm set by the church: a holistic quest for knowledge and progress operating under a religiously attuned set of absolute behavioral and philosophical guidelines that, in the view of the Unification Church, highlighted peace, piety, and progressivism.

The Unification Church in seeking to direct American science through conferences represented an extreme but representative religious approach to science: the desire to *guide* it. Thus, Unificationist leaders and members took a pro-science position. But they did so with the hope and aspiration that their religious movement would guide science toward what the movement considered its divinely mandated goal, the discovery of knowledge, the progress of human material life, and ultimately, alongside the efforts of religion, the creation of a heaven on earth. This included support of American's scientific establishment, upon which the Unificationists looked positively. Like many other American Christians,[12] Unificationists believed religion to be compatible with a modern scientific worldview, envisioning science and religion as separate spheres that did not impinge upon the other. At times science presented problems to religion, for example the often thorny issue of human evolution and natural selection. Yet overall, Unificationism saw science as a powerful force for good. The Unification Church embodied a progressive millennialism in keeping with the American postmillennial tradition. Like the Social Gospelers a half century earlier, the Unification Church saw science and technology as tools of establishing a model Christian society. Believing themselves responsible for fostering a heaven on earth, Unificationists looked to science as a valuable asset and to the scientific community as a natural ally.

1

Science and the Foundation
of Unificationism

Reverend Sun Myung Moon and the
Genesis of Unificationism

Sun Myung Moon[1] was born on February 25, 1920, in a Korea that stood at the cusp of modernization. Ten years earlier the Japanese Empire had annexed Korea and begun a forced process of infrastructure and economic development. The young Moon encountered the same industrial and technological revolution that overtook the United States a few decades earlier: railroads, electricity, factories, and the advent of modern business and industry. The Korean historian Bruce Cumings places what he calls the "profound" transformation of Korea at "[t]he period from 1935 to 1945," during which "Korea's industrial revolution began, with most of the usual characteristics: uprooting of peasants from the land, the emergence of a working class, widespread population mobility, and urbanization."[2] This era coincided with Moon's formative teen years and early adulthood. Between Moon's birth and his twenty-third birthday, his native Korea witnessed a 343 percent increase in industrial employment as well as profound social displacement due to falling agricultural prices and rising demand for industrial workers. The railroad in particular, Cumings notes, "penetrated" and "integrated" Korea, ferrying raw materials, finished products, and Korean workers throughout the peninsula.[3]

Moon's early religious upbringing is uncertain, but then much in colonial Korea was uncertain. Alongside modernizing the Korean economy, Japanese colonial authorities also sought to "modernize" native Korean religious and social norms. Combined with the social and geographic dislocations owing to industrial development, Korea experienced what Adrian Buzo calls a "profound cultural loss." Buzo argues that under Japanese colonial rule, "Koreans lost an entire edifice of faith that had undergirded the life of the country for 500 years, linking people and their daily thoughts and activities to [the

Korean] monarch, country and beyond to the universe. . . . Sense of identity, purpose in life, and the significance of daily activities became crowded with unanswerable questions, and neither spiritual leaders nor colonial authority could offer guidance to people disturbed and uprooted by momentous change. For some, Christianity and other new religions filled the spiritual void."[4] Christianity held the allure of looking to the Occident, rather than Japan, as its spiritual center. The year before Moon's birth, Korean Christian leaders joined with nationalists in a short-lived rebellion against the Japanese colonizers.[5] The Moon family, and Sun Myung himself, were among the spiritually uprooted people of Korea, converting to Christianity when the future founder of the Unification Church was ten years old, one of many families to convert in Korea's fastest-growing Christian regions.[6] Moon adopted his new Christian religion with gusto. Later biographies chronicle that by the age of fifteen or sixteen Moon claimed the abilities of a religious visionary, communicating with spirits and receiving divine revelation. Moon himself taught that while praying as a young teenager, Jesus Christ manifested before him, asking him to pledge to end human suffering on Earth.[7]

Around the same time that Moon claimed to receive his first revelations, he also began scientific and technological training. Moon's muddled experience of education in fact linked to his mixed religious experiences: the traditional Korean Confucian system during the winter and modern subjects under a Presbyterian missionary during summer.[8] At the age of eighteen he left his parents to enroll at a technical high school in Seoul, where he took an interest in electricity. While in Seoul he also began to attend a Pentecostal church; his family reported that during his return visits he would pray feverishly and frequently.[9] A Pentecostal emphasis on healing and works of the spirit would become prominent characteristics of his later movement. Deciding to pursue an advanced degree, Moon enrolled at the junior college associated with Waseda University, a prestigious private university in Tokyo, continuing his study of electrical engineering.[10] Moon continued to experience religious visions in Japan.

The educational and religious trajectory of Sun Myung Moon encapsulated a number of cross-cultural flows and importations. Raised in Korea during Japanese colonial occupation, Moon encountered the scientific and technological modernization that the colonial power introduced to the peninsula. Japan itself had imported this modernist impulse from the West during its early Meiji period (1868–1912) before subsequently exporting it to Korea. During each step of cross-cultural flow, individuals and groups filtered science through native categories, such as Shinto nationalism in

Japan and Confucian ideals of scholarship in Korea. Moon, unlike the Hare Krishna founder Swami Bhaktivedanta (see chap. 3), accepted the scientific modernism that he learned from the colonial power. Yet Moon combined his acceptance of the scientific worldview propagated by Japan with his embrace of another import, the religion of Europe, Christianity. Moon himself then filtered Christianity through his own Korean norms and sensibilities, which led him to create the Unification Church. Completing the cycle of transnationalism, Moon and his followers exported their understanding of religion and science to Japan and then to the West. The Unification Church's perspectives on science reveal these global cross-cultural flows.

Having completed his scientific training in Japan, Moon returned to Korea and began a career as an electrician. Following the conclusion of the Second World War and freed from his wartime industrial assignments, Moon transitioned from the world of engineering to preaching. In June 1946, not even a year after the United States ended the war with the atomic bombings of Hiroshima and Nagasaki, Moon left his wife and newborn baby to found a church in the northern Korean city of Pyongyang, obeying what he believed was a revelation directing him to do so.[11] There Moon gathered a circle of Christians through emotional public prayers and sermons wherein he preached the imminent return of Christ to Korea.[12] The outbreak of the Korean War and Moon's open defiance of communist authorities led to two and a half years of imprisonment, starting in 1948. While imprisoned, Moon continued to preach, converting other prisoners to his own view of Christianity, which increasingly emphasized Moon's personal revelations and hinted that Moon might serve some integral place in the coming advent.[13] The chaos of the American invasion and the outbreak of the Korean civil war permitted Moon and several of his followers to flee to South Korea.[14] Four years later in Seoul, in 1954 Reverend Moon founded the Holy Spirit Association for the Unification of World Christianity (HSA-UWS), the official name of the Unification Church. During the following decade, Moon and his growing Unificationist movement developed their ideas, texts, and understandings of their mission. Science came to occupy a growing role in this thought.

Science in Reverend Moon's Korean Unification Church

Moon's sermons during the first decade of the Unification Church's existence offers a glimpse into his movement's early thought on science and its relation to religion. They also reveal an underlying tension that later emerged in the Unificationist sacred texts, the Korean-language *Wolli Hesul* ("Explanation of the Divine Principle," 1957) and *Wolli Kangron* ("Exposition of the Divine Principle," 1966), and their English-language translations, notably *Divine Principle* (1973). In his sermons, Moon generally insisted that the best religion and best science operated as internally unified pursuits, two individually coherent spheres each considering a different aspect of life and the world. Moon, however, sometimes vacillated between this and another approach. The first, that of religion and science as separate spheres, showed Moon to understand the two as mutually valid but distinct approaches to the world. In his second approach to religion and science, Moon saw the two as parallel pursuits that needed to unify in accordance with his grand millennial vision for the future of Earth. Later, in their dealings with scientists Moon and his Unification movement would adopt the more moderate position that religion must guide science. Yet even during the ICUS era, the urge to unify religion and science persisted in the movement's religious discourse.

One of Moon's first explicit mention of science employed it as a point of comparison. A June 2, 1957, sermon represented this rhetorical use of science. In a reference not lost on a Korean audience deeply aware of the nuclear attacks (albeit utilizing atomic fission devices) on Japan, Moon declared, "just as today we have discovered the greatest force in the material world through nuclear fusion, in the future we will discover the same kind of force in the spirit world." Yet Moon integrated a judgment on the value of religion and science into the comparison, namely that religion's claims on the supernatural existed outside the critiques of science. "That is a force that cannot be explained with the present level of natural science. This force is transcendent and is applicable in the supernatural world, but it is surely possible for this force to reach all things of the universe through human beings."[15] Science cannot explain transcendental forces, Moon indicated, even though it possessed much value. Here Moon revealed a central tension within Unificationist thought. Science both "reach[ed] all things," but also fell short of offering religious truth. Science and religion ought to function as separate spheres, but they also must unify. This tension continued into American Unificationism.

Moon returned to science in two other sermons that year, both of which featured extended discussions on science's relation to religion and included implicit recognitions of religion and science as separate spheres. His September 29, 1957, sermon portrayed science and religion as simultaneously separate spheres, or paths, to use the sermon's nomenclature, as well as mutually unsuccessful approaches to the world that needed to come together under Unificationism's guidance. Basing his sermon on Psalm 23, which famously declared that the Lord led the psalmist on the paths of righteousness, "through the valley of the shadow of death" (RSV),[16] Moon pushed each member of his church to find his or her own path. "Yet that path will come in many different forms. There will be paths that rely on religion; there will be paths that rely on science. In each field in which you find yourselves, politics, economics, philosophy, etc., there will be a different path each of you walk." Such words indicate a relativism if not outright equality between the paths. But Moon continued, "[w]hen you reflect upon whether you have found the eternal value that will allow you to embark upon a new path from the position you are in today, you will find that no one has yet found that kind of value and purpose. In other words, in religion, science, culture or any other field, we were not able to find the universal value that could establish our new ideology of life and form the power of new life."[17] Equal only in terms of their inability to usher in the millennial era, neither conventional science nor conventional religion offered ultimate solutions to the problems of individual lives or the world as a whole. Later in the same sermon, Moon lamented that "solving this fundamental problem of human beings can never be accomplished with religion, philosophy or science, either those of the past or of the present." Strange words from the leader of a religious group, even a new religion! Moon clarified the matter somewhat in explaining why science failed to solve the problems of the world. He also prescribed the solution: "[b]ecause science today cannot work for the sake of peace for humanity or bring happiness in place of the whole purpose, science must also forge a bond with the one purpose of the whole. If those relations are not formed, then this world cannot be united as one."[18] The "one purpose of the whole" would have keyed Moon's audience that he referred to none other than Unificationism, with its goal of unifying the world's religions as well as sciences. Seen in this regard, both science and religion existed as inherently deficient categories in need of unification. Here the Unification Church's self-envisioned role of steward became clear: science needed help, and Moon and his church could provide it.

Moon revealed what I call the "radical but representative" position of Unificationism on science. Though the Unification Church took the radical position that it could actually redirect the aims of science, it was representative of many other postwar religions that hoped to guide science and technology, both in America and abroad. For example, the National Council of Churches (NCC)—comprised of representative of America's mainline Protestant denominations—called in 1966 for scientific research to "serve persons" rather than military interests, and encouraged research into basic science rather than defense-related technologies.[19] Though far more detailed in their demands of science, the Unification Church prefaced the bastion of mainstream American religion in calling for religious guidance of postwar science.

Moon believed that his religion ought to guide science because he believed the Unification Church able to access a form of knowledge inaccessible to science, a legitimating strategy surely not lost on potential converts. Invoking the concept of stewardship, Moon declared that humans developed science in accordance with a divine mandate to study and understand the natural world. But "religion," he indicated, considers "the world of the mind."[20] Moon envisioned science and religion as two separate spheres, each of which focused the human intellect on a different area of research, or as he declared in another sermon, "religion represents the field of metaphysical truth and the natural sciences represent the field of physical truth."[21] This reveals why the movement would later develop its efforts to bring the sciences together through the International Conferences on the Unity of the Sciences, just as it sought to unite the religious world. At its best, science existed as a single, unified sphere that studied the external world. As he would later show in his founder's addresses at the conferences, the fragmentation of science concerned Moon. Fragmentation complicated the boundaries and borders of science, making it less of a sphere and more of an amoeba, unsure of its center or boundaries. In contrast, within Moon's religious worldview, science served its divinely mandated function when it holistically considered the material world. Only when science existed as a single sphere could it clearly and neatly distinguish itself from religion, which considered the internal or immaterial truths of the cosmos. Further, the unity of science also implied the unity of religion, a central posit of Moon's vision of religious unification.

Ironically, Moon also posited unity between those two internally united spheres. The sermon continued, "although religion and science divided in the second half of the sixteenth century, in the last days today, we are crossing over to the state of union when we can again reach the one purpose."[22] The reference to the "last days" provides a crucial clue to understanding how Moon and Unificationism could concurrently uphold a belief in science and religion as separate spheres as well as hope to unify them. Moon based his October 6 sermon on 1 Thessalonians 5:1–11, an eschatologically oriented New Testament section that declares "the day of the Lord will come like a thief in the night" (RSV). Millennialism best explains the irony of two internally coherent pursuits requiring unification. In the normal world and in normal time, science and religion existed as separate spheres. But in the coming millennial age, the two would come together in service of a divinely mandated new world, a heaven on earth indeed. The sermon even included a messianic hint, the claim that "we can see that not only in the field of the natural sciences today, but also in the religious field, we have come to the point where we cannot move forward any more . . . we find that there must appear someone new who can remove obstructions and take responsibility for the people if they do not listen to the commands."[23] Such a call served not only to legitimate Moon's leadership—though it certainly did that—but also establish the Unification Church as more than just another ecumenical movement. Unificationism, as a steward of science, assumed a messianic role.

Millennialism served as the heart of this messianic vision of the stewardship of science. Like most living religious movements, simple theological categories such as post-millennial and pre-millennial fail to adequately distinguish Unificationism, which possessed characteristics of both. Pre-millennialism takes its name from the theological position that Christ's advent marks the initiation of the thousand-year period (millennium) of peace prophesied in the New Testament book of Revelation, to be followed by a cataclysmic battle with Satan and the permanent creation of the new heaven on earth. The Unificationism of the 1950s and 1960s—the church's millennial position shifted over time—stressed the key component of pre-millennialism, belief in the imminent arrival of a Christ-figure, in Unificationism's case identified as Moon himself. Like pre-millennialists, Unificationists looked to a millennial era of peace and prosperity to follow the new advent. However, Unificationism rejected the pre-millennial tenet of violent worldwide apocalypse (to use the common sense of the word), though it did warn that chaos and war might precede the millennium in some quarters.

Although theologically pre-millennial, Unification shared the general outlook of post-millennialists, a more optimistic brand of millennialism that claims the thousand-year peace is to precede the arrival of Christ. In the words of historian Paul Boyer, who chronicled the American millennialist tradition, post-millennialists "anticipated the gradual diffusion of Christianity until the Millennium almost imperceptibly became a reality."[24] Post-millennialism found its greatest expression in the turn of the twentieth-century American Social Gospel movement, which looked to social reform as the foundation of Christian religion and the Kingdom of Heaven on Earth. Rather than wait for the advent of Christ, humans must reform society themselves, explained Social Gospelers such as Walter Rauschenbusch, who bluntly declared that "[o]ne of the more persistent mistakes of Christian men has been to postpone social regeneration to a future era to be inaugurated by the return of Christ."[25] Unificationism, like the Social Gospel and wider post-millennialism, saw value in human work and the need to create model social institutions on Earth. However, they did so not in the hopes of preparing for the return of Christ, but because the millennial era had already dawned. Like post-millennialists, Unificationists looked to human activities as necessary and beneficial, but they performed them during the era of the Second Advent itself. Rather than pre-millennial or post-millennial, Unificationism was merely millennial.

In addition to the theological concepts of post-millennialism and pre-millennialism, the more phenomenological categories of catastrophic and progressive millennialism, as devised by scholar of new religions Catherine Wessinger, help explain the Unificationist view of science. Wessinger writes:

> Catastrophic millennialism involves a pessimistic view of humanity and society. We are so corrupt and sinful that the world as we know it must be destroyed and then created anew. This will be accomplished by God (or by superhuman agents such as extraterrestrials), perhaps with the assistance of human beings. The millennial kingdom will be created only after the violent destruction of the old world. Progressive millennialism involved an optimistic view of human nature that became prevalent in the nineteenth century. Humans engaging in social work in harmony with the divine will can effect changes that non-catastrophically and progressively create the millennial kingdom.[26]

Unificationism lacked the essential characteristics of catastrophic millennialism. Though Moon did warn of an impending confrontation between good and evil, in the guises of democracy and communism, famously declaring that "the time bomb is ticking," the movement encouraged its members and outsiders to work toward establishing an ideal world.[27] Theologically speaking, within Unificationism the dawning of the Second Advent freed human beings of their sinful natures, as optimistic a view of human nature as one can expect from a Christian-oriented group that accepted the reality of original sin. As Moon declared in his October 6, 1957, sermon, "Only when the ideology of unification is established on this earth and its tasks are brought to pass can Jesus complete his mission."[28] Unificationists dedicated themselves to bringing the world's religions and cultures together, creating world peace, and ending human suffering such as hunger, poverty, and disease.

Progressive millennialism explains the Unificationist view of science. Later Unificationist thought would explicate the place of science in the pursuit of the millennium, but Moon's early sermons only hinted at it, often conflating scientific progress with spiritual progress without explanation. He declared in a January 12, 1958, sermon, "[n]ow that the Last Days have come, everything will come to a conclusion. Philosophy will come to a conclusion, science will come to a conclusion, and the world economic system based on material will also come to a culmination point. At one point in the future, due to infinite progress in science, scientific research will invent improved food. Furthermore, you who are living in the last concluding era today must repent about your faith until now and try your best to live according to the words Jesus gave us."[29] The sermon does not clearly indicate the possible relevance of the invention of improved food to the need to repent and live according to the Gospel, but the juxtaposition of these two statements, along with similar ones in other sermons, shows that Moon considered science as a parallel to religion. Scientific progress mirrored religious progress.

Moon did clearly explicate the place of science in the coming millennial era, namely in alliance, sometimes union, with religion. Alone, science could not solve the problems of the world. "In other words," Moon explained in a March 30, 1958, sermon, "there will come a time when one cannot stand firm only with a horizontal [i.e., not heavenly] world ideology. No matter how much one boasts of the scientific civilization of today, it cannot cause the happiness of humankind."[30] Science lacked the guidance and value-orientation of religion, and therefore floundered. It also studied an incomplete universe, since it focused on purely the material world. But the merger of religion and science, enacted under the guidance of the Unification movement, offered a solution. "Consequently, no matter what you do now, you cannot produce the works of harmony which can link with the laws of the heavenly principle. . . . We must establish the new religious ideology that can forge relations with the universe."[31] Just a few years later, the "new religious ideology," as Moon called it, took root in the United States.

Transitions: The Unification Church Comes to America

Within seven years of the formation of the Holy Spirit Association for the Unification of World Christianity, four Unificationist apostles left Korea for the United States. These missionaries, Young Oon Kim, Sang Ik Choi, David Sang Chul Kim (no relation to Young Oon Kim), and Colonel Bo Hi Pak each founded independent Unification communities throughout the States. Although the groups would eventually merge with each other, for almost a decade several distinct Unificationist communities operated autonomously from both each other and the control of Moon.[32] A variety of factors separated the groups, including ideological, geographic, and cultural differences. Partially, demographics separated the groups, but so did personal loyalties. A member of Kim's Oakland-based Unification movement recalled the need to avoid members of Choi's San Francisco community, explaining that "[f]ollowers of different groups did not speak to each other, each believing that their leader was the only one who was doing what Father [Moon] wanted." He noted that his own avoidance of members of the rival group ceased only when Moon arranged for him to marry a woman who was "one of [Choi]'s most faithful followers."[33]

Ideological and theological differences also explained the gulf between the groups, each of which possessed its own version of the Unification sacred text. While the sub-movements within Unificationism had merged by the early 1970s, throughout the 1960s it is appropriate to discuss several competing Unificationist movements in America. In their treatment of science, the four groups varied. Young Oon Kim's movement, which absorbed the one founded by Colonel Pak, relegated science to the background. Appealing primarily to Pentecostals, Kim treated science as a foundation of Western culture but not directly relevant to religion. Instead Kim emphasized miraculous works of the spirit. She did however note that her Unificationist message appealed to the new "Atomic Age" and rhetorically declare her own movement modern, and therefore in keeping with science.[34] David S. C. Kim, who missionized a wider evangelical audience, similarly expressed ambivalence toward science. He denigrated scientific knowledge as less helpful than religious knowledge, but also recognized science's role in an eventual millennial union with religion. Choi reversed those positions. Working in San Francisco among the youth of America's counterculture, Choi critiqued conventional religion and looked to science as an alternate model, a modern foundation for the new Unificationist religion.[35]

With the multiple leaders, movements, and theological positions, American Unificationism lacked organizational, theological, institutional, and charismatic cohesion. Only one person could provide the unity that the three competing evangelists lacked, and in December 1971, the Reverend Sun Myung Moon arrived in North America to stabilize, solidify, and encourage the growth of the American movement. Other scholars have chronicled the history of Moon's efforts to unify the group, which included centralizing outreach efforts, rotating members through different centers, and reforming Unification institutions.[36] However, these histories, generally produced by sociologists, tend to ignore one crucial factor in the solidification of the movement: the emergence of a unified theology as codified in a new translation of the Unification sacred text *Wolli Kangron*, titled in English as *Divine Principle*. Translated by Dr. Won Pok Choi (unrelated to Sang Ik Choi), *Divine Principle* brought the disparate Unificationist groups under a single theological roof, one that contained the presuppositions and positions of the earlier translations used by the Young Oon Kim, David S. C. Kim, and Sank Ik Choi. Like Young Oon Kim's movement, the new *Divine Principle* assumed a Pentecostal emphasis on gifts of the spirit. Similar to David S. C. Kim, the new text exalted the Unificationist religion as the best system of values, one that ought to guide the world's other religions and sciences. And like Sank Ik Choi, the *Divine Principle* reached out to secular audiences by declaring science the basis of human cognition and preaching the need for a new scientifically oriented religion for the future. The new *Divine Principle* served as authoritative for the group for the next twenty-five years. It also reveals how the Unification Church understood the nature of science and its relation to religion, demonstrating remarkably continuity with wider American culture.

Religion and Science in Divine Principle

The 1973 *Divine Principle* not only solidified North American Unificationism, it also greatly expanded the theological base of the movement, providing a detailed English-language philosophy with roots in Korean Christianity, Daoism, and Confucian thought, as well as influences from modern philosophy. It also contained a close English translation of Moon's words, which allowed a direct examination of science in his thought, albeit as channeled through the translation of Dr. Won Pok Choi.[37] Moon's history as an electrical engineer shaped the language that *Divine Principle* employed. Scientific metaphors, philosophy, Christian theology, and allusions to particle physics commingled within the text.

The relationship between humans and God serves as a representative example of how Moon utilized science in his treatment of Unificationist religion. Fundamentally, the human/divine relationship required two unequal but necessarily reciprocal parties. In the text, Moon first employed aesthetics as a point of comparison. The relationship between human and God paralleled the appreciation of beauty, *Divine Principle* explained, because both sprang from "the circular movement between a subject and an object, occurring on a horizontal level [that] becomes a spherical one through a three-dimensional orbit. That is, the beauty of the things of creation exists in infinite variety, and this is due to their varied orbit, form, state, direction, angle, and speed of individual give and take action."[38] Restated in somewhat less arcane language, both beauty and the relationship between human and God owed their existence to an ever-changing subject perceiving an ever-changing object. If the comparison to aesthetics did not satisfy the reader, then *Divine Principle* offered another explanation, one predicated on the physical sciences. The subject/object interaction that gave rise to both the divine/human relationship and the aesthetic of beauty paralleled the relationship of subatomic particles within an atom: "When a proton and an electron, by forming a reciprocal base, enter into give-and-take action with the proton as the center, there occurs a circular movement which makes the two into one unit, and thus an atom is produced. The proton and the electron also have dual essentialities which are engaged in continuous individual movement."[39] Moon employed comparisons to other scientific disciplines such as botany and human biology throughout the text, but as befitting his technical training, he turned to electricity and magnetism most frequently. Here, Moon demonstrated his willingness to use scientific metaphors, and even rephrase theology in a scientific manner. Yet, Moon's specific choice of scientific metaphor invokes another influence: Daoism.

Although the *Divine Principle* did not differ from the Christian-oriented theology of the movement's origins, its underlying philosophy bore a strong resemblance to Daoism, specifically the Daoist sensibility of balance and interrelation between two opposites. Though most frequently associated with Chinese culture, Daoism expanded into Korea during the first millennium, sometime between the fourth and seventh centuries.[40] Although in Korea it did not assume as highly an institutionalized form as in its Chinese homeland, Daoist sentiment percolated through Korean culture. Daoism envisions the universe as infused by an invisible but real energy or force called the *qi*, which internally exists as a union of two cosmic opposites, the principles of *yin* and *yang*. The Daoist expert Isabelle Robinet explains that Daoism postulates "a basic dynamic, Qi, which is neither matter nor spirit, existed before the world did, and everything that exists is only an aspect of it, in a lesser or greater state of condensation."[41] Within the qi, yin and yang represent the opposite forces that define each other and together create the various forms and essences of the cosmos. Yin and yang exist as the opposites such as female and male, dark and light, Earth and Heaven, and passivity and activity, that together form the various substances of the universe. The two, Robinet writes, "testify to the basic Oneness that underlies the world, by the close correlation that binds them together. They illustrate the dynamic of opposites, a dynamic that can be seen only in pairs whose opposition shows in the law of alternation that governs their functioning."[42] From yin and yang, Daoism sees the many elements that comprise the world. That is, Daoism envisions a unity behind a duality (yin/yang), beyond the elements of the material world. Much of Daoist thought and practice considers how to achieve harmony between the two cardinal opposites, for example extolling the virtue of *wu wei*, the ideal of actionless action. In lived practice, Daoist practitioners engage in geomancy (*feng shui*), oracles (using the *I Ching*), and alchemical practices meant to lead to longevity and eventually even immortality.

Rather than look to such everyday practices, the *Divine Principle* assumed the balanced dualism of its Korean Daoist background, but recontextualized it in a Christian framework. As the text itself stated,

> [T]he "Book of Changes (*I Ching*)," which is the center of Oriental philosophy . . . emphasizes that the foundation of the universe is Taeguk (ultimacy) and from this comes Yang and Yin (positivity and negativity). From Yang and Yin come the "O-haeing" (five elements: metal, wood, water, fire and soil). All things were created from O-haeing. Positivity and negativity together are called the "Tao" [Dao]. The "Tao" is defined as the "Way," or "Word." That is, Taeguk produced the word (creative principle) and the Word produced all things. Therefore, Taeguk is the first and ultimate cause of all existence and is the unified nucleus of both positivity and negativity. By comparing this with the Bible (John 1:1–3), "The Word was God . . . and all things were created through him," we can see that Taeguk, the subject which contains positivity and negativity, represents God, the subject who contains dual essentialities.[43]

Using the language of physics, Moon attempted to unify Daoism and Christianity. Science, as a transnational and transreligious language, could rhetorically bridge the gap.

The union of particle physics with Daoism and Asian conceptualizations of interdependence would have resonated with a subset of American readers of *Divine Principle*. Just two years after the publication of the Unification text and during the height of the Unification Church's early phases of growth in the United States, the American scientist Fritjof Capra's *The Tao of Physics* swept through academic, scientific, and countercultural circles. Capra described the book as his own attempt to "overcome the gap between rational, analytic thinking and the meditative experience of mystical truths," which he first attempted through hallucinogenic drugs and later developed through examining mysticism and quantum physics in light of one another.[44] Like *Divine Principle*, Capra's book accepted science as a new foundation of human society but hoped to unify the religious and scientific halves of individual and societies. In a sentiment that echoed those of Sun Myung Moon in *Divine Principle*, Capra declared that he intended *The Tao of Physics* "to suggest that Eastern thought, and, more generally, mystic thought provide a consistent and relevant philosophical background to the theories of contemporary science; a conception of the world in which man's scientific discoveries can be in perfect harmony with his spiritual aims and religious beliefs. The two basic themes of this conception are the unity and interrelation of all the phenomena and the intrinsically dynamic nature of the universe."[45] Though the millennial pragmatism of Unificationism frowned on mysticism, Capra and Moon could agree that Daoist inspired notions such as "unity," "interrelation," and the "dynamic nature of the universe" bridged the divide between religion and science. Capra ultimately appealed to a far greater audience than did Unificationism, but both spoke to the same Americans who respected science and scientific-sounding language but looked to religion, specifically Asian religion, for guidance as well. By tapping into the same spirit as Capra, Unificationism broadened its appeal.

Despite the need to bring science and religion together, the distinction between the worlds of spirit and physicality and an ensuing spirit/body dualism characterized the Unification worldview, particularly its understanding of science. The Unification Church insisted that the universe contained more than merely the physical reality accessible through our senses, which hardly distinguished it from most other religious movements. Yet the *Divine Principle* moved beyond merely asserting the reality of the spiritual (i.e., dualism) to promoting a form of parallelism between the material and spiritual. Fundamentally, the spiritual world functioned analogously to the material world, and therefore must be ascertained and studied in a similar manner. *Divine Principle* envisioned the "spirit world"—as the text called the invisible world—as a parallel cosmos to the material one that humans routinely sense and experience, a realm of angels, demons, souls of deceased individuals, and other intelligent aware entities. As real, Moon insisted, as the visible world around us, in fact individuals could observe this spiritual realm using methods analogous to their experience of the physical world. "The invisible world," *Divine Principle* explained, "like the visible world, is a world of reality. It is actually felt and perceived, through the five spiritual senses."[46] Here, Moon provided a hint to the Unificationist view of science and its relation to religion. Science provided the tools to study the visible world. In the spiritual world, religion could do the same. Science therefore paralleled religion as a mode of accumulating knowledge.

The Principle envisioned the dual existence of mind and body as proof of the invisible spirit world, since few would deny that mind and body together make up a whole person, nor that form (external) and substance (internal) together create the visible physical world.[47] Moon labored to demonstrate the reality of the spiritual world for two reasons. First, the authority of *Divine Principle* and Moon himself rested in the spiritual world, particularly in the revelations passed to Moon from the spiritual forms of Jesus and John the Baptist. Second, Moon defined science as the empirical study of the physical world, and religion as the study and engagement with the spiritual world. Only if the spiritual world were as real as the physical world could religion claim the sort of legitimacy as could its sister, science. James R. Lewis calls this use of science to buttress a new religious movement's worldview a "legitimation technique," since it appeals to the authority of science to legitimate the movement. In the case of Unificationism, the parallelism between spirit and material means that the authority of science implied the parallel authority of Unificationist religion.[48] This parallelism of the material and spiritual worlds contained the kernel of the Unification Church's three fundamental positions on science and religion: (1) the inherent value and legitimacy of science in its investigation of the material cosmos; (2) the nature of religion as a parallel or sibling to science that investigated the spiritual realms just as science did the physical world; and (3) the underlying compatibility of and need for both religion and science. Throughout its growth and history in the United States, the Unification Church demonstrated these three basic positions, which culminated in the attitude that religion, and Unificationism especially, must guide science in its methods, aims, and moral bearings. All three positions appeared in *Divine Principle*.

The Unification movement accepted science as a valid, legitimate, valuable, and divinely mandated endeavor. Valid and legitimate, because science aimed to overcome the unnatural condition of human ignorance. Divinely mandated, because ignorance existed through an unintended violation of the divine order, and the removal of that ignorance represented a restoration of the Edenic state of order, and therefore part of humanity's redemption. Like the postwar American scientists who gushed in Walt Disney and Haber's *Our Friend the Atom* that science would spread the wonders of the modern world to all humanity, the *Divine Principle* envisioned science as a means toward creating a heaven on earth. That is, the Unification Church transformed science from a merely human endeavor to a godly one. Here Unificationism again demonstrated a radical but representative approach to science: accepting the progressive scientific American zeitgeist but transposing it into millennial religious language.

Such a position emerged from the Unification view of ignorance: according to the *Divine Principle*, the primordial fall of humanity in the garden of Eden injected ignorance into the cosmic order. "Seen from the viewpoint of knowledge," *Divine Principle* indicates, "the human fall signifies man's descent into the darkness of ignorance."[49] Ignorance requires a predicate—one must be ignorant of something—and on this topic Moon is somewhat vague. Humankind became ignorant of the intended divine order of things, but seemed to also have developed an innate ignorance that characterizes human society. The crucifixion of Jesus, for example, was born of such ignorance. At times Moon indicated that the world itself has become a place of ignorance, a claim that relied upon the Daoist-inspired notion of correspondence between internal and external realities. Individual human internal ignorance sowed the seeds of global social ignorance.[50]

Despite the prevalence of ignorance, *Divine Principle* understood it to be an unnatural state of affairs, one that humanity inherently sought to overcome. Since ignorance interrupted the divinely mandated order of the cosmos, the struggle against it assumed a religious meaning akin to the millennial quest to reestablish the Edenic state.[51] Because the world is intrinsically dualistic, characterized by visible and invisible (or material and spiritual) realities, ignorance must be dispelled on two fronts. Within this endeavor Unificationism recognized the value and purpose of science: "due to the fall, man fell into ignorance of both the spiritual side and the physical side [of reality]. From this point, man's spiritual ignorance has been enlightened by religion while his ignorance of physical reality has been overcome by science."[52] Or, as the introduction to the *Divine Principle* grandiosely stated,

> However, due to the fall, man fell into ignorance without being able to attain a highly developed society. Since then, he has striven to restore the ideal world of scientific development which was purposed in the beginning, by overcoming his ignorance by means of science. Today's highly developed scientific world is being restored externally to the stage directly prior to the transition into the ideal world.[53]

Lest the reader remain unclear as to the nature of science, the *Divine Principle* explicitly declared it the attempt to "overcome this ignorance and restore the light of knowledge . . . the path taken toward the discovery of external truth."[54] Such an approach clearly functioned as a legitimating strategy, demonstrating Unificationism's own perceived value. But it also spoke to the movement's self-understanding as possessing something akin to a scientific epistemology.

Reverend Moon certainly did not invent the notion of science as an activity intended to dispel ignorance and spread the light of knowledge, nor would anyone greet that as a new revelation. A classic understanding of science, this view developed throughout the Enlightenment, became prevalent among many nineteenth-century intellectuals and remained powerful in the late twentieth century as Unificationism spread to the United States. Enlightenment thinkers such as David Hume and Jean-Jacques Rousseau basked in the light of science, envisioning ignorance as a darkness that would disappear if only science could more brightly shine. In the nineteenth century, social scientist Augustus Comte founded the school of positivism, or the "religion of humanity," as he called it, which declared empirically observable scientific facts the basis of all philosophy and theology. Comte declared that the old beliefs of religion, Roman Catholicism especially, faded under the observation of science.[55] In the twentieth century, scientists such as the astronomer Carl Sagan continued to look to science in the same way. Sagan appropriately titled his 1996 book *The Demon-Haunted World: Science as a Candle in the Dark*, since the author hoped to employ the tools of science to dispel popular ignorance about subjects ranging from UFOs to ESP to Atlantis to some forms of religion itself. The Unification Church shied away from the scientific triumphalism of Comte and Sagan, but like Comte and Sagan, Moon imagined science as a great light that dispelled the darkness of ignorance.

Within Unificationist thought, science and religion offered a two-pronged attempt to overcome ignorance. If science represented the pursuit of material knowledge, then religion, in a parallel endeavor, considered the spiritual world. As a result of this position, *Divine Principle* portrayed religion as something between a twin of and a type of science. Unificationism posited that religion and science complemented each other, that while science considered the visible and external worlds, religion studied the internal and invisible worlds. Equally real worlds, the *Divine Principle* insisted on the study of each as necessary to dispel the ignorance foisted upon humanity by the Edenic fall. Of science, the *Divine Principle* declared: "[o]n the [one] hand, man's physical ignorance has been greatly overcome by the scientific research of the 'world of result,' the natural (or physical) world which is familiar to everyone." In terms of religion, it continued, "man's spiritual ignorance has gradually been overcome as he searched for the invisible 'world of cause' through religion."[56] Parallel developments, both religion and science sought answers to questions about the dualistic world. Science asked questions such as "What is the basis of the material world?" and "What are the natural laws of physical phenomena?" Religion asked "What is the origin of humanity?" "What is the purpose of life?" and "What is good and evil?"[57]

Here the *Divine Principle* treaded on well-worn ground, reiterating the classic argument that religion and science exist as separate spheres. During the heyday of Unificationism's rise in the United States, the paleontologist and Harvard professor Stephen Jay Gould (1941–2002) perhaps best represented the mainstream appeal of the separate spheres approach. An accomplished scientist, Gould also thrived in the role of a public intellectual, and his *Rock of Ages: Science and Religion in the Fullness of Life*, published in the waning years of his life, succinctly summarized the ideological positions that he held throughout the decades. Gould coined his own term, "non-overlapping magisteria," (NOMA) to explain why religion and science could coexist as mutually distinguishable realms of human knowledge and activity. Borrowing the Latin term *magisteria* from its Catholic context, where it means a domain of authoritative teaching, Gould's NOMA doctrine limited religion and science to two mutually exclusionary separate spheres. "Science tries to document the factual character of the natural world, and to develop theories that coordinate and explain these facts. Religion, on the other hand, operates in the equally important, but utterly different, realm of human purposes, meanings, and values—subjects that the factual domain of science might illuminate, but can never resolve."[58] Although this argument has its advantages, especially for those who willingly turn to science for factual data and to religion for moral guidance, it failed to impress critics who insisted that their religion possessed empirical truths, which could range from the age of the Earth, to the manner in which humans and animals appeared on the Earth, or when human life begins. In the eyes of critics, Gould's position and similar separate-spheres approaches limited religion to near irrelevancy, effectively emasculating its ability to present truth-statements in the public sphere. Yet the *Divine Principle* in adapting this approach retained a much stronger position for religion, because it accepted the reality of the spiritual world, a cosmos beyond the ability of science to comprehend. "A sailor making a voyage on the sea of the material world under the sail of science in search of the pleasures of the flesh may reach the coast of his ideal," the *Divine Principle* admitted, "but he will soon find it to be nothing more than a graveyard to hold his flesh. But when the sailor who has completed his voyage in search of external truth under the sail of science comes into contact with the sea-route to internal truth, under the sail of religion, he will be able to end his voyage in the ideal world, which is the goal of the original mind's desire."[59] That only the sail of religion ultimately brought seekers to the port of truth indicates why Unificationism looked to itself as a guide for its fellow vessel science.

Such a position created a paradox. It admitted a valid sphere of research for religion, but it also implied that the best religion looked and acted like science. That is, Unificationism saw religion as needing to adopt the methodology and techniques of science but to then apply them to the spiritual realm. The best religion therefore employed rationalism, empiricism, and logic, and not, as Kierkegaard would have it, faith. A true heir to the Enlightenment-era Protestant Reformers, the *Divine Principle* admitted that previous generations might have accepted miracles and wonders as evidence of divine favor, but such an age had passed. The book's introduction explained, "Jesus' performance of miracles and his revelation of signs were to let the people know that he was the Messiah and enable them to believe in him. Knowledge comes from cognition, and man today cannot cognize anything which lacks logic and scientific proof."[60] In classic Protestant form the text implied that miracles functioned as proof for earlier eras, yet could no longer do so in the modern scientific world.[61] It continued, "[t]o understand something, there must first be cognition. Thus, internal truth also requires logical proof. Religion has been moving through the long course of history toward an age in which it must be explained scientifically."[62] The *Divine Principle* explicitly assumed that potential converts to Unificationism wanted a scientifically grounded religion, one that appealed to their cognitive abilities rather than to emotions or faith. Here the Unification Church demonstrated a very savvy awareness of its potential converts in the English-speaking world: the modern, college-educated youth of the 1970s.

Unificationism competed with other religions for the same converts. *Divine Principle* recognized that, and in a not-so-subtle jab declared, "[i]t is thus impossible to satisfy completely man's desire for truth, in this modern scientific civilization, by using the same method of expressing the truth, in parables and symbols, which was used to awaken the people of an earlier age. In consequence, today the truth must appear with a higher standard and with a scientific method of expression in order to enable intelligent modern man to understand it."[63] Such a position impacted the methods and rhetoric of Unificationist proselytizing, and also explained what the movement saw as the declension of Western religion. *Divine Principle* explained such decline as the result of two factors. First, individual church leaders acted immorally, casting shame on the whole of religion. Second, religion failed to keep up with the times. "Another factor has fated religion to decline. Modern men, whose intelligence has developed to the utmost degree, demand scientific proof for all things. However, religious doctrine, which remains unchanged, does not interpret things scientifically. That is to say, man's interpretation of internal truth (religion) and his interpretation of external truth (science) do not agree."[64] The Unification movement looked to possible solutions to this problem. It would sponsor events designed to bring religious groups together, as well as the conferences meant to shepherd science toward a common goal of serving humanity. Behind those attempts, the Church held onto the millennial hope of finally bringing together science and religion.

If Unificationism saw science and religion as a two-pronged attempt to overcome ignorance, then much of the creative tension in the Church's engagement with science emerged from confusion over whether science and religion were two prongs of the same fork, or two individual utensils descending upon the same morsel of truth. That is, must science and religion act in complete parallel, or ought they remain totally independent? Generally, the *Divine Principle* and Unificationism adopted a two-spheres approach to science and religion, seeing each as necessary. Simultaneously it held hope for guiding science in accord with its own religious positions. In most cases, the text clearly portrayed science and religion as separate, though perhaps not equal, spheres. Just as "[n]either can there be a spiritual world apart from a physical world, nor spiritual happiness apart from true physical happiness," Unificationism declared the need for both religion and science.[65] In a statement that admitted to the power of science yet sought to stake a claim for religion as well, the introduction to *Divine Principle* declared that humanity "has been approaching a solution to the fundamental questions of life by following two different courses. The first course is to search for the solution within the material world. Those who take this route think it to be the sublime path. They yield to science, taking pride in its omnipotence, and seek material happiness." Yet, *Divine Principle* asked, "can man enjoy full happiness when he limits his search to external material conditions centered upon the physical body? Science may create a pleasant social environment in which man can enjoy the utmost in wealth, but is such an environment able to satisfy the spiritual desire of the inner man?"[66] Though science without religion offered only limited happiness, religion without science provided equally unsatisfying results. "Religion has until now de-emphasized the value of everyday reality; it has denied the value of physical happiness in order to stress the attainment of spiritual joy. However strenuously man may try, he cannot cut himself off from reality, nor can he annihilate the desire for physical happiness that follows him always like a shadow."[67]   This approach indicated the need for both religion and science, but a tension remained over how the two ought to relate. This tension, and the ironies that it entailed, carried through into Unificationism's outreach efforts. It is to those efforts, culminating in the International Conferences on the Unity of the Sciences, that we now turn.

2

Science and the American Unification Church

This chapter traces the major Unification positions on science though the *Divine Principle* and the Unification institutions that the group founded in the 1970s and 1980s. Through their texts and organizations, the Unification Church upheld several basic positions: respect for science as a positive force for humanity; consideration of religion as a parallel endeavor that ought to follow similar methods as science; valuation of religion generally and Unificationism specifically as offering ultimate solutions that could serve as guides to both science and religion. These positions assumed the basic approach of envisioning religion and science as separate spheres, as well as supported the movement's millennial perspective that it needed to shepherd science and religion together in order to restore the Edenic kingdom of heaven on earth.

Reaching Out: Science and World Transformation

Unlike many new religions, the Unification Church generally eschewed sectarianism and separatism. As a "progressive millennial movement," to use Wessinger's term, they sought to engage and transform society rather than retreat from it.[1] In their study of Unificationism, David Bromley and Anson Shupe labeled the Unification Church a "world-transforming" movement, that is "one that aims at total change of the social structure through employing persuasion as its primary strategy."[2] As opposed to "world-denying" movements that isolate themselves from what they consider the polluting or irredeemable elements outside their own group, world-transforming groups engage the world in hopes of remaking it according to their own ideals.

The Unification Church indeed aimed to transform the world and looked to science as a tool toward that end. Among the ways in which Unificationism sought world transformation, they established semi-independent agencies and institutions to spread Unificationist ideals outside the movement itself. As critics have charged, some of these "front" organizations failed to clearly reveal their association with the Unification Church, while others even intentionally misled people, although the majority publicly disclosed their affiliation.[3] By definition they promoted a type of indirect proselytizing, hoping to spread the Unificationist message, even if most of the agencies did not seek converts. Fundamentally, the Church envisioned its organizations as actors in the establishment of the new millennium, and individual Unificationists looked on their involvement in these agencies as part of their religious service. Many of the semi-independent Unification agencies looked to science as an aid to establishing that heaven on earth.

As one of the largest of those semi-independent groups, the Unification-financed student organization, the Collegiate Association for the Research of Principles, more commonly known by its acronym CARP, brought Unification principles to college campuses and the youth subculture more broadly. CARP primarily worked through a widely available newspaper, the *World Student Times*, rather than through face-to-face dialogue. The newspaper did not officially reveal its relationship with Unificationism, though most issues in their back pages printed summaries of Unification principles alongside a picture of the Reverend Moon labeled "Rev. Sun Myung Moon—the inspiration of CARP." CARP also provided a good example of the way in which a Unificationist organization looked to and utilized science in its world-transforming mission. The *World Student Times* frequently published stories related to science, often stressing the key points of Unificationism's position on it—the value of science, the compatibility of science with religion, the need for religion to become more scientific and rational, and of course the value of Unificationism in guiding the two.

CARP sometimes employed its *World Student Times* to subtly hint at the Unification view of science, rather that declare it outright. The *World Student Times*'s coverage of the 1978 Nobel Prize in Physics provides a representative example. The three-column story detailed the prize given to Arno A. Penzias and Robert W. Wilson for their work on the Big Bang theory, specifically on cosmic background radiation. After summarizing the theory and the scientists' research, the article's third column focused on its relevance to religion. "Questions arise such as: What cause produced this effect? Who or what put the matter and the energy into the universe? Was the universe created out of nothing or out of some pre-existing matter? For the first time there seems to be substantial evidence for a First Cause." Here the *World Student Times* article alluded to a time-honored philosophical proof of the deity's existence, in this case the cosmological argument. As stated by Aristotle and later Aquinas, the existence of the universe implied a Prime Mover or

First Cause, which both philosophers identify as God. Science, the Unificationist newspaper claimed, had now provided "substantial evidence" for the cosmological argument. The article continued, "[t]heologians were generally delighted but the astronomers were curiously upset by this." Such a subtle jab at scientists, following a prolonged discussion of the research's importance, served to simultaneously highlight the value of astronomical science itself in providing evidence of God's existence, while reinforcing the value of religious answers over and against the authority of individual scientists. Lest the reader forget that there were good scientists as well, the article approvingly cited Albert Einstein as endorsing of the concept of a "beginning," which the article implied was equivalent to the First Cause. The article concluded with a reminder that CARP and the *World Student Times* asked only for evidence, implying a distinction from other religious groups, which in the Unificationist view depended upon faith.[4] Such a position allowed the Unification Church to use science to positively position itself vis-à-vis other, competing, religious groups.

Other *World Student Times* articles more directly and forcefully made the connection between Unificationism and science. An October 1980 article, "An Introduction to the Divine Principle: What the Moonies Believe," highlighted the scientific nature of Unificationism. It introduced *Divine Principle* as "a framework in which to order, interpret, and give meaning to the empirical data of our daily life. Its unique appeal to idealistic, intelligent young people rests firmly in its teaching of the complementary importance of faith and reason." Few religious movements would refer to their sacred texts as "frameworks" for interpreting "empirical data," and of course the Unification Church more commonly characterized *Divine Principle* as a revelation that completed the Christian Bible. Yet the *World Student Times* portrayed the movement's text using explicitly scientific terminology. Clearly, the church sought to portray itself as modern, scientific, rational, and entirely compatible with the contemporary world. Adopting an almost apologetic tone, the article explained: "[o]ur physical universe is an effect, as [the] result of some 'unknown' cause. Let us call this invisible cause 'God.' This is the same line of reasoning that allows us to 'believe in' and even utilize X-rays by observing the effect (exposed film) of these invisible causal agents. Thus, science, logic, and reason all support the existence of an invisible causal agent for our visible, resultant universe. *Divine Principle* simply calls this causal agent 'God.'" With "belief," "God," and even "unknown," safely cordoned off by quotes, alongside a technical metaphor that invoked modern particle physics, the text made its explicitly religious message more palatable to the authors' intended audience: idealistic, intelligent, scientifically attuned young people. This article concluded along the same lines as the previous one on the 1978 Nobel Prize in Physics, with a rhetorical insistence on Unificationism's authority. *Divine Principle*, it explained, offered both practical guidelines as well as the answer to the scientific question of "the origin of the physical universe."[5]

In transposing religious concepts into more secular language, Unificationism again offered a radicalized but representative glimpse into postwar American religion. Norman Vincent Peale, who transformed Christianity into "the power of positive thinking" stands out as representative of this strain of religious thought. In his discourse Peale avoided not just theological jargon but any overtly religious language. As R. Laurence Moore has written, "[f]aith, prayer, and Scripture, Peale said, existed for one thing—to help individuals overcome their feelings of insecurity and inferiority."[6] The same social forces that led to Peale's tremendous success also led the Unificationists to employ nonreligious language in their proselytizing. Though the Protestant theological "Death of God" movement was perhaps even more radical in this regard than Unificationism, its desire to completely convert Christianity into a nontheistic belief system similarly points to the growing power of secularized religious language in postwar America.

Many other Unification outreach groups similarly invoked science, either offering unifying solutions or situating themselves as scientifically attuned organizations. For example, the Freedom Leadership Foundation (FLF), a Unification anticommunist agency led by future Unification Church president Neil Albert Salonen, published a pamphlet in the mid-1970s trumpeting that "[t]he Freedom Leadership Foundation does not meet the Communist challenge in a passive or defensive way. It projects a positive alternative, a dynamic synthesis of religious and scientific thinking—the Unification Ideology." A page later, the pamphlet explained that "[t]he Unification Theology overcomes outdated Marxist theory by showing scientifically that cooperation and harmony—not contradiction and struggle as Marxism asserts—are the motivating forces of human progress."[7] Like Sang Ik Choi's San Francisco–based Re-Education Foundation a decade earlier, the FLF minimized its religious orientation in this example of its proselytizing material. One might view the pamphlet as evidence of a cover-up or intentional deception. Yet given that the FLF publicly revealed its association with Reverend Moon and the Unification Church, a better explanation sees the pamphlet as evidence of a group that highly valued science and sought in a competitive religious marketplace to convey its compatibility with the modern, scientific world.

Turning In: Science and Institutionalization

During the early to mid-1970s the Unification Church not only sought to transform the world through the Collegiate Association for the Research of Principles, the Freedom Leadership Foundation, and other outreach agencies, it also institutionalized itself. With a unifying sacred text, *Divine Principle*, a more centralized organizational structure led by Moon himself, and a rising cash-flow from its increasing membership, the Unification Church turned toward establishing institutions that served the movement's members themselves rather than recruit new ones. Of these, the Unification Theological Seminary (UTS) provided a crucial educational center to train Unificationists and serve as intellectual hub of the American movement. Unification scholars associated with the UTS further developed English-language Unification theology, while seminarians formally engaged the study of their movement's ideology and worldview. Given its prevalence in their sacred text, unsurprisingly its faculty and students considered science and its relation to Unificationism.

Purchased in 1974 from the Christian Brothers, a monastic Roman Catholic educational order, the campus that became Unification Theological Seminary in the small town of Barrytown, New York, sits approximately one hundred miles north of New York City along the Hudson River. It occupies a fortuitous geography for a center of a new religious movement. A decade earlier and thirty miles to the southeast in the town of Millbrook, Harvard professors and counterculture protagonists Timothy Leary and Baba Ram Dass (né Richard Alpert) conducted their (in)famous mid-1960s LSD experiments. Seventeen miles to Barrytown's west sits the town of Woodstock, the utopian Catskill mountain town and namesake of the music festival. Unification Theological Seminary began operation in September 1975 with a faculty of five full-time professors and fifty students.[8] Unificationist pioneer David S. C. Choi assumed the presidency of the new institution. In his written welcoming message to seminary students, Choi explained the role of the new institution with reference to the offspring of science, technology. "Man's spiritual development has not kept pace with the dramatic technological advances of recent years," warned Choi. Following the *Divine Principle*'s lead in understanding spiritual and material as parallel world and pursuits, Choi justified the new UTS as a solution to that problem.[9]

Following their president's lead, a number of the seminary faculty turned to questions of religion and science. Five years after UTS's birth, Dr. Kurt Johnson, a part-time instructor at the Unification Theological Seminary, outlined and taught an elective course titled The Scientific Basis of Divine Principle, which repeated the following academic year, and drew from Johnson's own expertise in biology as well as that of four other scientist-lecturers.[10] The UTS course catalog described the new course as a "survey of contemporary scientific information and philosophy and its corroborative relation to Sun Myung Moon's Principle of Creation, with a view to developing the student's ability to apply Divine Principle models to his or her particular professional interest."[11] In the preface to his course-pack, Johnson explained that "the materials have been prepared as a beginning toward an understanding of 'The Principle' and its relation to science." However, that science "corroborated" Unificationism, as the course description indicated, became a theme of the course, hence its name, The Scientific Basis of Divine Principle.[12]

Johnson's course covered the history of science as well as the relation of Unification thought to particular scientific fields, such as genetics, health sciences, evolutionary biology, and political science. Like many other instructors, he stated his goals in his syllabus, included in the course-pack: "The course will have several goals: 1. To develop an itemization of topics in which Divine Principle can be in dialogue with science. 2. To set goals about developing statements concerning Divine Principle and its particular relationships to various scientific disciplines and their applications. 3. To develop a curriculum of science and religion at the Seminary. 4. To become conversant about science and the Divine Principle in a credible way."[13] Generally, Johnson looked to science as a form of knowledge that paralleled religion and provided valuable support to the Unificationist perspective. The same basic Unificationist approach to science found in *Divine Principle* also underlay Johnson's course. Similar to other Unificationist texts, the course-pack included a chart that related science and religion to each other, setting up two neat columns or separate spheres. In the case of the Johnson course's booklet, the chart appeared on the first page of readings for the first lecture:

TABLE 2.1

Religion	*Science*
internal experience	external experience
language of expression of truth through "myth" and abstraction	language based on recording observations and ideas about what these mean
based on personal experience and otherwise not testable	concerned with nonpersonal, testable experiences[14]

In keeping with wider Unificationist perspectives Johnson envisioned religion and science as parallel but compatible entities. The instructor also provided a more theoretical basis to the separate spheres approach, explaining that science and religion fundamentally differed because science "[h]as traditionally been 'inductive,' assembling many small observations and using these to reason to a larger generality." Religion, on the other hand, "[h]as traditionally been 'deductive': it tells you what is true and everything is patterned from that point of view."[15] Yet this distinction, Johnson declared, proved illusionary. Leaning on the philosopher of science Karl Popper, Johnson explained that science also followed a deductive system of hypothesis that sought out data, rather than blindly assemble data and then create a hypothesis. Alluding to Thomas Kuhn (whom he discussed in a later lecture), Johnson indicated that sets of such hypotheses form the basis of science for a time, but that "these can change as science progresses."[16] Science, like religion, offered a paradigm to the world.

The fact that the two shared an epistemological foundation indicated to Johnson that one could combine them to solve the problem of resolution. "How is reality to be observed, how is it to be talked about, how is it to be described? Here science and religion are both seeking answers. Therefore, the marriage of science and religion in a deductive mode is a major step forward in the relation of science and religion."[17] Johnson and his guest lecturers dedicated much of the semester to explaining how science and religion could marry, specifically how science supported, or "corroborated" in his terms, Unification thought. Quantum physics, Johnson noted, "is consistent with the Divine Principle," as were molecular and evolutionary biology, and political science.[18] Yet the course offered far more than a scientific rubber stamp of Unificationism. Johnson introduced philosophy and history of science as well as basic scientific theories to his students, ranging from Popper to Kuhn to quantum physics. He also insisted that his students take science seriously, for example encouraging them to think about ways in which one might read the Principle's narrative of Adam and Eve alongside evolutionary biology. He concluded the lecture on creation and evolution, the last of three classes that considered Unificationism and evolutionary biology, with a call to his students to incorporate modern science with religion. "It will behoove Unification members to work as hard as possible to help deal in a credible way between science and Divine Principle. If the restoration of the world is actually an agenda of the Unification Movement, short cuts in relation to science, such as distorting, not understanding, misrepresenting, or oversimplifying concepts in science will only work against the cause."[19] Invoking the movement's millennial ambitions of world transformation, Johnson insisted on an underlying compatibility between religion and science, even on the sticky issue of evolution.

As a scientist-theologian, Johnson was not alone in seeking to rectify the relationship between science and religion. Fritjof Capra's work on *The Tao of Physics* certainly reflects a similar intent, though Capra made little impact among other scientists. The efforts of the scientist-theologians of the Institute on Religion in an Age of Science (IRAS) offers a wider parallel to the work of Johnson and the Unification Church. Throughout the late 1950s and 1960s, the Institute on Religion hosted retreats for scientifically attuned theologians and theologically attuned scientists to meet and discuss the relation and possible fusion of religion and science. Culminating in two books—*Science Ponders Religion* and *Religion Ponders Science*—as well as a journal on religion and science still in publication—*Zygon: Journal of Religion and Science*—the IRAS revealed that mainstream scientists and theologians similarly hoped to bring their fields into closer contact and friendship.[20] Johnson and the Unification Church's goals of demonstrating the two's compatibility hardly differed from the Institute on Religion in an Age of Science. Only the Unificationists' millennial vision of the eventual union of religion and science marks the new religion as more radical that the position of IRAS's scientist-theologians.

The International Conferences on the Unity of the Sciences

The Unification Church was not unique among new religious movements for sponsoring science conferences—both Transcendental Meditation and the Hare Krishnas held such events—but in terms of time frame, scale, and academic rigor, the Unificationist movement's International Conferences on the Unity of the Sciences (ICUS) outshined the other religions'. The ICUS conferences also revealed the group's overarching view of science: that religion, and the Unification Church specifically, must *guide* science in order to create, in secular terms, an ideal future, or in religious terms, the millennial realization of a heaven on earth. Such a position evidenced itself in the manner in which the Unification Church organized and managed the International Conferences, as well as in Reverend Moon's founder's addresses, speeches that he presented at each of the ICUS gatherings.

The Unification Church created the International Conference on the Unity of the Sciences, but it adopted ICUS from another organization, the utopian Council for Unified Research and Education (CURE), which held the first, and only, "International Conference on Unified Science," in 1972. The brainchild of Edward Haskell (1906–86), CURE dedicated itself to synthesizing all knowledge into a single coherent body of "unified science." Though the Council existed as little more than the project of the independently endowed Haskell, who had never completed his PhD nor worked within the world of academic, government, or industrial science, CURE peaked in 1972 with the publication of a book, *Full Circle: The Moral Force of Unified Science*. The book urged the world's scientists to adopt a new standard, that of unified science, "the convergence of insights from all fields," which would unite all knowledge under a single rubric. Haskell went so far as to develop a chart that collected and organized atoms, molecules, stars, galaxies, and human cultures under a single rubric.[21] The same year, CURE held the International Conference on Unified Science in order to spread its position. One year earlier, the Unification Church had asked Haskell to lead a symposium on unified science, which the church naturally saw as an ally in its utopian ambitions. Moon personally took an interest in Haskell's work and approached the scientist to offer his movement's financial support of a conference on unified science. On the condition that CURE retain sole authority over "subject, persons, discussions, and so forth," in Haskell's words, he accepted the offer.[22] Thus was born the International Conference on Unified Science (ICUS I), held in New York's Waldorf-Astoria Hotel on Thanksgiving week, 1972, with Moon giving a keynote address on "The Role of Unified Science in the Moral Orientation of the World." Though some anti-cult activists later accused the Unification Church of bankrolling CURE or running it as a front organization, after the second ICUS conference Haskell and CURE went their separate way from Moon and the Unification Church. The Unificationists, however, adopted ICUS as their own and began planning for the conferences' future. The Council for Unified Research and Education languished and eventually disappeared following Haskell's death.

Moon and the Unification Church transformed the ICUS from a onetime event founded by an avant-garde scientific outsider to a thirty-year series so scientifically mainstream that it regularly attracted America's top-clearance nuclear scientists and tenured academic professors from throughout the global community of physical and social scientists. They also changed its name to the International Conferences on the Unity of the Sciences, eschewing the more sectarian notion of "Unified Science" that Haskell upheld, and instead suggesting the broader "Unity of the Sciences" as its goal, using the word "sciences" in the plural form. The second conference, in Tokyo (1973), served as a transition, with Haskell still in attendance alongside a preponderance of philosophers of science and a few physical scientists. The third

International Conference (1974), now fully under the wing of the Unification Church, attracted numerous mainstream and highly regarded scientists, with one hundred twenty-eight in attendance, including seventeen Nobel laureates. The Chancellor of Cambridge University, the neurologist Lord Edgar Adrian, Baron of Cambridge, chaired the conference, with British scientists R. V. Jones, England's former head of wartime science and personal scientific advisor to Winston Churchill, and Kenneth Mellanby, head of the Institute for Terrestrial Ecology at Monks Wood Experimental Station, as vice-chairs.[23] The third ICUS set the tone for the future conferences: the Unification Church's sub-organization, the International Cultural Foundation, subsidized the meeting, and individual Unificationists, primarily students, served as the administrators and support personnel for the conference. Moon kept a low profile, speaking during the opening banquet for a founder's address but otherwise absenting himself from the meetings. In fact, the most notable controversy appeared when some of the scientists, including Lord Adrian himself, admitted to not knowing who Moon was or what connection he had with the conference.[24]

TABLE 2.2

Conference	Year	Location
ICUS I	1972	New York City, NY
ICUS II	1973	Tokyo, Japan
ICUS III	1974	London, England
ICUS IV	1975	New York City, NY
ICUS V	1976	Washington, D.C.
ICUS VI	1977	San Francisco, CA
ICUS VII	1978	Boston, MA
ICUS VIII	1979	Los Angeles, CA
ICUS IX	1980	Miami Beach, FL
ICUS X	1981	Seoul, South Korea
ICUS XI	1982	Philadelphia, PA
ICUS XII	1983	Chicago, IL
ICUS XIII	1984	Washington, D.C.
ICUS XIV	1985	Houston, TX
ICUS XV	1986	Washington, D.C.
ICUS XVI	1987	Atlanta, GA
ICUS XVII	1988	Los Angeles, CA
ICUS XVIII	1991	Seoul, South Korea
ICUS XIX	1992	Seoul, South Korea
ICUS XX	1995	Seoul, South Korea
ICUS XXI	1997	Washington, D.C.
ICUS XXII	2000	Seoul, South Korea[4]

Although to what degree Moon and his church influenced the proceedings would become a point of contention, throughout the history of the conferences the attending scientists uniformly reported that the Unificationists did not intrude or limit the scientists' presentations.[25] Though Moon himself decided on the overall theme for the event, committees of academic scientists, none of them Unificationists, decided on the nature of the panels and sessions and invited participants to present papers at the conferences. Some committees followed the overall conference theme more tightly than others, with the result that the individual papers sometimes had nothing to do with the theme of the overall conference, a reality that became especially prevalent as the conferences grew in size.[26] Most of the papers at the third ICUS somehow considered the theme of "Science and Absolute Values," some narrowly and other broadly. For example, Committee IV, which focused on science, values, and the university, featured papers ranging from "Ideology and Practice of the Democratic University of the Netherlands as Instituted by Law of 1970" (Arthur Rörsch) to "Word and Thought: Towards a Harmony of the Sciences" (Hans Popper).[27] The twelfth ICUS (1983), by contrast, focused on "Absolute Values and the Reassessment of the Contemporary World" and featured everything from a historical paper on Michael Faraday's apprenticeship to assessments of nuclear deterrence strategies to a session on the metaphysics of eco-philosophy.[28]

Moon and the Unificationists realized that few scientists would attend a conference with obvious religious overtones, certainly not if confronted with overt proselytizing. Rather than hope the ICUS series would convert scientists to the movement, the Unificationists looked upon the International Conferences as part of their millennial quest of establishing a heaven on earth. The church and the scientists attending its conferences concurred that science offered opportunities for social, individual, and global progress, and the Unification Church focused on this agreement. Reverend Moon's proposal at the 1981 Tenth International Conference on the Unity of the Sciences provides a good example. Moon's address at ICUS X held special significance among the many speeches he gave at the ICUS events because for the first time, Moon discussed in depth the Unification Church and its relation to the conferences it subsidized. In explaining his religious movement to scientists, he stressed its millennial ambitions: "religion's purpose is the salvation of the world rather than just the salvation of individuals or families. . . . Then what is the Unification Church? It is the new religion destined to carry out this historic mission."[29] He then made a startling declaration: the path to world peace and millennial perfection lay in building a transnational highway system that would unite all cultures, religions, and ideologies, beginning with a underwater highway linking China, North and South Korea, and Japan. Science and technology could serve the world by supporting this endeavor. In the written proposal that the Unification Church later produced, based on Moon's speech at the ICUS, the movement's founder explicitly linked the religious theme of millennial tranquility to the development of a technological solution:

> Towards realizing this ideal of "humanity as one family and all men as brothers," I propose the building of an International Highway which will link the countries of the East and West. . . . This proposal is part of a concrete plan to realize the ideal world of the future as quickly as possible. Such a plan calls for the realization of Heaven on Earth by developing a network of highspeed transportation which will bind the peoples of the world into one.[30]

Moon concluded by calling for scientists and technologists to support his proposal, which would include an invention of long-range "pneumatic tube system" of freight links throughout the world. The scientists in attendance responded by unanimously voting for a resolution supporting "the spirit behind" the proposal, though not the proposal itself, the feasibility of which many of the attendees doubted.[31]

Although Moon downplayed the unification of science in this particular proposal, he nevertheless revealed why the Unification Church continued to support the ICUS conferences: they served its millennial goals of creating the ideal world, which required the support of science and technology in addition to religion. As the church's International Cultural Foundation declared in the sixteenth ICUS's "Statement of Purpose" (1987), "[i]nsights from science, religion, and culture should be harmonized into one worldview as the foundation for a new, global culture transcending the national, religious, racial and ideological biases present within culture. Given this vision of the integral wholeness of the world, it is believed that there can emerge a unified, comprehensive worldview consistent with the human knowledge derived from scientific inquiry as well as from religious and cultural experience."[32] This statement directly paralleled the perspective of the movement's sacred text, *Divine Principle*, as previously discussed, in its hope for a unified ideology drawing from both science and religion. Unificationist millennialism also explained why the ICUS conferences, like *Divine Principle* and other Unification texts, assumed two mutually exclusive paradigms, the first that science and religion existed as separate spheres, and the second that they ought to merge or unify. The first paradigm held in normal time, but the Unificationists looked to the second as the ideal relationship of religion and science destined by the advent of the millennial age.

An interplay between these two paradigms became evident in Sun Myung Moon's founder's addresses, the speeches he presented during the opulent opening banquets of the International Conferences on the Unity of the Sciences. Moon generally stressed the separate spheres approach, implying the need for the distinct coexistences of both science and religion. For example, when addressing the sixth ICUS (1977), held in San Francisco, the birthplace of the American Unification movement, he declared that science and religion each asked different questions, in words that Stephen Jay Gould would have felt comfortable speaking. "Religion and philosophy concern themselves with metaphysical and moral questions that have long occupied man's consciousness." Conversely, "[s]cience limits itself to concern with the regularities of the universe and understanding things in space and time."[33] Rather than conflict, Moon saw innate compatibility between religion and science, both of which sought truth and explanation: "[f]urthermore, in contemplating the mystery and wonder of man and the universe, religion and science, through inspiration, logic, and observation, both seek to explain, or at least point to, the Cause that brought into existence the universe and mankind."[34] Two years later, in a somewhat more defensive note, Moon insisted that science ought not intrude upon religion's sphere. He singled out questions of the nature and cause of existence as outside science's purview. Science could study the makeup, function, and behavior of DNA, he allowed, but only religion could comment on how it came to exist. On the matter of origins, science needed to cede to religion.[35]

As such a warning indicates, Moon did not abdicate to science the role of sole arbiter of truth. He did not, in other words, follow Gould in declaring *factual statement* the domain of science, and he certainly disagreed with Carl Sagan, who looked to science as the only candle capable of illuminating the darkness of human thought and society. Returning to the basic positions throughout Unification sacred texts, Moon accepted the value of science, and even the need for religion to be scientific, but he also posited the ultimate value of religion over science. In his addresses before the scientists gathered at the ICUS events, Moon would emphasize the first of these perspectives, imply the second, and put the third into practice. The third of these positions, the belief that religion offered value that science could not, underlay the purpose of the International Conferences. Science, the Unificationists hoped, would follow the lead of religion, which offered a standard of absolute value around which science might unify itself.

Perhaps working under the sound psychological assumption that one offers praise alongside critique, Moon frequently reiterated the value of science throughout his founder's addresses. Like the *Divine Principle* and its predecessor texts, Moon saw science as a force of human progress, one that offered an increase in quality of life. In the opening of his ICUS IV (1975) address, Moon extolled "the original motivation and purpose of science, which is to bring about human happiness."[36] Several years later at the eighth International Conference, held in 1979 in Los Angeles, Moon praised science in the sort of glowing language that one expects of a true believer in scientific progress. "Scientists who have had a sense that theirs is a crucial mission as contributors to mankind have continued, on the one hand, to pursue ultimate scientific truth and, on the other, to apply scientific technology in almost every field of human endeavor. The resulting benefits have been fantastic economic growth, material affluence, and physic[al] well-being such as mankind has never before known."[37] Each of his founder's addresses included similar accolades to science, though sometimes qualified with language similar to that of the eighth ICUS, that only some scientists have dedicated themselves to the noble aims of true science.

Moon also, no doubt to the elation of the scientists, remarked on the need for religion to look more like science. Contemporary religion failed, he insisted during his address to the eleventh ICUS (1982), because it could not satisfy the modern scientifically attuned person. In language echoing that of *Divine Principle*, here Moon explained that "[u]nless reasonable and consistent answers are available and given, today's intellectuals are not willing to accept religions such as Christianity."[38] Because intelligent people demanded religions that appealed to their intellects and completely accorded with modern scientific finding, the world needed a new religious ideology, one at peace with science. Lest any of the scientists attending the conference doubted to which religion Moon referred, he explicated it: "[i]t is the Unification Church that emerged to solve various problems of the absolute value perspective. This value perspective can, in turn, resolve the great confusion of the world. The Unification Church is comprehensive, logical, and reasonable, and its teachings known as the Unification Principle and Unification Thought have the power to engender total spiritual awakening to all men of conscience and intellect."[39] Like CARP and the other Unification Church proselytizing endeavors, Moon stressed the scientific nature of Unificationism, amplifying and revealing its continuing appeal to young Americans.

Yet Moon's founder's speeches did far more than merely parrot the standard Unificationist position as developed decades earlier by himself and other Unification leaders, namely that his own movement needed to guide science in order to establish a millennial future. He also commented on timely scientific matters, paralleling the wider discussions among scientific circles and the view of science in the larger society. He regularly touched on issues of pollution, population growth, nuclear contamination, fears of technology out-of-control, questions of who should determine science policy, and whether science needed limits on its methods and ambitions. Like many other religious leaders, Moon and his Unification Church looked to themselves as guides for science, particularly in matters related to growing environmentalist concerns. During the heyday of the ICUS events, the American ecological consciousness was rocked by both the near-nuclear disaster at Three Mile Island and the environmental catastrophe at Love Canal. As Robert Booth Fowler has indicated in his *The Greening of Protestant Thought*, during the 1970s and 1980s both mainline and evangelical Protestants came to see themselves as stewards of the environment, and felt that they needed to offer guidance to the techno-scientific establishment on how to treat the created natural world.[40] Moon's desire to direct—*guide*—the aims of science and technology exists within this pattern of growing stewardship.

Moon's address to the second ICUS (1973), provided an example of how Moon invoked Unification theology and thus hoped to guide contemporary science. Recalling the Daoist-inspired notions of duality between subjects and objects that infused his movement, Moon lamented that "[a]s I see it, men of today are losing their subjectivity over science, and it looks as though man's ability to control scientific technology, which he himself has developed, is gradually being weakened."[41] Within Unification theology, God and humanity relate as subject and object, just as husband and wife, parents and children, masters and disciples, ancestors and descendents all similarly relate according to the binary hierarchy. For humanity to lose its subjectivity over science implied a breakage of the natural order. Although Moon did not specifically elaborate how humanity had lost control over technology, a few minutes into the speech he cited pollution as one example of science and technology out of control.[42] He also offered a solution to the broader problem: Moon insisted that science needed to unify around a standard of value, "to establish a true standard of value for the common benefit and welfare of all mankind" based on the universal value of love, specifically that of "the one absolute Being who is the only subject of this absolute love."[43] Throughout the 1970s, Moon would periodically return to environmental concerns in his founder's addresses as examples of science not controlling its technological output. For example, his speech to the third ICUS (1974) specified the problems caused by resource scarcity, population growth, pollution, nuclear testing, and ozone depletion.[44]

The Unification Church reserved the ability to direct and guide science because—despite his acceptance of science as the epistemological foundation of modernity, as evidenced in the founder's address and mirrored in the Unification texts—Moon insisted that religion, and the Unification Church specifically, offered solutions that science needed. Religion tendered a yardstick with which to measure science, as well a "standard of value" to guide science. Moon concluded his address to the fourth ICUS (1975) in millennial language reminiscent of both secular utopian dreams and religious visions of the heaven on earth, explaining that science had a role to play in the coming ideal world, a role mediated by religion. "Science policy must be determined in consideration of society as a whole. We must not lose the very central point of the whole purpose: science is not for science itself but for the welfare of humanity."[45] Though he spoke as the founder and leader of a new religious movement, Moon's insistence that science must serve wider society reverberated among the wider population. A National Science Foundation funded study a year later showed that a third of all Americans thought society needed to exert more control over science and that a majority felt science needed to contribute to alleviating the world's problems.[46]

The decade before, the initial ICUS conferences had witnessed numerous social critics lamenting the loss of human control over science. On the popular front, American movie audiences had flocked to watch Stanley Kubrick and Arthur C. Clark's *2001: A Space Odyssey* (1968), with its tale of an out-of-control intelligent computer that murdered its users, a situation only rectified when its sole surviving operator disconnected it. Alongside its iconoclastic message, the movie's psychedelic technicolor end sequence popularized *2001* among the emerging American counterculture.[47] The year of the second ICUS, Ernst Schumacher provided a more literary condemnation of technology run amuck in his *Small is Beautiful* (1973), which called for a redirection of "technology so that it serves man instead of destroying him."[48] Science and technology, Schumacher wrote, in words that reinforced other critics and would echo through the counterculture, dehumanized individuals and groups when it failed to operate for the general good of humanity. "In the excitement over the unfolding of his scientific and technological powers, modern man has built a system of production that ravishes nature and a type of society that mutilates man."[49] Surveys from the late 1960s and early 1970s showed a small but noticeable population of Americans—ranging from 10 to 20 percent—who worried that science had advanced too quickly, ravaged human relations with the environment, and failed to adequately consider the human ramifications of scientific and technological development.[50] Sociologists also found a majority of Americans concerned with science's dehumanizing aspects, particularly the tendency of people to feel isolated from their "human side" and "nature."[51] Moon and the Unification Church reflected such perspectives when they called on science to first and foremost serve humanity's happiness through allegiance to absolute values.

Turning from Moon to the scientists themselves, how did the ICUS participants internalize the messages broadcast by their Unification hosts? Certainly the Unification Church did not succeed in its millennial ambitions of building a new society with science's help. Nor did science unite, either around absolute values or any other central pole. However, the attending scientists did respond to Moon and the Unificationist movement's cue, discussing the nature of science, its place in the modern world, its relation to religion, how science might be unified, and how it should relate to values. With hundreds of participants over its two-decade history, no consensus emerged. Even the scientists serving as chairpeople, committee chairs, and keynote speakers failed to agree on not only answers but even what questions to ask. Some raised similar issues to Moon. André Cournand, Nobel laureate and American medical scientist, explained in his address at the second ICUS that the fragmented world needed to overcome its divisions. Unlike the Unificationist leader, however, Cournand declared science the best solution. "Because of its universalism, reflected in its traditions as in its methods of operation, science more than any revered [revealed?] religion is suited to assist in this task." This, he explained, would not only heal global rifts, but also defend against the "recent expressions of hostility toward science" and "the decline of public support for science."[52] Along similar lines, Robert Mulliken, the Nobel Prize–winning molecular chemist, declared at ICUS IV that "[w]ith regard to scientific values, as a scientist, my religion is truth, all kinds of truth." Marshalling a symbolic demonstration of science's ultimate truth value over and against religion Mulliken directly followed this statement with the bold declaration: "As humans we are part of the biological world, therefore the fact of biological evolution is a central truth for us. I say fact, not theory, because the evidence is so completely convincing."[53]

Other scientists considered pointed issues of the day. For example, in his 1975 ICUS paper the University of Chicago sociologist Morton Kaplan focused on the need to consider the ethics of scientific research by calling attention to drug testing procedures, alluding to the thalidomide drug scare in his description of "new horrors, drugs thrown upon the market, deformed children, people dead."[54] Seven years later, the Jewish theologian Richard Rubenstein, serving as chairman of the ICUS committee on "responsibility of the individual in world society," devoted much of his chairman's address to highlighting economic insecurity. "In the United States, for example," he declared, "many men and women have begun to lose faith in the banking system. They prefer to accept a lesser return on their investment by purchasing Treasury bills and notes rather than certificates of deposit from the banks."[55] Rubenstein spoke during the heart of the nation's Savings and Loans scandals, during which the deregulated industry imploded under the weight of bad loans and forced billions of dollars of deficits onto the federal government. Several years later, as the U.S. Congress looked to axe the federal science budget, Alvin Weinberg turned to questions of science funding, arguing for the need for scientific efficiency and a unified ideal of scientific merit.[56]

In other words, the ICUS series had little real effect on scientists or American science. Individuals presented papers and addresses on whatever topics seemed most relevant to themselves and their work, but no consensus emerged. However, the Unification Church, through the International Cultural Foundation, continued to fund the conferences into the twenty-first century, though they occurred less frequently in the waning days of the millennium. Since the ICUS had little impact in the scientific community, critics often wondered why the church continued to fund the enterprise. Such detractors most often accused Unificationism of using the ICUS to purchase legitimacy. These criticisms along with the Unification Church's deep involvement with ICUS cannot be separated from the "cult wars," the battle between new religious movements and their detractors.[57] People opposed new religions for a variety of reasons, ranging from the theological (they have bad theology), to the social (they break up families), to the psychological (they disrupt free will). The cult wars played out in court rooms, academic associations, state legislatures, and the media. Some critics accused the Unification Church of employing a variety of "magic" to ensnare its victims; others argued that the movement employed normal methods of persuasion to gain new adherents. Such detractors pointed to the ICUS conferences as part of the Unification plan to entrap America's youth. For example, K. H. Barney, head of the Ad Hoc Committee of Concerned Parents, one of the major anti-Unificationist groups, charged that "[t]he Moon organization uses movies and photos of Moon surrounded by smiling scientists to recruit new members."[58] Similarly, the *Boston Globe* reported that in a news conference coinciding with the seventh ICUS in 1978 in Boston, Barney's group "warned scientists attending the unity of the sciences conference that their pictures and words would be used for public relations purposes in Korea and elsewhere. They said Moon tries to make his movement more acceptable by aligning it with important people such as winners of Nobel Prizes."[59]

At the heart of such arguments, these critics argued that Unificationism used the ICUS, and therefore science, to purchase legitimacy. The conferences, another anti-Moon activist declared, represented "one more instance of Reverend Moon buying respectability for the church."[60] Such positions point toward the tremendous power of science, and its legitimacy in the public eye. Surveys of the general American population show that of all vocational fields, the pursuit of science regularly ranks among the most respected.[61] Much like priests, scientists tap mysterious and explainable powers, and promise technological miracles and other aid. They lend credibility, prestige, and legitimacy to any endeavor. Critics of the conferences recognized this fact. Of Reverend Moon, the highly respected journal *Science* wrote: "[p]erhaps if any of the scientists took him seriously, they would not be so quick to lend him the prestige of their presence."[62] Toronto's *Globe and Mail* also complained that "[t]he presence of a distinguished group of academics lends legitimacy to a conference whose sponsorship is questionable and problematic."[63] Even the *Christian Century*, bastion of mainline Protestantism, declared that "[f]reedom of speech . . . is not the issue. Lending your name to the Moon game of acquiring credibility is."[64] Certainly these critics had a point. The Unification Church did use photos of ICUS for publicity purposes, and as a means of projecting an air of legitimacy to their enterprise. However, the church has a much broader reason for sponsoring ICUS: its millennial quest to provide guidance to science and scientists. Ironically, if there was one thing that Moon and his critics could agree upon, it was the need for scientists to consider moral values in their professional lives. One former member of the Unification Church who became a leading anti-Unification crusader complained of the ICUS scientists, "I think it's high time these scientists considered their moral responsibilities." To that sentiment, ironically Reverend Moon would concur![65]

Guiding Science

In its treatment of science, the Unification Church mirrored much of broader American society's complaints and criticisms of science, but also the general societal acceptance and respect toward science. Science could be too big, too immoral, or too destructive, but overall it was a good thing. At times, like religious commentators on science far removed from new religions, the Unification Church called on science to cede to the moral power of religion and accept its guidance. At other times, Unificationists themselves borrowed the rhetoric and legitimacy of science for their own movement, again paralleling wider currents outside new religions.

Fundamentally the Unification Church accepted science as a positive force in American cultural, social, political, and economic life. In fact, they embraced science in its most institutionalized form, creating science conferences and inviting professional scientists to attend and discuss the state of their fields. Yet Unificationism also offered two critiques of science. First, science lacked unity, existing in fragmented form across a multitude of projects, centers, and disciplines. Second, unaided by an authoritative set of absolute values, science floundered in relativism and threatened the stability, peace, and health of human individuals and societies. But Moon's Unification Church reached out to science with a solution: scientists themselves must realize the need for centering their disciplines on solving human problems in accord with absolute values. At its International Conferences on the Unity of the Sciences, Unificationism offered a ready-made set of these absolute values, ready for immediate use by scientists. In its understanding of the relationship between religion and science, the Unification Church saw itself indeed as a *guide* for science.

Part II

Science and the Hare Krishna Movement

You scientists, you say some jugglery of words: proton, atoms, this, that, and hydrogen, phoxygen, oxygen. But what benefit people will get? Simply they'll hear this jugglery of words. That's all. What else you can say?

—Swami A. C. Bhaktivedanta Prabhupada,
recorded conversation (April 28, 1973)

Introduction

The merchant vessel pulled into Boston harbor to deposit its unusual passenger, an exotic charismatic public preacher hailing from foreign shores. Seventeenth- and eighteenth-century religious leaders John Winthrop and George Whitefield had tread the same ground, as had the native-born Cotton Mather and Henry David Thoreau. The Indian *swami* (religious leader) A. C. Bhaktivedanta Prabhupada, who arrived by steamboat from Calcutta at 5:30 a.m. on September 17, 1965, had a similar mission: to introduce to America a new religious perspective, and to create a model religious community. No less so than Winthrop, who so famously declared the Puritan intention of founding "a city upon a hill" for the whole world to see, Bhaktivedanta hoped to establish in America an ideal religious society, albeit one predicated on Hinduism rather than Christianity. Like Whitefield, the Indian swami traveled from city to city spreading his gospel, speaking on streets, in theaters, and anywhere else he could attract crowds.[1] In doing so, Swami A. C. Bhaktivedanta Prabhupada founded the International Society for Krishna Consciousness, known to members and scholars by its acronym ISKCON and more popularly as the Hare Krishna movement.

Bhaktivedanta, also called by the honorific Prabhupada by his disciples, arrived in America with very few personal possessions. His suitcase contained changes of clothing, a letter of introduction to an Indian family in Pennsylvania, forty rupees in Indian currency, dried grains for making his own vegetarian food, reading material, a diary, and an umbrella.[2] More importantly, as far as the swami was concerned, he brought two hundred three-volume sets of his own English-language translation of the Indian devotional classic, the *Srimad Bhagavatam*, a central religious text in the Hindu sect that Bhaktivedanta followed. Besides his personal effects and the text he hoped to disseminate to American converts, Swami Bhaktivedanta carried one other item: a stack of five hundred single-page pamphlets to promote the *Bhagavatam* and his mission of spreading it.

The pamphlet itself suggested the purpose of the Indian monk's mission. First, it described Bhaktivedanta himself and the book that he carried. With a large photo of A. C. Bhaktivedanta at its center, the pamphlet declared, "'Sri-mad Bhagwatam' [Bhagavatam] // India's Message of // Peace and Goodwill // Sixty Volumes of Elaborate English Version by // [photograph] // Tridandi Goswami A. C. Bhaktivedanta Swami." Next, it explained how the swami had arrived in America, in doing so fulfilling the additional role of reflecting Bhaktivedanta's sponsorship, namely the steamship company that had donated his room and board for the swami voyage's as well as paid for the printing of the pamphlet. In a large font, it declared, "Carried by the Scindia Steam Nav. Co., Limited // Bombay." Finally, the pamphlet explained why Swami A. C. Bhaktivedanta had traveled to America, and why he hoped to distribute his books in the United States: "All over the world for scientific knowledge of God."[3] From his first moments in America, the founder of the Hare Krishna movement carried a physical statement on science, religion, and the relation between the two. ISKCON, its founder declared, possessed "scientific knowledge of God."

This pamphlet revealed a fundamental assumption of Swami A. C. Bhaktivedanta Prabhupada, one that shaped the religious movement that he founded—that human beings could know God scientifically and could teach this process to others. Bhaktivedanta insisted that anyone who investigated with an open mind would find a more perfect explanation for human life and the universe itself in his Krishna Consciousness movement than in any other religious or scientific option. However, at other times he declared that the religion he brought to America, a sect of Hinduism known in India as Gaudiya Vaishnavism, itself represented a science. At other moments Bhaktivedanta thundered against science as wrongheaded, immoral, and arrogant. All of these positions represented a single overarching view of science and religion in the Hare Krishna movement: that Western science had failed, and that a more religiously attuned alternative, that proffered by the Hare Krishna movement itself, needed to replace it.

Within a year of arriving in the United States, the swami had created a small religious community in Manhattan, at first in borrowed space on the Upper West Side of the city, and later in his own rented quarters in the more bohemian Lower East Side. The exotic Hindu street preacher attracted crowds as he publicly chanted the *mantra* (meditative prayer) that his particular sect of Hinduism upheld as most central. The words of the mantra, "Hare Krishna, Hare Krishna, Krishna Krishna, Hare Hare, Hare Rama, Hare Rama, Rama Rama, Hare Hare" gave a name to the group of mostly countercultural followers who flocked around Bhaktivedanta. Before long the media paid attention to this new group of "Hare Krishnas," as they had been dubbed. When the reporter Jerry Erber of the small newsweekly *National Insider* asked followers of Bhaktivedanta if the Krishna Consciousness espoused by their International Society was a "religion, a cult, a philosophy, or what?," they responded to him by not only equating their practice to science but invoking scientific analogies and language. "Krishna Consciousness is not a religion but rather a science," one explained. "According to this science we are samples of God." Bhaktivedanta himself appealed to science in order to defend the legitimacy of the group. When Erber asked if the small size of his following concerned him, the swami responded, "a science is a science no matter how many followers it has."[4] While clearly also a legitimating strategy, ISKCON-as-a-science functioned as an important mark of identification for the movement's members.

From its earliest days, observers, followers, and leader alike all understood the religion of the International Society for Krishna Consciousness with reference to science and scientific terminology. For example, the first mainstream publication to discover the Hare Krishnas, the *New York Times* in 1966, featured the poet Alan Ginsberg, whom the *Times* cited as an authority on the group. Ginsberg, an unofficial spokesman for the counterculture, explained Bhaktivedanta's religious teaching using both religious and scientific language, alluding to the biological changes that accompanied the chanting of the Hare Krishna mantra. Ginsberg explained, "[i]t brings a state of ecstasy. For one thing, the syllables force yoga breath control; that's one physiological explanation."[5] Here, a publicly recognized figure—though certainly not a scientist—employed explicitly scientific terminology, the "physiological explanation," to explain a central ISKCON ritual.

Science and religion remained a central concern of Bhaktivedanta and his International Society for Krishna Consciousness. Through pamphlets, books, regular articles in the movement's glossy magazine, speeches, and more ephemeral materials, Swami A. C. Bhaktivedanta and the American converts who became fellow devotees of the Indian god Krishna emphasized the place of science in their religious system. Like the Reverend Sun Myung Moon's Unification Church, which preceded ISKCON in missionizing America, the Hare Krishnas understood themselves as possessing a scientifically valid worldview that could hold up to any scientific scrutiny. Further, both systems believed science supported their religious positions and contentions. Unlike the Unificationists, however, the Hare Krishnas took a very dim view of Western science and technology, openly and explicitly rejecting both Western science and America's science establishment as irredeemable and fatally flawed. ISKCON declared that it offered an alternative: an Indian, spiritual, textually grounded science that was neither Western, materialistic, nor empirical, yet nonetheless both more fully explained the world and better served humanity's moral and religious needs than conventional science. The Hare Krishna movement looked to their formulation of an alternative science in order to *replace* modern Western science and technology.

NOTE: This section makes use of a number of Sanskrit terms, all of which must be transliterated into roman characters. The leaders and members of ISKCON sometimes use variant transliterations of Sanskrit words, for example "Bagawatgita/Bhagavad-Gita" and "Krishna/Krsna." While I have not changed direct quotations, I have provided a bracketed explanation when the transliteration of a Sanskrit term strongly varies from the conventional academic norm. In all cases I have avoided the use of diacritical marks, which are more likely to confuse than elucidate the reader untrained in Indology or philology.

3

Science and the Foundation of the Hare Krishnas

The Origins of ISKCON

The Hare Krishna movement, known more formally as the International Society for Krishna Consciousness (ISKCON), developed out of a preexistent Hindu devotional sect transplanted to the West. Yet ISKCON represented something radically new: a Hindu devotional sect transplanted to, and transformed in, America, where it appealed primarily to Western converts and drew inspiration from—and simultaneously rejected—the postwar American, and subsequently Euro-American, counterculture.[1] Though equivalent in doctrine to the Gaudiya Vaishnava sect of Hinduism, ISKCON's founder Bhaktivedanta innovated in how he introduced the religion to Americans and how he positioned it vis-à-vis the wider culture. The American Hare Krishna converts rejected what they saw as the corrupt outside world and crafted a sectarian religious world for themselves, a hybrid culture drawing from Indian as well as countercultural norms. In constructing this hybrid worldview, the American devotees of Krishna turned to science and their view of it to define themselves and their movement.

Abhay Charan De and the Origin of the Hare Krishnas

Like the Reverend Sun Myung Moon, Bhaktivedanta's early exposure to industrialization and modernization shaped his later life, and he employed modern technological and technocratic methods in propagating and operating his religious society. Unlike Moon, however, the young Abhay Charan (A. C.) De, as Bhaktivedanta was known before adopting the religious life, did not embrace the idea of modernization and the Western scientific worldview behind it. At most willing to accept the modern scientific world as a tool for spreading his religious message, even before sailing to the Americas and leading a new religious movement, Abhay demonstrated both attraction and ambivalence toward science and technology.

Born September 1, 1896, the future Hare Krishna founder witnessed half a century of British colonialism and the rise of a modern and independent India. The child of high-caste middle-class parents in Calcutta, Abhay Charan De grew up literally across the street from a Hindu temple of the Gaudiya Vaishnava lineage, the variety of Hinduism professed by his parents and other members of his immediate family, and that later defined the theological moorings of the Hare Krishna movement. Biographical sources portray a religiously centered child whose daily life revolved around home and temple worship activities dedicated to the Hindu god Krishna, the central deity of Gaudiya Vaishnavism, and one of the most popularly worshipped Hindu gods.[2] The official biography produced by ISKCON, which also serves as the most thorough source on the early life of Swami Bhaktivedanta, details his parents' successful efforts to inculcate religious devotion in their young son. By the age of six, Abhay had become an informal religious leader among his siblings and friends, gathering them for worship and even organizing a children's version of the eight-day-long religious festival Ratha-yatra. Although the biography, which tends toward the hagiographic, admits that Abhay mimicked the religious activities of the adults around him, clearly the boy had internalized the Hinduism of his parents.[3]

In addition to a foundation in traditional Hindu religiosity, Abhay Charan De's parents sought a modern Western-style education for their child, turning to the British colonial educational system. Like Sun Myung Moon, who studied traditional Western subjects among Presbyterian missionaries, Abhay Charan De undertook his schooling under the guidance of Western Christian institutions, the prestigious school operated by the Church of Scotland, the Scottish Church College of Calcutta, which he attended from 1916 to 1920.[4] The college had a reputation for excellent scholarship, training students in English culture, and as a center of Bengali intellectualism. Swami Vivekananda, the Hindu missionary who spoke at the 1893 Chicago Parliament of World's Religions, attended the college, as did Paramahansa Yogananda, another guru who spread Hinduism to the West. Swubhas Chandra Bose, the future president of the Indian National Congress and Indian military leader, attended Scottish Church College in the class ahead of Abhay.[5] Though the college required study of the Christian Bible and theology, Christianity did not interest Abhay Charan De, whose religious world his parents had bequeathed him. The future founder of ISKCON dutifully attended classes and studied the standard British colonial curriculum—British history, modern science, classical literature—but he would come to reject it. Much of Abhay Charan De's later work directly criticized the material that he learned at Scottish Church College, rejecting Western culture, history, literature, and of course science as pale comparisons to what he considered India's ancient glorious civilization.

Alongside internalizing Hindu religiosity and a Western education, during his childhood, adolescence, and college years Abhay Charan De also witnessed the modernization of India. British colonial administrators in the nineteenth century had already established an efficient technological infrastructure linking India's major cities, but targeted most of their development toward entrenching their political and military dominance and transporting resources for export. What British governor-general Lord Dalhousie called "the three great engines of social improvement, which the sagacity and science of recent times had previously given to the Western nations—I mean Railways, uniform Postage, and the Electric Telegraph" successfully linked upper-class Indians and British bureaucrats in Calcutta, Bombay, Madras, and Delhi by the end of the 1850s.[6] However, outside of these socially and geographically limited corridors of power, India remained a pre-modern society, at least when judged by Western notions of economic and scientific development. In his encyclopedic history of modern India, Claude Markovitz argues that "[u]p to 1905, modern Indian industry was more or less limited to the textile sector, both cotton and jute. From then onwards, partly under the influence of the *swadeshi* [nativist] movement, industrial diversification began to crystallize, essentially through Indian initiatives. Cement factories, chemical factories, paper mills, all oriented towards the domestic market, emerged, but, in the absence of tariff protection, they often faced considerable difficulties."[7] During the dawning years of the twentieth century, India slowly emerged into the modern world. Abhay Charan De grew up right in the middle of it.

Abhay's childhood coincided with the emergence of modern Indian economic and technological society. After decades of stagnation, in part due to global economic factors but primarily the product of colonial control, the Indian economy picked up during his first few years of life, peaking during his teen years (the early 1910s). Abhay witnessed the effective creation of a natively operated (rather than colonially imposed) export market, at first mostly agricultural, with jute (a native Indian fiber), tea, and opium predominating. Economic figures show steep increases in all those products during the final decades of the nineteenth century and first decade and a half of the twentieth centuries. The rate of construction and expansion of factories likewise rose, with 1913 witnessing the first domestic production of Indian steel from natively mined iron sources.[8] Electricity and telegraph began to penetrate the countryside and the older areas of the cities, rather than merely the centers of colonial power. Of the changes wrought by the modernization of India, electrification personally impressed the young Abhay Charan De the most. Piecing together oral histories, interviews, and diaries, ISKCON biographer Satsvarupa Dasa Goswami wrote of his movement's founder:

> Abhay turned ten the same year the rails were laid for the electric tram on Harrison Road [on which he lived]. He watched the workers lay the tracks, and when he first saw the trolley car's rod touching the overhead wire, it amazed him. He daydreamed of getting a stick, touching the wire himself, and running along by electricity. Although electric power was new in Calcutta and not widespread (only the wealthy could afford it in their homes), along with the electric tram came new electric streetlights—carbon-arc lamps—replacing the old gaslights. Abhay and his friends used to go down the street looking on the ground for the old, used carbon tips, which the maintenance man would leave behind.[9]

Although enamored as a child by the advent of electricity and modern technology, Abhay Charan De would later react against these very innovations, complaining that Western science and technology distracted from the religious or spiritual pursuits upon which he believed Indians and all people should base their lives. Just as he rejected the Whiggish notions of British civilization he learned at Scottish Church College, Abhay Charan De did not embrace Western technology or science. Tellingly, however, the place of science and technology reappeared throughout his religious writings as he attempted to rectify the ideal of Indian Hindu religious centeredness and the reality of Western technological and scientific modernization that he witnessed as a ten-year-old child.

In accordance with Bengali tradition, Abhay married a high-caste woman whom his father selected for him, and a year after graduating from Scottish Church College started a family and a business career, becoming a part-time pharmacist and manager for a small pharmaceutical company owned by a family friend.[10] Although a competent manager and chemist, questions of ultimate meaning concerned Abhay Charan De far more than business interests. While in college, he embraced Mahatma Gandhi's religiously inspired Indian nationalism, so much so that Abhay adopted the simple handmade tunic that publicly declared him a follower of Gandhi, and later refused to participate in his own graduation ceremony as a protest against the colonial nature of Scottish Church College.[11] He had made his choice in favor of

Indian culture, Indian values, and Indian religion. Yet the ecumenical liberalism of Gandhi's movement failed to satisfy Abhay, who even as a Gandhian showed a renewed interest in the religion of his childhood, the more conservative Gaudiya Vaishnavism of his family and the temple under whose shadow he had grown.

The religion that Abhay Charan De followed, and subsequently became the most influential exporter of, grew out of two sets of Hindu revivals, one led by the sixteenth-century Indian mystic Chaitanya, and the other by Bengali reformers of the nineteenth century, who worked under the influence of British colonialism. Gaudiya Vaishnavism's roots, however, derived from the traditional Hindu worship of Vishnu, who along with Shiva and Brahma compose the threefold godhead of Hinduism. The term *Vaishnavism* itself refers to the worship of Vishnu (a *Vaishnava* or *Vaishnavite* is a person who worships Vishnu). Of these three major gods, Hindus most frequently worship Vishnu, whom tradition associates with guiding and preserving human society. A majority of Hindus believe that Vishnu periodically takes physical forms, called *avatars*, in order to guide and preserve human society. Such forms vary depending on the need of human society, but among Vishnu's avatars, Hindus most frequently venerate the cowherd prince Krishna (sometimes transliterated "Krsna"), a slayer of demons and savior of villagers as well as friend and companion to the mortal Arjuna, a noble warrior facing the gruesome task of warring against his own kinfolk.

In keeping with their reading of Hindu sacred texts, Gaudiya Vaishnavism reverses the more common Hindu understanding of Krishna as an avatar of Vishnu, and proclaims that Krishna is the most intimate name and identity of the one true God who creates and sustains the universe, who then creates the triune godhead of Brahma, Vishnu, and Shiva (some schools within Vaishnavism explain that Krishna separates himself into the triune Godhead, rather than creating it ex nihilo), and then further manifests himself in the form of avatars. Of the many avatars that Vishnu takes, Gaudiya Vaishnavism recognizes Krishna as most central, since only during that incarnation did the one true God manifest with his true name and personality. As Graham M. Schweig, a scholar of Gaudiya Vaishnavism as well as intellectual leader within the tradition writes, using the technical Sanskrit terminology, "within those Vaishnava traditions for whom the form of Krishna is considered the supreme and ultimate form of the divinity, he is both an *avatara* [avatar] and the *adi-purisha devata* (the original person of the godhead). He is the supremely intimate deity from whom the more powerful and cosmic forms emanate."[12] Krishna, therefore, is both the single cosmic God of the universe as well as a specific incarnation that God takes. Singular devotion to Krishna, whom his worshippers consider the creator and sustainer and the entire cosmos, characterizes Gaudiya Vaishnavism.

Gaudiya Vaishnavism differentiates itself from other forms of Vaishnavism in a second way, its attachment to the Indian mystic reformer Chaitanya (1486–1533), understood by members of the Gaudiya sect as not merely a reformer, but an incarnation of Krishna himself. Chaitanya taught that the best form of worship is that of emotional or ecstatic devotion, particularly communal chanting and joyful singing of hymns and prayers. In this way, Chaitanya stressed the path of Hindu religiosity called *bhakti*, or devotion. Unlike some of the more intellectual forms of the religion, such as the disciplines of physical yoga, meditation, or study, bhakti appealed to a wider audience. Like the Jewish Chasidic movement or Protestant pietism, Chaitanya de-emphasized social class, educational level, and intellectual sophistication, and subsequently brought his form of Vaishnavism to the uneducated masses. Edward C. Dimock Jr., the West's premier scholar of Gaudiya Vaishnava history, wrote that such bhakti-centered movements as Chaitanya's "spoke to the people of the non-high culture, as well as those participants in the Sanskrit culture who for their own reasons were no longer satisfied with the rigid and highly formulaic religious system represented by brahmanism [Hindu orthodoxy]."[13] Influenced by Islamic notions of community, Chaitanya ignored the strictures of caste, preaching to mixed audiences and publicly declaring that all people could equally participate in the devotional bhakti worship.

Chaitanya's reform efforts succeeded to such an extent that during his own lifetime, followers began to see Chaitanya as a literal godsend, that is an incarnation of Vishnu sent to reform and reinvigorate religious devotions. The movement that he founded, taking its name from the geographical region of Gauda where he preached, became known as Gaudiya Vaishnavism, and unlike other forms of Vishnu-worship, envisioned its founder Chaitanya as an avatar. The singular piety to Krishna that Chaitanya demonstrated, which itself reflected Bengali popular religiosity and devotionalism, also installed within Gaudiya Vaishnavism the doctrine of Krishna as the sole cosmic God, thus further differentiating the sect from other forms of Hindu Vaishnavism.[14]

Before it reached Abhay Charan De, Gaudiya Vaishnavism filtered through another era of reform, that of the nineteenth-century Bengali reformers who reacted to both British colonialism and the modernization of India. Even though reformers differed, they all agreed that Hinduism needed to adapt to the modern world, especially in light of their personal and collective exposure to British culture and religion. Further, they declared that a suitably modernized Hinduism equaled the Christianity of the British and other Western religions in terms of theological and philosophical sophistication. One of the earliest of these Bengali reformers, Ram Mohan Roy (1772–1833), influenced by liberal Protestantism and the Hindu philosophical traditions, founded the Brahmo Samaj, which emphasized the nonpersonal monotheism of the Hindu sacred texts called the Upanishads.[15] A subsequent wave of reformers, including Ramakrishna (1836–86) and Swami Vivekananda (1863–1902) applied a more theistic or personal perspective, emphasizing worship of the supreme Goddess, Sakta, alongside philosophical introspection.[16] Finally, reformers within Gaudiya Vaishnavism, namely Bhaktivinoda Thakur (1838–1914) and Abhay Charan De's own spiritual master, Bhaktisiddhanta Sarasvati (1874–1937) focused reform efforts on the worship of Krishna.

The reformers looked to India and Hinduism for their religious identities, encouraging Indians and Westerners alike to consider the religious and philosophical traditions of Hinduism as a font of religious knowledge. As Thomas J. Hopkins argues, "[b]oth symbolically and practically, these Western-educated intellectuals were affirming in the late nineteenth century a new message: that Hindus had little to learn from the West in terms of spirituality, whereas everyone—themselves included—had much to learn from Hindu spiritual masters."[17] In light of social, economic, and religious colonial dominance, the Hindu reformers exerted Indian self-confidence and Hindu pride.[18] ISKCON would do the same.

Abhay Charan De traced his lineage to Bhaktisiddhanta Sarasvati and his father Bhaktivinoda Thakur, two leading lights of the Bengali reform movement as well as devotees of Gaudiya Vaishnavism. Bhaktivinoda Thakur not only served the British Raj as a professional magistrate but also produced nearly one hundred translations and commentaries on Gaudiya Vaishnava themes, with the intention, in Jan Brzezinski's words, "to rationalize Gaudiya Vaishnavism and bring it into the modern age."[19] He set the pattern for his son and later Bhaktivedanta by focusing on translating Gaudiya Vaishnava sacred texts, producing written commentaries on the scriptures, and lecturing to mixed audiences, specifically those comprised of Hindus of multiple castes. Although one must treat with caution any declension-themed narrative propagated by reformists, the scholarly consensus does indicate that the more egalitarian notions of Chaitanya had declined by the nineteenth century.[20] Bhaktivinoda Thakur and his son Bhaktisiddhanta Sarasvati set out to reinvigorate Gaudiya Vaishnavism through appealing not only to its compatibility with modern modes of thought, but to its openness to Hindus of the lower castes and stations. Like Chaitanya's efforts under the shadow of Muslim dominance, the latter-day Vaishnava reformers responded to Anglo-Christian criticisms of Hinduism as mired in the unjust Indian caste system. In 1911, while the young Abhay Charan De still attended secondary school, Bhaktisiddhanta published a booklet declaring caste effectively irrelevant, pronouncing that a person's caste depended on their actions and qualities rather than birth or their father's occupation, as Hindu society traditionally understood it.[21]

Abhay met Bhaktisiddhanta in 1922, two years after graduating from college. Years after the fact, A. C. Bhaktivedanta recalled of the experience, "I accepted him as my spiritual master immediately. Not officially, but in my heart."[22] Recognition of Bhaktisiddhanta Sarasvati as his *guru*, or spiritual teacher, followed a decade later in 1932, when Abhay requested and received initiation as a householder (congregational member, as opposed to monastic) of the Gaudiya Vaishnava lineage. His guru expected that Abhay, as a householder, would continue to support his wife and children, but would also devote as much effort, energy, and expenses as possible to religious causes such as hosting visiting teachers, sponsoring the building of temples, and leading gatherings of other Vaishnavas for discussion and study.

Abhay fulfilled these requirements, and he also honed his skills at preaching. Unlike most of his fellow Gaudiya Vaishnavites, Abhay had benefited from an education at Calcutta's premier colonial college and spoke almost naturally in English as well as Bengali. In February 1935, he accepted the opportunity to speak to a small gathering of fellow disciples of Bhaktisiddanta in honor of the guru's birthday. Abhay spoke in English, reciting a poem of his own invention and a speech that critiqued Western material culture as a pale comparison to what he considered the traditional Vaishnava spirituality. He declared "the darkness of the present age is not due to lack of material advancement, but that we have lost the clue to our spiritual advancement which is the prime necessity of human life and the criterion of the highest type of civilization. Throwing of bombs from aeroplanes is no advancement of civilization from the primitive, uncivilized way of dropping big stones on the heads of the enemies from the tops of hills. . . . [W]hile others were yet in the womb in historical oblivion, the sages of India had developed a different kind of civilization which enables us to know ourselves. They had discovered that we are not at all material entities, but that we are spiritual, permanent, and nondestructible servants of the Absolute."[23] The theme of Indian spirituality versus Western materialism, of ancient Hindu truths against modern

Western destruction would endure in Abhay's work both before and after he founded the International Society for Krishna Consciousness.

Abhay's fellow Vaishnava devotees responded enthusiastically to his message and rhetoric, leading the future ISKCON leader to publish the address in his guru's periodical, *The Harmonist*. Bhaktisiddhanta apparently approved, and in a letter that he sent Abhay shortly before the elderly spiritual leader died, he charged Abhay with a specific missionary endeavor: the duty of spreading Gaudiya Vaishnava religion to English-speakers. In a passage of a letter that Abhay considered his new vocational charge, Bhaktisiddhanta wrote, "I have every hope that you can turn yourself into a very good English preacher if you serve the mission to inculcate the novel impression of Lord Chaitanya's teachings in the people in general as well as philosophers and religionists."[24] This letter, along with an earlier instruction that he should use what funds he had to publish tracts and books in support of Vaishnava causes, led Abhay Charan De to immediately shift his focus to translating central Gaudiya Vaishnava texts into English and publishing English language periodicals.

Science and Religion in Abhay Charan De's Early Material

Following his spiritual master's instructions, in February 1944 Abhay Charan De published in Calcutta the first issue of *Back to Godhead*, an English-language forty-two-page juggernaut of a pamphlet. *Back to Godhead* contained ten articles, each either written or translated by Abhay Charan De. Abhay set the tenor of the periodical in its masthead, with the first and each subsequent issue declaring "Godhead is Light, Nescience is darkness. Where there is Godhead there is no Nescience." The word "nescience," which conveys a meaning of both agnosticism and ignorance, provides a key to understanding how Abhay Charan De and his *Back to Godhead* approached science. The light of Krishna, which Abhay frequently referred to as transcendental science, would dispel both skepticism and ignorance. According to Abhay, modern Western science, that is science based on empiricism and the study of the material universe, idolized skepticism and stymied itself in ignorance. Representing both types of nescience, materialistic science offered nothing to the modern world, *Back to Godhead* insisted.

Each of Abhay's articles in the first issue of *Back to Godhead* directly confronted science and its relation to religion, an appropriate symmetry since the final article in the ultimate issue of the Indian run of the periodical also discussed science. The roots of the sectarian approach to science demonstrated by the American Hare Krishnas existed inchoate in even these early sources, as evidenced by approaches to science in Abhay Charan De's first articles: a rejection of Western-style materialistic science as futile and impotent, and simultaneously a conviction that his own Gaudiya Vaishnava movement offered a scientific solution to the world's problems. This mirrored the author's own rejection of Western modernity and simultaneous embracing of Hindu traditionalism.

The first position, the rejection of Western scientific materialism, emerged forcefully in his article "Godhead and Potentialities." He began by summarizing a passage from the Bhagavad Gita, which had long served as the foremost scriptural source in Gaudiya Vaishnavism and many other forms of Hinduism, as well as fascinating Americans (such as transcendentalist Henry David Thoreau). Abhay explained that "the soul or the spirit of the living entity is never born nor does it ever die. It was never created in the past nor it is created at present neither it shall be created in the future." Nearly every form of Hinduism accepts such a position on the immortality of the spirit, making its appearance in his article rather unremarkable. Yet the future leader of the Hare Krishnas moved beyond the traditional ascription of the passage to demonstrate the eternality of the human soul to take a jab at the validity of modern science. Immediately after this passage, Abhay provided an asterisk that pointed to a note at the bottom of the page. Without additional explanation, the footnote declared: "It is futile attempt therefore to produce life-substance in the laboratory of scientists."[25] One might view this negative assessment of science as standing out as apparently unrelated to the article itself, which considered issues of the soul and its relation to God. However, Abhay understood it as directly related: the Bhagavad Gita and Vaishnava tradition preached one set of ideas about the soul and God, and scientists, particularly Western materialistic ones, preached a different set of ideas. This dualistic approach the science and religion would reappear throughout Abhay Charan De's work.

Abhay's next articles in the first issue of *Back to Godhead* provide the context to the author's earlier denigration of science. On the surface, the article "Theosophy Ends in Vaishnavism" encapsulated the author's critique of the nineteenth-century Hindu-inspired religious movement Theosophy, founded by H. P. Blavatsky, Henry Steel Olcott, and others in 1875, which Abhay rejected as nontheistic and therefore erroneous. Within his critique, however, he turned to the issue of whether scientists and philosophers outside his own theistic Vaishnava tradition could discover the truths of God using differing methodologies. Abhay said no. He wrote, "God is Great and He reserves the right of not being exposed to the mundane speculationist and dry philosophers but He appears Himself by His own Will and Independence when He is offered transcendental loving services in all respects. The Sun appears in the morning just out of His own accord and not being bound up by the extraneous effort of the scientist. The scientist will fail to make appear the Sun at night by the discovery of all searchlights and scientific instruments."[26] This passage offered two arguments: first, those who used the wrong methodologies, i.e., mundane speculation and dry philosophy, could not understand the divine. Abhay would repeatedly employ those descriptions, "dry philosophy" and "mundane speculation," as descriptors of those who did not share his particular Gaudiya Vaishnava religious views, specifically those with less theistic understandings of religion ("dry philosophy") or those who worked purely in materialistic or empirical science ("mundane speculation").[27] In neither case could the practitioners of these methodologies grasp the truths of the divine, Bhaktivedanta insisted. Second, science was impotent, or in his own words, "extraneous." Scientific instruments, machines, and theorems could not cause the sun to appear. The sun, like all parts of nature, transcended the abilities of science. This second argument, that of science's futility, encapsulated the specific case of the first, namely that science could not study the divine. They combined to indicate that those who seek knowledge of the underlying truths of the natural world ought to consider nonscientific alternatives. This passage also reveals Abhay's objection to empiricism, the methodological basis of Western science. If God changes the material world on a whim, how could humans trust their observations, he reasoned.

Despite such negative assessments of science, Abhay insisted that the Krishna-based religion of Gaudiya Vaishnavism was scientific, a position that most clearly emerged in the article "The Science of Congregational Chanting of the Name of the Lord." This article demonstrated Abhay's frequent use of science as an adjective that applies to something else, namely the theology and practices of Gaudiya Vaishnavism. "Lord Chaitanya," he wrote, "has most reasonably and scientifically ordered us to chant the Name of the Lord as follows."[28] Or, as in an advertisement on the back cover of the magazine for his own translation of the Bhagavad Gita, he declared the text an "elaborate exposition of the world famous Hindu Philosophy—'The Bhagwat Geeta'— in its true, scientific, theistic interpretations."[29] In such cases the author never defined science, but rather used it as a parallel description to "reasonable" or "true," in effect accepting one of the wider understandings of science, that it is rational, truthful knowledge. In this approach to science, even when the word appeared as a grammatical noun it describes another concept. For example, Abhay Charan De wrote that "all people must be led to the Science of *Samkirtan* [group chanting] by all means and they shall be engaged in the culture of the science by *Samkirtan* only."[30] The very name of the article, "The Science of Congregational Chanting of the Name of the Lord," indicated this position. Here science meant something like a method or approach, though certainly not one based on materialism, empiricism, or positivism, three of the more common methodological assumptions of modern science. Abhay equated science and the practice of Gaudiya Vaishnavism.

Over the next sixteen years, until April 1960, Abhay Charan De would publish *Back to Godhead* as the English-language organ of Gaudiya Vaishnavism in India (Abhay hoped to distribute to Britain and the United States but was unable to do so). Of the more than two dozen issues during this period, nearly every one considered science and its relation to the Krishna-based religion of Gaudiya Vaishnavism. Of the articles that discuss science, most disparaged it.[31] Like his view of Western civilization more broadly, Abhay considered Western science a poor comparison to India's native culture and intellectual achievements. In various articles, he called science and scientific thinking futile, incorrect, useless, dangerous, wasteful, illusionary, and amoral. One typical criticism of science contrasted it with "transcendental modes of thinking," which the article equated to the religion of the Bhagavad Gita and Krishna. "Modern scientific thought is basically wrong, because such thoughts are products of the changing mind a subtle form of material elements. Transcendental modes of thinking is [*sic*] basically right because it emanates from the realm of eternal spirit or the deeper aspect of human personality," he explained in an April 1956 article.[32] In other articles, he implied that science operated immorally, as in the article "Definition of Vice & Its Scope," where Abhay wrote: "so-called scientific knowledge of the mundane scientist are different varieties of illusions only to bewilder from spiritual on the conditioned souls [*sic*] who have fallen from the pure state of existence. . . . The so-called scientific knowledge is prompted by a desire to lord it over the material nature which is the root cause of all vices as described above."[33] Abhay Charan De taught that materialism of any variety, scientific materialism included, distracted from the spiritual ambitions of life as taught by Gaudiya Vaishnavism.

Yet while he blasted science as illusionary, immoral, and wrongheaded, Abhay also insisted that Gaudiya Vaishnavism represented an alternative science. At times Abhay did not explain what he meant by science, allowing the word to function as a descriptor of something else. By this "adjectival" or rhetorical use of science, Abhay cast Gaudiya Vaishnavism as scientific without specifying what precisely the term "science" meant, or why Vaishnavism merited consideration as one. For example, the future ISKCON founder wrote in the article, "Who is a Sadhu?" (*sadhu* means "saint"), "[t]he Sadhu is a pure devotee of the Lord and he may not be a mendicant by dress. He knows the Supreme Truth scientifically. And he disseminates this transcendental knowledge to all out of his causeless mercy upon them."[34] No where else in the article did Abhay explain what scientific knowledge of truth might entail. The concept of science operated as a modifier or adjective only, describing Gaudiya Vaishnavism. This approach emerged most forcefully in Abhay's two-part article series on subatomic and stellar science, later published as *Easy Journey to Other Planets* (1960). Despite the title of this book, the articles focused on defending the reality of the soul and nonmaterial realms of reality, and the yogic practices designed to bring one closer to Krishna. Science served as a rhetorical model to defend these propositions, with scientific explanations of the nature of anti-matter paired with Abhay Charan De's defense of nonmateriality. However, the author also repeatedly declared his own approach as also scientific. Referring to Vaishnava devotees as "students of theistic science," Abhay seized on both the rhetorical power of science as well as its perceived legitimacy in order to support his movement's theological positions.[35]

Abhay Charan De no doubt spoke of science because he honestly believed that Gaudiya Vaishnavism was scientific. He did not attempt to define the term or explain why a potential adherent ought to consider the Krishna religion a science. Rather, Abhay invoked the cultural power of science, its aura of legitimacy and authority, especially vis-à-vis other forms of knowledge. Thus in describing the periodical of *Back to Godhead* itself, Abhay explained that "[i]t is not blind religious fanaticism neither it is [*sic*] a revolt of an upstart but it is scientific approach to the matter of our eternal necessity in relation with the Absolute Personality of Godhead."[36] Again, he did not explain what a scientific approach entailed or why *Back to Godhead* represented such methods. He did, however, contrast what he saw as the science of his journal, and hence Gaudiya Vaishnavism, with "religious fanaticism" and upstart revolutionary movements. Whatever science involved, it was neither fanatical or new but conventional and recognized, i.e., legitimate. The magazine represented science because, Abhay seemed to insist, Gaudiya Vaishnavism also was legitimate.[37] This case of using the mantle of science to legitimate a new religious movement follows the pattern explained by James

R. Lewis as a "rational appeal" to legitimation, since it roots the new religion in a perceived sense of rational belief. This in turn legitimates the new religion.[38]

At the same time that Abhay Charan De began to focus on publishing his *Back to Godhead*, he decided to pursue the religious vocation full time. On September 17, 1959, Abhay took initiation into the Hindu monastic orders (*sanyasi*) and became known as Swami A. C. Bhaktivedanta.[39] Becoming a sanyasi permitted the new A. C. Bhaktivedanta to leave behind his family so to devote himself to the religious mission. Freed of the social obligation to provide for wife and children, the new swami dedicated himself to writing and the dissemination of his work. In addition to his continuing work on *Back to Godhead* and translation of pivotal Gaudiya scriptures from Bengali and Sanskrit into English, Bhaktivedanta né Abhay Charan De began a very active correspondence with other leading Indian intellectual figures.

Bhaktivedanta's personal correspondences from this period support the contention that he simultaneously rejected mainstream Western science as well as clamored for its legitimacy and cultural power. Many of his letters include what I have called the "adjectival" use of science, in that he utilized the term only in describing something else. This approach highlights science from a rhetorical perspective, as a term that marks legitimacy and truth. For example, in a 1947 letter that he sent to Raja Mohendra Pratap, a renowned Indian anti-colonial revolutionary who had only recently returned from exile, Bhaktivedanta scolded Pratap for his apparent "pantheism," as evidenced by his essay, "Religion of Love." The swami admonished, "you have not quoted any authority for all your statements . . . the approach [to religion] shall be and must be authoritative, scientific and universal. Your delineations do not conform to all these necessary things. . . . My basis of arguments will be Bhagavad-gita which is the most authoritative, scientific and universal."[40] Here science functioned as a description of a preferred methodology, specifically the use of scripture as the basis of knowledge. Similarly, in a letter composed to Sardal Patel, the Deputy Prime Minister of India, Bhaktivedanta offered to establish an "organized, scientific" system of exporting Indian spiritual wisdom to the rest of the world. Without explanation as to what he might mean, ISKCON's founder insisted that he was "confident to organize this work in a scientific way if I am helped by the state."[41] Again, Bhaktivedanta utilized science rhetorically as a descriptor, in this case illustrating what he considered efficient, accurate, and valid methods of work.

Other correspondences reveal that Bhaktivedanta treated science as equivalent to Gaudiya Vaishnava religion, and sometimes Hinduism more broadly.

In a remarkable July 1947 letter to the revered Indian leader Mohandas Gandhi, Bhaktivedanta encouraged the man called Mahatma, or "Great Soul," to eschew his unguided reading of Hindu scripture and dedicate himself to a "bona fide Guru," in order "to learn the science of Absolute Truth."[42] Here, Bhaktivedanta equated science with his own Gaudiya Vaishnava lineage and implied that he would be willing to accept Mahatma Gandhi as a spiritual disciple. At the same time, Bhaktivedanta scolded Gandhi for accepting too many Western ideas and failing to follow what the swami considered the most valid lineage of traditional Hinduism, i.e., Vaishnavism. The swami's critique of what he saw as Gandhi's acceptance of non-Indian ideas further reveals how Bhaktivedanta's identification of his Vaishnava religion as a science functioned within a colonial context. The swami's identification of his lineage as a science functioned as a powerful marker in navigating colonial and growing postcolonial identities.

For an Indian spiritual leader who came of age in the shadow of colonialism, the representation of Gaudiya Vaishnavism as a science also positioned the nascent movement as both religiously and rationalistically superior to the West but also—as a science—universal. The science studies scholar Meera Nanda has described this approach as widespread among early Hindu nationalists, those Indians who looked to the ancient roots of Hinduism to found a new modern India and who hoped to find in Vedic science an alternative form of modern scientific legitimacy.[43] This theme emerged forcefully in another letter that Bhaktivedanta sent five years later, in a similar but more broadly pan-Hindu manner, to Gandhi's protégé Jawaharlal Nehru. "Absolute Truth is described in the Vedic literatures as Sanatana or Eternal. And the philosophy or science which deals in such eternal subjects is described as Sanatana Dharma."[44] Notably, Bhaktivedanta here used the term *sanatana dharma*, an indigenous Sanskrit name for the religion that Westerners call Hinduism, but one most frequently used at the time by Indians opposed to colonialism. In using the native term, Bhaktivedanta again revealed how his understanding of science developed within the Indian experience of colonialism. Not only did Bhaktivedanta treat science as synonymous with Hindu religion—as in his correspondence with Gandhi—but the swami further admonished Nehru in the letter for replacing Indian cultural, social, and governance norms with those drawn from the West. Bhaktivedanta's declaration of sanatana dharma as a science (and therefore rational and universal) enabled the swami to position himself and his movement as uniquely Indian and anti-colonial at the same time that he hoped to appeal to Western-educated English-speaking potential converts.

Bhaktivedanta's Mission to America and the Birth of ISKCON

In order to fulfill his guru's instructions to spread Gaudiya Vaishnavism to English speakers, Swami A. C. Bhaktivedanta decided to travel to the world's most populous English-speaking country and what had replaced Great Britain as the West's superpower, the United States of America. Having arranged for free transport aboard a steamship, the swami arrived in America in 1965. There he quickly set to work spreading Gaudiya Vaishnava teachings in America's most dense and populated metropolitan area, New York City. Finding the traditional churches, mainstream religious leaders, and intellectuals unreceptive to his message, the swami turned to the young men and women who mingled in the city parks and streets, the mainstays of the counterculture only then becoming popularly known as hippies. The counterculture positioned itself against the mainstays of American society, everything from consumer culture to the ideals of higher education, American exceptionalism, the value of work, respect for government, and of course technoscientific society.

The historian Theodore Roszak, whose assessment of the counterculture did as much to define as chronicle it, emblemized the countercultural perspective of science and technology. In his *Making of a Counter Culture* (1969), he complained that "scientists and technicians enjoy the freedom—indeed they demand the freedom —to do *absolutely anything* to which curiosity or a research contract draws them." To shock the reader into agreement, Roszak followed his critique with an imagined list of American scientists' ideal projects: creation of bird-baboon chimeras, synthesis of viruses for biological warfare, DNA research intended to allow parents to customize their children, and artificial intelligence computers that replicate not only human cultural endeavors but even "the mind of God."[45] Scientific arrogance, Roszak charged, endangered everyone. Another critic, the Catholic theologian and activist Jacques Ellul, declared that technology and the scientific mind-set "dehumanized" individuals and society, transforming people into servants of machine and technique.[46] Both Ellul and Roszak's accusations reverberated within the sector of the counterculture that turned to new religions (such as ISKCON) as an alterative. As one young Hare Krishna convert lamented, ever since the industrial revolution, "[t]he machine was to be the new God, and the scientists the priests."[47]

Among the hippies Bhaktivedanta found an audience willing and eager to disallow the mainstays of American religion—Christianity and Judaism—

and accept an Indian alternative. Bhaktivedanta's rejection of Western science fused with the counterculture's rejection of science as well as its members' distrust of traditional authority structures, resulting in a more strident opposition to the American scientific-technological society than the elder monk had demonstrated in his material produced in India. Consequently, the Hare Krishnas in America adopted a strongly anti-science position, openly rejecting Western science and calling for its replacement with an idealized Indian alternative, the Vedic science that Bhaktivedanta insisted offered older, more valuable, and more accurate knowledge. Here the American Hare Krishnas amplified the same themes that their founder had expressed in India: Western, materialistic science had failed, and needed to be replaced. Despite this position, the converts to the Hare Krishna movement and their guru continued to lean on the legitimacy and respect of contemporary science. Hence the ISKCON devotee Hayagriva Das Brahmacary could simultaneously attack the "mechanical chaos of the twentieth century" triumph of science, declare the 'Vedic background' of the Hare Krishnas—the Vedas are the ancient sacred texts of Hinduism—the ideal supreme science, and approvingly quote world-renowned Albert Einstein as a proponent of spirituality.[48]

In the United States, Bhaktivedanta continued translating Gaudiya Vaishnava sacred texts and authoring his own interpretations of them. But lecturing to potential converts and new disciples became his main pedagogical and religious practice. The distinction between what he began to call the Vedic science of Krishna Consciousness—"Vedic" implying that the science was rooted in the ancient Indian texts of the Vedas—and the materialistic science of the West occupied a premier place in his earliest lectures. One advantage of Vedic science, he insisted, was its populism. Following the lead of Chaitanya, the sixteenth-century mystic reformer whom the Hare Krishnas consider an avatar form of Krishna himself, Bhaktivedanta insisted that anyone could learn the Vedic science. Here the Indian swami paralleled the counterculture's disdain for formal education, perhaps hinting at why hippies so readily accepted his message. He explained in a September 13, 1966, lecture that "an ignorant person does not know of the science of God, but if he at least wants to hear of it, this is good. In fact, the Vedic literature is known as 'Sruti,' which means to learn by hearing. Spiritual science does not require a high education, nor a high intellect. Simply by hearing we can pass over the ocean of birth and death."[49] Rejecting the need for a higher education, Bhaktivedanta both accepted and reinforced the countercultural values of his audience. Additionally, he invested their preexisting opposition to the conventional American educational system with a religious explanation: the hippies who became Hare Krishnas continued to reject American high education (alongside Christianity), but now they did so with an additional, religious, rationale.

Bhaktivedanta continued the lecture by echoing another countercultural claim, that American materialism had failed its youth. "The atheists say that if we want to be happy we should get money so that we can have more food and material pleasures. However, in spite of all our material comforts and scientific advancements, we have not been able to stop the miseries of birth, death, old age, and disease."[50] Aligning himself with the romanticist critique of consumerism and materialism, Bhaktivedanta fused an opposition to science with an attack on what he saw as atheism and the too-comfortable lifestyle of Americans. While the DuPont corporation declared in its contemporary advertising slogan, "better living through chemistry," Bhaktivedanta insisted that the best of living came through Gaudiya Vaishnavism, rebranded in American as Krishna Consciousness—the Hare Krishna religion.

In keeping with the pattern he had established in the Indian issues of *Back to Godhead*, Bhaktivedanta also defined Krishna Consciousness as a science on its own terms. For example, in a 1966 lecture he insisted that "Bhagavad Gita is the science of God. In other scriptures, there is a concept of God. But, take this example: We can see that the flower is red, and the leaf is green. But a botanist will give you far more perfect and subtle knowledge. So, there is theoretical knowledge and practical knowledge. The science of God means that we should have, of course, knowledge of the Lord."[51] The Hare Krishna approach offered a science of God because it more perfectly described God, on both "theoretical" and "practical" levels. Or, as Bhaktivedanta bluntly declared in a January 1967 lecture, "The purpose of ISKCON is this: to understand the science of God."[52] Here the swami returned to one of the central points he emphasized in India, that Krishna Consciousness né Gaudiya Vaishnavism offered an alternative science to that of the West. Although perhaps new to the ears of Americans, none of this differed from the points he had earlier emphasized during his work in India.

What did change, however, was the context in which Bhaktivedanta worked to spread Krishna Consciousness. Rather than evangelizing to Indians enamored of Western science, he preached to Westerners enamored of Indian culture. Instead of countering the British colonial imposition of Western modernity, he spoke to American youth who also suspected the modern West and actively sought out an alternative. Bhaktivedanta therefore incorporated numerous Indian elements into his society, and Indian art, dress, and cuisine predominated in the International Society for Krishna Consciousness that he founded. This approach also appeared in Bhaktivedanta's written work, for example his twelve-page article, "A Study in Mysticism," published in the newly reconstituted *Back to Godhead*, now produced in America by the swami's disciples. The article, subtitled "An explanation of the mystic techniques offered by the great Teachers of Vedic wisdom—and their value to contemporary man," combined extensive use of Sanskrit, illustrations of *mandalas* (geometric designs used in meditation by Hindus and Buddhists), and language drawn from both Gaudiya Vaishnavism and the American counterculture. It also extensively invoked science and scientific metaphors. A single page, for example, criticized the American government for sending soldiers to die in Vietnam, questioned the value of higher education, rejected the ideal of technology as panacea, and called for the study of a "higher science," that of Krishna Consciousness.[53]

Just as revealing, in a 1969 issue of *Back to Godhead* Bhaktivedanta used his purport (explanation) of the tenth verse of the short Hindu text Ishopanishad, part of the more widely known corpus called the Upanishads, as a forum for attacking the Western scientific and technological establishment. The verse itself read, "The wise have explained to us that one result is derived from the culture of knowledge, and it is said that a different result is obtained from the culture of nescience." From this, Bhaktivedanta argued that "[o]ne should become a scientist or philosopher, and make research into spiritual knowledge—not material knowledge—recognizing that spiritual knowledge is permanent, whereas material knowledge ends with the death of the body." True scientists, he explained, pursue spiritual aims. Tellingly, however, Bhaktivedanta did not explain what such aims might entail. Instead, he launched into an attack on the American system of higher education. "The universities are, so to speak, centers of nescience only, and therefore the scientists are busy discovering lethal weapons to wipe out the existence of other countries. University students today are not given instructions on the regulative principles of Brahmacharya, the spiritual process of life, nor do they have any faith in the respective scriptural injunctions."[54] Four years after his arrival in the United States, the college-educated, former pharmaceutical chemist Bhaktivedanta had adopted the anti-establishment message of the countercultural youth to whom he had preached. Adding to his earlier themes of rejecting modern Western science and declaring Vaishnava science as superior, Swami Bhaktivedanta now declared the institutions of Western science, namely those of higher education, centers of ignorance and even, as he added in the same article, arrogance.[55]

4

Science and the Expansion of ISKCON

Bhaktivedanta's First Disciples on Science and ISKCON

As the decade of the 1960s came to a close, the Hare Krishnas strengthened their foothold in North America and extended their reach to Britain, France, and Germany as well. With temples in New York, San Francisco, Berkeley, Los Angeles, Boston, Montreal, Seattle, and an agricultural commune in West Virginia, ISKCON had achieved a wide geographic spread. It had also become an establishment in the American counterculture, with its saffron-garbed devotees and its Hare Krishna mantra easily recognized by both the hippies and the commentators who remarked on this colorful countercultural new religious movement. During the 1970s, ISKCON would both continue to expand as well as institutionalize itself, with larger temples, a bureaucracy operated by the new converts, and an attempt to outreach to the "straight" community outside the counterculture. Although one might expect the group's approach to science to have moderated during this era, the opposite happened. With the publication of several book-length collections and the spotlight of the media on its founder and his followers, the Hare Krishnas explicitly and vociferously attacked what Americans considered "science" and insisted that they offered an ideal replacement.

Thirteen months after Bhaktivedanta arrived on American shores, he had managed to convert a small cadre of former hippies to Gaudiya Vaishnavism, which he had incorporated in America in 1966 as the International Society for Krishna Consciousness. Of the duties Bhaktivedanta assigned his followers, he charged them with editing and publishing a new run of *Back to Godhead*, transformed from the irregularly published magazine of a Indian householder to the official organ of the society. Sensing the enormous value that their spiritual master placed on the written word and on publishing, many of Bhaktivedanta's most dedicated followers devoted themselves to writing and editing the journal. In producing the new American *Back to Godhead*, they fused their guru's religious teachings with their own intellectual and theological positions. To the Bhagavad Gita they added references to Tolkein and Whitman, LSD and marijuana. However, a critical position on science remained a core part of many of the articles that the first generation of devotees produced. On the one hand, the converts accepted their mentor's insistence that ISKCON represented an alternative science. On the other hand, they brought a vitriolic distaste for the American scientific establishment, the "new priesthood" of a scientific elite, as Ralph E. Lapp described.[1]

Two of Bhaktivedanta's new disciples, Hayagriva Das Brahmachary (né Howard Wheeler) and Rayarama Das Brahmachary (né Raymond Marais) took the reigns as editors and headlined the new American *Back to Godhead*, renumbered at volume 1, number 1.[2] Hayagriva came to ISKCON with a master's degree in English from New York University and a fascination with Hinduism and Buddhism that he gained from his courses in religion as an undergraduate at the University of North Carolina–Chapel Hill. Transcendentalist American poetry entranced him, and Hayagriva would later retire to the movement's Waldenesque rural West Virginia commune.[3] Much less is known of Rayarama, who contributed as editor to Bhaktivedanta's first American translations of the Bhagavad Gita but seemed to have left the movement after several years.[4] In the first article of the new magazine, the two men wrote of the Hare Krishna movement as one rooted in science and therefore irrefutably accurate. "True devotees of Krishna neither reason nor argue about Him. 'He who replies to words of Doubt, Doth put the Light of knowledge out,' wrote Blake. For the devotees, Krishna is an established fact. The devotees do, however, spread 'Krishna-consciousness' [*sic*] to others, to convince them of Krishna's existence through the 'science of devotion.' Devotion to God is a 'yoga,' a science, and it is to teach this science that Swami Bhaktivedanta has come to America."[5] Much of Hayagriva and Rayarama's rhetoric directly mirrored that of their guru, for example the references to yoga as a science, but they tentatively added to the message with the cited— but hardly integrated—reference to the mystic and romantic poet William Blake (1757–1827), a favorite poet of the counterculture. Each of the succeeding issues of *Back to Godhead* mentioned science, with the second issue declaring the "publication devoted to promulgating bhaktiyoga, the science of God as expounded by Lord Sri Krishna in the Bhagavad-Gita."[6]

The fifth issue, printed in January 1967, brought anti-science discourse to a new level, featured a disparaging and extended attack authored by Hayagriva Das on university learning, teachers, and students alike. It represented the new stridently anti-science perspective—at least when defining "science" as Western and materialistic—of a growing segment of the American Hare

Krishnas. In his "Krishna: The End of Knowledge," Hayagriva declared that science at best distracted from spiritual aims, and at worst led to self-destruction of the species. Combining the approach of his spiritual master Bhaktivedanta with the countercultural critics of science and technology, Hayagriva offered a strong critique of science:

> Furthermore, science has principally helped man to destroy himself most effectively. In the realm, science has proved itself most helpful and progressive. Extermination. . . . Always what [American poet] Hart Crane called "the iron dealt cleavage," iron, metal, science cutting flesh. It is a familiar story. Yet these madmen, masters of extermination, receive large financial grants from universities and foundations to further pursue the annihilation of the race. They are always trying to kill God, but God cannot be killed. Yet science, the pursuit of the firecracker, is considered knowledge. . . . Although modern man places all his hopes in science, the wise know this to be the knowledge of the madhouse.[7]

Over the next six pages, Hayagriva attacked the ignorance of scientists and academicians broadly and of university knowledge. The alternative, he implied, lay in Krishna Consciousness, what elsewhere he and other members of ISKCON insisted was a bona fide alternative science.

Hayagriva Das continued this theme in the next issue of *Back to Godhead*, with a twelve-page article titled "Doubt, Thy Name is Bondage," devoted almost exclusively to criticizing Western science as a worthless endeavor. Much of the article repeated similar charges from the previous issue's critique, but Hayagriva also offered a new charge, one aimed not at science itself but the practitioners of the methodology. Calling scientists "recalcitrant children of darkness," Hayagriva Das declared that "[v]ain men are trying to used [*sic*] their tiny brains to puncture a realm that can only be known through faith, devotion, and the grace of God. . . . Thinking the physical, material universe the all-in-all, they set about conquering it like children. . . . The scientist never acknowledge that he automatically accepts so much on faith—his very breath, for example, that makes it possible for him to pursue science and the empirical path."[8] Though Hayagriva certainly presented an extreme criticism, much of what he said—that scientists demonstrated arrogance and close-mindedness—reverberated not only with fellow members of the counterculture but with broader society. Hayagriva contrasted scientists with those who he considered more enlightened Westerners, the poets William Blake, Walt Whitman (1819–1892), and Hart Crane (1899–1932).

Nearly every subsequent issue of the first half-decade of *Back to Godhead* featured some discussion of science by the first-generation American Hare Krishna devotees. The pattern followed that set by Bhaktivedanta himself in the Indian run of the periodical, with the majority of cases using science as a term to describe something else that the Hare Krishnas supported (e.g., science of God-consciousness, science of controlling the mind, science of God, scientific writings of the great Hindu mystics, etc.),[9] but with a large minority of articles critiquing science, technology, and the scientific mind-set that predominated in the United States. In the latter cases, authors often combined both perspectives. Only the science of Krishna Consciousness differed. As Hayagriva's coreligionist Nayana Bhiram Das Brahmachary declared, "because of the scientific presentation of spiritual knowledge characteristic of the Vedic literature, Krishna Consciousness also offers somthing [*sic*] new to people of the West."[10] Ironically, the something new that ISKCON offered the West was something they declared to be quite old in the East.

Considering synoptically the early writings of Bhaktivedanta's first American disciples, science functioned as a rhetorical mark of identity. By calling their adopted Vaishnava tradition a true science, these converts claimed for themselves the legitimacy of the science in the modern world. Yet their rejection of what they disdained as Western science allowed them to position themselves in opposition to what they perceived as the materialistic, rationalistic, technological Western culture. Similar to the Unification Church's position, the early ISKCON converts demonstrated a radical but representative approach. As the avant-garde of the growing American counterculture, the Hare Krishnas represented a wider reappraisal of the centrality of science in the modern world. The aforementioned social critics Theodore Roszak and Jacques Ellul offered a somewhat more mainstream assessment, though each still spoke primarily to the growing counterculture. One might easily mistake Roszak's critique of science with that of Hayagriva when he wrote that "[w]hatever enlightening and beneficial 'spin-off' the universal research explosion of our time produces, the major interest of those who lavishly finance that research will continue to be in weapons, in techniques of social control, in commercial gadgetry, in market manipulation, and in the subversion of democratic processes."[11] ISKCON's growth in the United States represents a more radicalized version of the same assessment, adding a theological condemnation of the modern world as well as utopian vision for an idealized Indian alternative.

"Life Comes From Life": Bhaktivedanta and His Disciples on Science

In 1973, between April 16 and May 17, then again from December 2 to December 10, Swami A. C. Bhaktivedanta engaged in a set of impromptu conversations on issues of science during morning walks with his disciples. The ISKCON members joining their guru on these walks tape-recorded the exchanges, eventually producing a set of seventeen transcripts. The Hare Krishnas published a shortened version of the first of these (recorded on April 16, 1973) in their movement's organ, *Back to Godhead*, two years later as "Life Comes From Life." With the exception of that five-page excerpt, the movement reserved the transcripts until 1979, two years after Bhaktivedanta's death, when his disciples published the remaining sixteen collected and edited conversations as *Life Comes From Life*. Bhaktivedanta spent much of the time during these talks insisting that all life, human or otherwise, originated from Krishna, the source of life. He specifically targeted the scientific view that it originated from nonliving organic chemicals ("the primordial soup") as "unscientific and incorrect," in his terms. Darwinian evolution also troubled him, since it contradicted some of his Vedic assumptions, as did the general tendency of scientists to insist that they knew better than religious sources.

Bhaktivedanta's "Life Come From Life" conversations with his disciples underwent so many changes and edits that many of his original words have become lost.[12] The newest transcriptions of those tapes that remain, made available in 2003, demonstrate that Bhaktivedanta's disciples heavily redacted the text before publication in the 1970s, leaving the book and intermediate manuscripts extremely unreliable in terms of revealing the original 1973 conversations. (Bhaktivedanta had encouraged his followers to "manipulate and expand" the morning walks for their own purposes, so they were in effect following his advice in editing them.[13]) Nevertheless, the sources that are available demonstrate Bhaktivedanta and his disciples' extreme opposition to Western science, which emerged as the clearest theme in the conversations. A typical exchange, and Bhaktivedanta's opening words from the October 18 conversation, has the swami stating what he takes to be a Vedic truth, noting that science and scientists disagree, and dismissing them as wrong: "Even on the sun there are living entities. What is the opinion of the scientists? [Disciple: 'They say that there is no life there.'] That is nonsense."[14] Bhaktivedanta maintained such distinction between science and Krishna Consciousness as a refrain in the conversations. Science accepted Darwinian evolution, but

ISKCON knew that Krishna predefined all species at the moment of cosmic creation; science proclaimed that life on Earth originated from chemicals, but ISKCON understood that life came from Krishna; science denied miracles, but ISKCON recognized the miraculous powers of the yogis; and so forth.

The *Life Comes From Life* book and identically titled article in *Back to Godhead* portrayed Swami Bhaktivedanta as both a font of wisdom and prophet of caution against the false gods of science. The book's back cover, for example, called the contents "a brilliant critique of some of the dominant policies, theories and presuppositions of modern science and scientists. *Life Comes From Life* will break the spell of the materialistic and nihilistic myths which, masquerading as science, have so bewitched modern civilization."[15] The surviving tapes and transcripts reveal ISKCON at a point of transformation: a cadre of senior disciples literally leading their aging leader through his morning walks, sometimes responding to his pronouncements, and at other times prompting them. These disciples—Indian-born chemist Thoudam Damadara Singh and American-born former hippies Karandhara Dasa, Brahmananda Swami, and Hrdayananda Dasa Goswami—all of whom had become Hare Krishnas in the previous decade—would soon adopt the mantle of leadership in the movement. Though each platform varied, with Singh the most positive toward modern Western science, as a whole they showed tremendous distrust for the American scientific establishment, scientists, and science generally. Each also insisted that ISKCON offered a better and more scientific solution to the nation and world's needs.

Whereas in interviews with outsiders, Swami Bhaktivedanta emphasized the scientific nature of Krishna Consciousness in order to appeal to Americans' innate (as he understood it) attraction to science, the "Life Comes From Life" talks represented internal conversations among committed leaders of ISKCON. Hence Bhaktivedanta and his disciples discussed how their own movement differed from science, focusing on what they considered the most problematic issues in science and their group's relation to it. They specified science's methodological empiricism that devalued textual evidence, and what the Hare Krishnas took to be the arrogance of scientists toward alternative sources of truth. In both cases, scientists disregarded what ISKCON's leaders believed were central repositories of truth, the Vedic texts. Scientists assumed that they knew more than did nonscientists, and particularly that they had better access to the truth than did the ancient Indian Vedas. This not only troubled Bhaktivedanta and his followers, but offended them, as demonstrated by their abusive language toward scientists. During the walks the swami and his disciples called scientists thieves, demons, animals, rascals, and asses, among other terms of reprobation.[16] Other times, Swami Bhaktivedanta threatened to "kick in the face" the scientists who repudiated his tradition. Beneath this acrimony, the Hare Krishna leadership distrusted what they considered the arrogance of scientists in refusing to take religious accounts seriously. During the April 28 conversation, the normally well-spoken Bhaktivedanta became almost exasperated at scientists' refusal to accept textual, rather than empirical, evidence. Putting one of his disciples in the role of scientist, he confronted science in the second person. "Vedas says: 'Here is the original cause,' you won't take it. . . . Veda means knowledge, perfect knowledge. But when gives you [sic]: 'Here is the original cause.' You won't take. You shall stick to your imperfect knowledge. This is your disease."[17] While Bhaktivedanta certainly refrained from calling scientists "diseased" to their faces, in internal discussions he and his followers admitted to their anger with scientists' refusal to take seriously what ISKCON held most dear, the texts of the Vedas.

The most extreme rhetoric against scientists, however, Bhaktivedanta and his disciples reserved for those who attempted to create life in laboratories or claimed that life originated from nonliving organic matter, i.e., the theory of the origins of terrestrial life from a "primordial soup" of nucleic acids and other hydrocarbons. To these scientists, the elder swami reserved his harshest criticism and one of the few recorded mentions of, as one nondevotee attending the morning walks described, "physical violence of a most unpleasant type."[18] Such scientists, Bhaktivedanta stated on several occasions, ought to be "kicked in the face with boots."[19] Such fiery language indicates the degree of tension that ISKCON leaders felt between their own movement and the materialistic assumptions of most mainstream scientists. Again, Bhaktivedanta addressed science in the second person, but spoke to his disciples as well:

KARANDHARA: There's a miss. . . .They say there's a missing link [between DNA and organic chemicals].

BHAKTIVEDANTA: A missing link? Then I kick on your face. You're missing this kick. Now learn it. Nonsense. Here is the missing point. Just learn it. Write vigorous articles to kick on the face of these rascals. All of you. You have got so much advanced laboratories, advanced knowledge. You do not… even you are defying the authority of God. You have become so great. And you cannot prove that life is coming out of matter. That you are leaving aside for future. And I have to believe such a rascal? Do you think it is nice? You are talking all nonsense, and I have to believe you?

KARANDHARA: They say they have almost proof that some acids, they make some acids and it's almost like an animal. Just about, not quite, but almost.

BHAKTIVEDANTA: Asses, asses?

KARANDHARA: Amino acids.

BRAHMANANDA: Asses.[20]

Swami Bhaktivedanta, Singh, Karandhara, and Brahmananda repeated these claims throughout the "Life Comes From Life" conversations. Science could not scientifically prove its contentions, they insisted, whereas Krishna Consciousness offered the truth, encapsulated in the perfect Vedas of ancient India.

Again one must notice that the ISKCON leadership offered an assessment of American science that while surely radical, was representative of a wider critique. In challenging the ability of science to function as sole arbitrator of truth in the realm of the origin of life, the Hare Krishnas had numerous parallels in American religion. Creationists, young-earth geologists, and the intelligent-design movement (ID) offer just three examples. In 1963, during the same decade that the Hare Krishna movement came to America, a group of moderate evangelical scientists uncomfortable with the materialistic assumptions of most biological theories of the origin of life created the Creation Research Society (CRS). For decades, the CRS's high school textbook *Biology: A Search for Order in Complexity* represented the group's attempt to offer a new scientific approach to supplant evolutionary biology. With Gallup polls during the late twentieth-century showing upwards of 40 percent of Americans holding similar positions, ISKCON's rejection of Western scientists as "defying the authority of God" and call for their "kicking in the face" must be read as a radical rendering of the same sentiments.[21]

Science Among ISKCON's New Leadership

As he aged and his movement grew, Bhaktivedanta passed the reigns of authority to his most senior male disciples, people like Karandhara, who would become the leader of the Los Angeles Hare Krishnas, and Singh, who was to become the first director of Bhaktivedanta's institute for religion and science issues. As they traveled more extensively and served as intermediate religious teachers, or gurus, to new converts, they in turn became the intellectuals of the ISKCON movement. Many of them took their first steps as intellectual leaders within the Hare Krishna movement by publishing in the group's *Back to Godhead*, whose pages serve as guides to the transition in power. While Bhaktivedanta himself published fewer articles, his disciples published more, for example, the three representative articles published by the following three members of the ISKCON's new leadership: Yogesvara Dasa, Bali Mardan Dasa, and Pancaratna Dasa.[22] Between them, they led the Hare Krishna's new mission to France (Yogesvara), the movement's publishing arm of Bhaktivedanta Book Trust (Bali Mardan), and the movement's outreach to academics (Pancaratna). They also demonstrate three differing perspectives on science within the Hare Krishna movement: a limited acceptance of Western science as a support for ISKCON's own positions, the rejection of Western science because it conflicted with Vaishnava beliefs, and the perspective that ISKCON itself was scientific. These combined with other approaches, most notably Hayagriva's continued countercultural (or neoromantic) critique of science, which he issued from the movement's rural commune in West Virginia.

Some in the new cadre of ISKCON leaders adopted more cautious approaches to science, such as the young American called Yogesvara Dasa (né Joshua Green), an American-born convert who during his studies of comparative literature at the Sorbonne encountered Krishna Consciousness. Bhaktivedanta appointed him the leader of the French branch of ISKCON.[23] Though Yogesvara had joined the movement only four years earlier, his five-page article in *Back to Godhead* forcefully differentiated between the Western paradigm of science and what he called the "Vedic conception," but which recognized science as a positive activity of understanding the world, albeit one that could not achieve its ends. The article, "Primal Origins," proposed that cosmologists needed to accept the Vedic scriptures if they had any hope of understanding the origins of the universe and the nature of the cosmos. Complete with an image of a spiral galaxy, Yogesvara's article positioned true science as a variety of Vedic knowledge. "The Vedic conception of the forthright man of science is one of an individual bent on extending the perimeters of empirical knowledge to bring about a fusion with transcendental truth. Real science, according to the Vedic conception, is not unspiritual, but rather, unrestricted, truly experimental—even to the extent of experimenting with the chanting of ancient *mantras*, for example."[24] True scientists had nothing to fear in Krishna Consciousness, he explained, and would willingly sample the movement's proscribed forms of devotion, or bhakti, if they truly wished to follow an open-minded research agenda. Yogesvara, of course, had no doubts that ISKCON's bhakti-centered practices would prove efficacious.

Scientists who sought answers could find them in ISKCON's texts, Yogesvara maintained. Here the empiricism of Western science contrasted with the textual basis of Vedic science, at least as ISKCON imagined it. The Hare Krishna's texts offered knowledge of the origins of life and the cosmos that science would otherwise find impossible to obtain, Yogesvara insisted. He wrote, "Krsna consciousness, as a practical program for implementing the conclusions of spiritual science, may offer some valuable insights into primal origins, or the beginnings of the creation, which might not otherwise be available to sincere men of science. This information is drawn from authentic Vedic texts, and, as we shall see, it finds convincing supportive evidence in modern logic and scientific discovery."[25] Yogesvara's concluding sentence in this selection, that modern logic and science "support" Vedic conclusions, demonstrates the primacy of Vedic texts in his thinking. Like some textually oriented Jews or Christians, science might "support" the positions drawn from the scripture, but in the event of contradiction or confusion, the text remains the primary source of data.[26] Science could only confirm Krishna Consciousness, or else it was incorrect and therefore bad science. Hence, Yogesvara insisted that "this article is an attempt to present basic scientific information that will help sincere inquirers understand Krsna to be the cause of the universe—and help them understand Krsna's causeless nature."[27] Science offered value in as much as it supported Krishna Consciousness's own views and beliefs.

While Yogesvara emphasized the consensus of science and Krishna Consciousness, albeit within the rubric of science corroborating ISKCON's own positions, other young intellectual lights within the movement took the opposite approach. Bali Mardan Dasa, whom Bhaktivedanta had appointed a trustee of the ISKCON's new publishing arm, the Bhaktivedanta Book Trust, authored an attack on Darwinism in *Back to Godhead*, sections of which could just as easily have come from a fundamentalist Christian opponent of evolution. Echoing the words of the nuclear physicist Ralph Lapp, who warned in *The New Priesthood* of science becoming "the Great Dictator of our times," Bali Mardan accused Darwinian science and evolutionary biologists of "attack[ing] man's faith in God and establish[ing] science as the new deity with themselves as its priests."[28] While Lapp's accusations of the priesthood of science evoked a latent Protestant anti-clericalism and focused on science's danger to democracy, Bali Mardan warned of science as an alternative religion, one that sought to establish its practitioners as the new religious leaders of society.

Like some Christian and Jewish opponents of Darwinism, Bali Mardan argued that ultimately the evolutionary biologists used bad science to reach bad conclusions. These scientists, he noted, "cleverly rearrange their theories to fit the changing evidence," and create theories such as evolution, an "unscientific claim to satisfy the minds of atheistic men."[29] The reason for his critique of Darwinism also paralleled that of most Jewish and Christian opponents of evolution who reject evolutionary theory because they believe it contradicts statements of their sacred texts. Christians and Jews concern themselves with the biblical description of creation in Genesis, but one of the main problems for Bali Mardan and other members of ISKCON lay in the Vedic claim of a thriving ancient human civilization, hundreds of thousands, or even millions, of years before evolutionary biology accepts the presence of *Homo sapiens*. Bali Mardan raised this point directly in his article by accepting the fossil evidence of ancient Neanderthals and Cro-Magnons but insisting that these variant species existed alongside fully developed human beings who left no physical evidence. "Excavated bones come from aboriginal tribes living side by side with the advanced Vedic culture," he explained. But since the Vedic peoples cremated their dead, they left no fossil evidence of their ancient civilization in India, leaving empirical materialistic scientists to assume that human beings evolved only within the past two-hundred thousand years.[30] Bali Mardan concluded his article with a forceful defense of the authenticity of the Vedas, which he regarded as the bedrock of the ISKCON worldview and therefore its science. "The infallible source of knowledge is the Vedic scriptures which, unlike the speculative postulates of empirical scientists, are spoken directly by the Supreme Lord Himself."[31] Science offered no value, Bali Mardan argued, because it disagreed with the fundamental Vedic texts and therefore demonstrated its unreliability.

In 1974 Pancaratna Dasa, an American convert then serving as vice president of ISKCON's New York temple and contact person for outsiders, joined a nondevotee and recent graduate of Fordham University's PhD program in Asian religious studies to co-teach an experimental course in Krishna Consciousness at Fordham.[32] Pancaratna and his fellow instructor J. Frank Kenney offered the course to ten students at Fordham University's campus in Manhattan in the spring 1974 term.[33] As a team, Kenney and Pancaratna Dasa assumed three objectives, namely (1) the fostering of an "in-depth understanding of the religious experience" of Krishna Consciousness; (2) a "broad critique of Krishna Consciousness from a variety of [academic] viewpoints," such as sociological, psychological, and phenomenological studies of the movement; and (3) "active student involvement" in learning. None of these three goals stand out as overly remarkable for a college seminar. However, each instructor also approached the course with his own objectives. Kenney sought to use Weberian sociology and the psychological approaches of Carl Raschke to study ISKCON.[34] Pancaratna explained his approach as follows: "in order to convey some understanding of Krishna Consciousness I thought it necessary to emphasize the following points: (1) Krishna Consciousness is not a religious faith; it is a science; (2) Krishna Consciousness is neither sectarian nor dogmatic but rather scientific because it involves a practical, 'fool-proof' technique for achieving God-consciousness; (3) the scientific nature of Krishna Consciousness is most clearly demonstrated by the process of distinguishing matter and spirit; and (4) as a consequence, the first step in Krishna Consciousness realization (and the first point presented for class discussion) was the concept 'I am not this body,' a concept which is scientifically verifiable in view of the ever-changing body."[35]

Each of Pancaratna's four emphases highlighted what he considered the scientific nature of ISKCON. A tension existed, however, between Pancaratna's insistence on the nature of Krishna Consciousness and the reality that he and Kenney taught the course in the university's Department of Religious Studies and thus described the class as "the study of this new American religion" of Krishna Consciousness. Implicitly, Pancaratna Dasa even accepted the reality that students would compare ISKCON to other religions, explaining that the course "made available the vast philosophical and religious understanding of the Vedic literature and challenged the students to investigate their own religious values and attitudes." Kenney likewise noted that the students attempted to understand the Hare Krishnas by "baptizing them into one's own religious frame of reference."[36] Given the location of the course in a religious studies department, statements of both professors, and their evaluations of student involvement, clearly all involved recognized the religious nature of Krishna Consciousness. Nevertheless, Pancaratna Dasa focused so heavily on science because he not only accepted Bhaktivedanta's teaching on the scientific nature of the Hare Krishna religion, but also ISKCON's desire to demonstrate its scientific nature to a wider audience.[37]

These three voices—Yogesvara Dasa, Bali Mardan Dasa, and Pancaratna Dasa—reveal three different positions on science taken by leaders of the Hare Krishna movement: that it provided value in as much as it corroborated ISKCON's ideology, that it conflicted with Vaishnava beliefs, and that ISKCON itself represented a scientific alternative. Although each obvious differed, the differing perspectives did operate under a wider umbrella. Krishna Consciousness, all agreed, offered the best solutions to individual and global problems, provided the best information and data on the workings of the universe, and most perfectly fit within a modern scientific approach to life. Ultimately, all insisted that their own religious movement offered much more than conventional Western science.

The Bhaktivedanta Institute and The Scientific Basis of Krsna Consciousness

In 1974, as Pancaratna Dasa attempted to demonstrate the scientific nature of Krishna Consciousness to undergraduate students, Swami A. C. Bhaktivedanta Prabhupada created an institution within ISKCON to do the same thing on a broader scale. The swami hoped that this new center, the Bhaktivedanta Institute, would propagate what he considered the scientific nature of Krishna Consciousness. Its charter declared, "[t]he main purpose of the Institute is to explore the implications of the Vedic knowledge as it bears on all features of human culture, and to present its findings in courses, lectures, monographs, books and journals of high scientific standard."[38] Though it would require several years before the Institute produced any such findings, publications, or conferences, eventually during the 1980s (after its namesake's death) it would become the intellectual center for science and religion within ISKCON. A decade after that, it splintered into several competing Bhaktivedanta Institutes when its leaders assumed fundamentally different positions on science. But in the 1970s, it served as a catalyst that further involved one of ISKCON's few leaders with a doctorate in science, Svarupa Damodara Dasa, in bringing Krishna Consciousness to scientists.

Svarupa Damodara Dasa served as the Bhaktivedanta Institute's first director in 1974, even though he had converted to ISKCON only three years earlier.[39] Svarupa, who also published under his birth name of Dr. Thoudam Damodar Singh, had taken part in the 1973 "Life Comes From Life" conversations between Bhaktivedanta and his disciples, and at the time of those talks he was also studying for his doctorate in organic chemistry at the University of California–Irvine. Despite his Sikh surname, Singh had been raised a Hindu, and like Bhaktivedanta he studied chemistry at a prestigious Indian university, though in Singh's case at two, both Gauhati University and Calcutta University. Unlike Bhaktivedanta, Singh found science far more attractive than religion and dedicated himself to a career in chemistry during his young adult years, which brought him to doctoral studies in the United States. His conversion to ISKCON followed a typical pattern, beginning with a spiritual crisis brought on by a personal loss (the death of his mother), a chance meeting with Hare Krishnas singing and dancing on the street, and eventually a visit to an ISKCON center. Singh, who adopted the religious name of Svarupa Damodara Dasa during his initiation into the Hare Krishna movement, differed from many of the other American converts by remaining in higher education and continuing his advanced studies in science. As an Indian who had embraced his Hindu religion, though trained in science under first the British and then American educational system, he shared with Bhaktivedanta a liminal location in regard to science and religion.

Bhaktivedanta recognized Svarupa né Singh, one of the movement's first PhDs, as a potential intellectual leader within ISKCON, and appointed Svarupa head of the new Bhaktivedanta Institute. Svarupa's ascendancy as intellectual and scientific leader within ISKCON resulted in an immediate windfall, the production of a book-length treatment of religion and science. With a first print-run of thirty thousand copies, Svarupa's *The Scientific Basis of Krsna Consciousness* (1974) attempted to directly confront scientists' materialistic and empiricist assumptions. Its author hoped it would lead to a wave of scientists accepting Krishna Consciousness: "This booklet is primarily directed to our scientific friends," he wrote in the book's first chapter. "Instead of centering one's consciousness around temporary machines, one should transfer his consciousness to Sri Krsna, the supreme scientist, knowing that He is the central point for all activities. . . . [A]ll activities have no value unless Krsna is included within these activities. Thus we can understand that the science of Krsna is the only real science which is to be learned and practiced."[40] Svarupa's confrontational approach—calling the Krishna Consciousness the "only real science"—encapsulated ISKCON's wider perspective on Western science, namely that the movement's own approach ought to replace that of normative American science. Three basic themes dominate *The Scientific Basis of Krsna Consciousness*: a teleological argument for God's existence; a dismissal of normative scientific methodologies; and a defense of the value of the Vedas. The net effect minimized the value of Western science and maximized the Vedic science that ISKCON promoted.

After a brief introduction, Svarupa's book turned to demonstrating the evidence for the existence of God. He utilized a classic approach, that of teleology, the study of the order inherent in nature. Teleological arguments claim that the existence of order in the cosmos implies the existence of a creator, and have been a fixture of theology since the works of Plato and Aristotle. Thomas Aquinas authored a teleological argument for the existence of God, the American evangelist Jonathan Edwards used teleology in his work, and the Intelligent Design movement that originated in late twentieth-century Christian circles also relies upon a teleological approach. Yet perhaps the most famous of such teleological arguments for the existence of God is that of British theologian William Paley (1743–1805), who formulated what later students of philosophy named the watchmaker argument. The complexity of nature, Paley argued, implied a creator, just as did the complexity of a watch.[41]

Svarupa's teleological argument followed a similar vein. The "systematic path" of planetary orbits, he argued, provided evidence of a designer, as did the orbits of electrons around an atom's nucleus. Both planets and particles traced perfectly looped orbits around their centers, thus demonstrating the presence of an author of the natural law of rotation, a law that governed everything from planet to electron. "Thus," Svarupa explained, "from the submicroscopic reaches to the galactic objects, this material universe is running like intricate, well-oiled clockwork according to great natural physical laws and principles."[42] Such laws and principles, he insisted, demonstrate a law-giver and origin. On a biological level, Svarupa noted, the social patterns of honeybees and their ability to build sturdy and intricate hives revealed a similarly complex order within nature, as did the physical laws of optics and gravity. Each demonstrated the presence of a supreme creator, "Lord Sri Krsna, the supreme scientist and supreme engineer, under whose kind will the whole cosmos is working."[43] Illustrations provided additional evidence, with one picture showing the familiar double helix of deoxyribonucleic acid (DNA) alongside a peg-and-ball diagram of the genetic molecules that readers might recall from college or high-school chemistry kits. The drawing included such scientific details as molecular chains labeled as cytosine and guanine, two of the four chemicals that form base pairs in DNA, as well as the structural formula for the compounds, the coded diagram that allows chemists to physically represent molecules.[44]

Having established the existence of God using the teleological argument, he moved to dismiss the value and power of contemporary Western science and its practitioners. First, Svarupa targeted the abilities of scientists to both understand and accurately observe the natural world, requirements of the empirical foundation of modern science. Scientists lacked the power to comprehend the full nature of the universe, he explained, and even if they could, they did not have the faculties to glimpse it.[45] Even more damning, Svarupa argued, scientists insisted on the ability to prove all conjectures, using what he had already dismissed as limited power of reasoning and observation. This resulted in the inability of scientists to accurately describe the natural world as well as their refusal to accept the textual evidence that ISKCON insisted offered the solution.[46] Svarupa's critique of empiricism echoes those of Bhaktivedanta, written thirty years earlier in India.

Yet Svarupa insisted that he and his movement offered the medicine for this disease: the ancient Indian texts, the Vedas. Seizing a story that his guru Swami Bhaktivedanta told him during the "Life Comes From Life" walks, Svarupa compared empirical scientists to frogs living in wells. Just as the frog in the well could not imagine the size of the Pacific Ocean, human scientists cannot understand the true nature of the universe. Only outside knowledge could enlighten the frog. Complete with an illustration of "Dr. Frog, PhD," Svarupa explained that the frog's belief that it accurately perceived and understood the nature of its own well revealed only its hubris and ignorance. Even if one removed the frog from the well, it would remain mired in "well-consciousness," unable to grasp the world outside its formative experiences. Better, he explained, if the frog accepted the teachings of a wiser and authoritative teacher.

A defense of the Vedas and their relevance for modern science occupied much of the remaining pages of the booklet, particularly the Vedic texts on creation and cosmology called the Puranas. After a two-page dismissal of Darwinian evolution as "mental manipulation" predicated on a "poor fund of knowledge," Svarupa turned to the Puranic description of creation, which he called "complete and perfect knowledge (science)" as well as "infallible" and "the Supreme Judgement."[47] Having already established the veracity of the Vedas and the need for acceptance of religious authority, Svarupa summarized the Puranic explanation as the "complete and perfect knowledge of evolution in minute detail," and chided scientists for not accepting what he insisted was self-evidently perfect.[48] Only arrogance and a misguided belief in the supremacy of human rationality and senses could explain scientific rejection of Vedic truth, Svarupa maintained.

The author concluded his book by dismissing "most modern scientists" as "demoniacs" and proponents of "less than animal civilization," and restating the need for all people, scientists included, to seek out "a bona fide spiritual master, initiator, or teacher of the science, . . . the science of Krsna, Krsna consciousness."[49] It is doubtful that many scientists reached the end of Svarupa Damodara Dasa's *The Scientific Basis of Krsna Consciousness*, which its author intended for his "scientist friends," without being offended. The text denigrated scientists as small-brained, visionless, demoniac, animalistic, obstinate, and diseased. Its author concluded the text with an image of a leering scientist pushing a button while a mushroom cloud rose from an annihilated city, indicating both his movement's strong animosity toward the scientific establishment as well as wider position that ISKCON's Vedic science ought to replace Western science.

Spiritual Revolution

Despite ISKCON's hopes and intentions, most of its future adherents did not come from scientific backgrounds but from the American youth culture that rejected wider society's establishments of science, education, and government.[50] While these potential adherents might read a few articles in *Back to Godhead*, they probably would not (and did not) take the time to digest entire books when first confronted by Krishna Consciousness. ISK-CON therefore adopted the religious tract as a broadcast method of communicating with and attracting potential new devotees. Some of the tracts took the form of trifold pamphlets, while others resembled short newsletters. The ISKCON San Francisco and Los Angeles communities produced one of the first of the latter variety in 1975, titled *Spiritual Revolution*, a four-page tract distributed on college campuses in the San Francisco area. Like other sources produced by the Hare Krishna movement during the 1970s, *Spiritual Revolution* spoke the language of science: it defined Krishna Consciousness as a science, rejected the dominant paradigms of Western science, and portrayed ISKCON as scientific in scope and character. *Spiritual Revolution* also included the same Manichean rhetoric of Svarupa's *Scientific Basis of Krsna Consciousness*, of Vedic science vs. Western science. But in keeping with Bhaktivedanta's recognition that America valued science, *Spiritual Revolution* attempted to show the forward-thinking nature of ISKCON's Vedic science by indicating its compatibility with the cutting edge sectors of modern science, quantum physics and relativity.[51]

Two of the unique contributions of the *Spiritual Revolution* pamphlet were a one-third-page cartoon titled "The Conversion of Doctor Mud" and a brief editorial ("The Grand Illusion") on the back page of the tract. The first of these items positioned scientists as tools of a fascist state, whereas the second tried to demonstrate the compatibility of recent scientific findings with Vedic science. Together, they indicated the simultaneous effort within ISKCON to replace Western science as well as defend the movement itself as scientific.

The "Doctor Mud" cartoon contained eleven frames, which told the story of a professor indoctrinating students with materialism. The unnamed cartoonist drew Doctor Mud as a caricature: he wears a suit and eyeglasses, has receding curly hair and a big nose, and looks like an overeducated egghead. Representing the arrogant material scientist, he propounds to a rows of students, "Meet your origin! The primordial mass of matter, the 'chunk!' If you do not accept the 'chunk,' you will fail this class, and never succeed in life. Matter is all in all. Seek no more." In an Orwellian twist, a hitherto invisible loudspeaker then addresses the professor:

> Very good, Dr. Mud, our potential opposition, all the intellectuals and students, are now robot slaves of materialism. Now we can continue to exploit the natural resources and peoples of the world without opposition. The military-industrial states will cover every inch of the globe. Even if it means the death of freedom and the earth, we shall enjoy our perverted senses at all costs! Cut down the trees! Pollute the skies! Fill the cities! Build factories! Destroy spirit! Kill soul! And then, everything will be under *our* control! Thank you, Prof. Mud![52]

Potential readers could no doubt recognize the allusions within the cartoon to environmental devastation and government wrongdoing. The years preceding 1975, when ISKCON published the cartoon, witnessed an explosion of interest in ecology, including the first Earth Day and the founding of Greenpeace in 1970 and 1971 respectively.[53] Similarly, the recent events of Watergate, culminating in the resignation of President Richard Nixon in 1974, reminded readers of government corruption and selfishness. The tract's readers, addressed as "students and intellectuals" on the first page of the pamphlet, would also have recognized the implication that their college classes indoctrinated them into materialism, perhaps a subtle jab at ISKCON's foes who accused the Hare Krishnas of indoctrinating its own members into a foreign religious cult.

The cartoon climaxes in the grace of Krishna causing a "stirring in the heart" of the students, followed by their complete "liberation" from "illusion and bondage" through the "transcendental sound" of the Hare Krishna *mantra* ("Hare Krishna, Hare Krishna, Krishna Krishna, Hare Hare . . ."). Finally, the students confront Dr. Mud, accuse him of "brainwashing us with material sound," and declare, mimicking the words of ISKCON founder Swami Bhaktivedanta, "Now we demand that you teach the truth about life. Life comes from life, not matter." Doctor Mud then rejoices, having been freed of materialistic bondage by Krishna's "liberating spirits," and himself begins singing the Hare Krishna mantra.[54]

The message of the Doctor Mud cartoon combined anti-establishmentarianism and environmentalism with the strong tradition of opposition to materialistic science within ISKCON. The cartoon ultimately portrayed Dr.

Mud as more a naive tool than a nefarious demon, in notable distinction to the illustrations in Svarupa's *Science Basis of Krishna Consciousness* and Bhaktivedanta's dismissals in "Life Comes From Life." "I was never satisfied at heart by teaching materialism, but I went to their schools, they paid my salary and so . . . ," explained the character.[55] That the cartoonist titled the piece "The Conversion of Doctor Mud" recognized the possibility that individual scientists might accept Krishna Consciousness, and therefore exempt themselves from the wholesale rejection of their Western materialistic methodologies. In other words, the tract demonstrated a more moderate view of science than many other ISKCON sources, perhaps in keeping with the movement's attempt to reach the widest possible audience of college students. Nevertheless, Doctor Mud's pronouncement also makes it clear that the rejection of both materialism and the mainstream scientific establishment accompanied conversion to the Gaudiya Vaishnavism of ISKCON.

The final page of *Spiritual Revolution* featured a short commentary titled "The Grand Illusion." The placement of images contextualized the piece, which discussed the similarities of nondeterministic quantum physics and Vedic science. Above the article an image of a smiling A. C. Bhaktivedanta Swami Prabhupada positioned the story (and indeed the entire pamphlet) as a part of the guru's authoritative tradition. "The Grand Illusion" itself featured an in-line image of the God Krishna surrounded by the electron orbits of an atom, a easily recognizable symbol that postwar Americans recognized as representing nuclear science. Readers could also understand the message of this iconography before reading the accompanying article: Krishna Consciousness, and Krishna in particular, had *something* to do with modern subatomic science.

The brief text of "The Grand Illusion" explicated the details of that relationship, explaining that modern science had finally recognized the cosmic truths long ago revealed in the Vedas, a theme which Swami Bhaktivedanta had stressed since the 1950s. Both Vedic science and quantum physics rejected Newtonian mechanism and materialism. Alluding to physical theory, the article explained, that though matter appears solid, it comprised mostly empty space, with only the raw energy of nonmaterial forces providing reality. Scientists called these forces electrical and nuclear attraction, and the Vedas call them *sakti*, the Sanskrit word for vital essence or energy. Both suggest a nonmaterial conception of reality, the article argued. Further, the new scientific field of quantum physics discredited traditional Newtonian mechanism, which the article equated with the impersonalistic view of a clockwork universe created by a distant and uncaring deity. On this matter, "The Grand Illusion" declared, cutting-edge Western science and Vedic science agreed.

> All matter or unconscious things have been reduced by the scientist to some kind of energy or sakti, it is obvious that this energy can only be referred to [as] some conscious principle. Scientists like Einstein, Eddington, James Jeans and J.B.S. Haldane have already recognized this.[56]

Even scientists now recognize the foundation and basis of life in consciousness rather than gross material matter, the editors of *Spiritual Revolution* insisted. The article summarized the findings of all four scientists mentioned in the quote as "almost identical to that of the five-thousand-year-old Srimad Bhagavatam," one of the books that ISKCON considers part of the Vedic corpus. Citing the work of O. B. L. Kapoor, PhD, a physicist associated with the Hare Krishna movement, the editorial concluded by recommending the structuring of society around the scientific details discovered in that text.[57]

But the editors of the pamphlet did not end "The Grand Illusion" with a positive evaluation of science. Rather, they cautioned that most scientists did not accept the discoveries of their own vanguard, since materialism had mired them in mechanism and impersonalism. "The social implications of the scientific discoveries of such great men as [Albert] Einstein, [Arthur Stanley] Eddington, J. B. S. Haldane, and Sir James Jeans are being suppressed in favor of the views of their more ordinary and short-sighted colleagues. The pernicious influence of politics can even be found in the so-called spotless halls of science."[58] The overall thrust of the article, and indeed all of the *Spiritual Revolution* newsletter, remained that the Hare Krishnas offered a scientific alternative to the destructive, dangerous establishments of the West. Famous scientists themselves supported this contention, the tract's authors maintained, and confirmed the ancient truths of Gaudiya Vaishnavism.

ISKCON After Bhaktivedanta

The International Society for Krishna Consciousness brought to America a message opposed to the norms of Western science, namely empiricism and methodological materialism. Once in the United States, Swami Bhaktivedanta attracted mostly disaffected youth associated with the counterculture, whose resistance to the establishments of education, government, religion, and economics fused with the swami's view of science, producing a movement demonstrating strong antagonism toward the institutions and ideals of American science. Through articles, books, lectures, interviews, and other media, the leaders of the Hare Krishna movement explicitly criticized science and called for replacing it with what they believed to be a better, more authentic alternative rooted in the ancient Indian texts of the Vedas.

Swami A. C. Bhaktivedanta spent most of his adult life attempting to create an alternative to Western modernity grounded in the Indian Vedas. From his earliest exposure to Western civilization at Scottish Church College, he rejected the Occident as materialistic and lost, and science as culpable in that process. After Gandhi's Indian nationalism failed to capture him, Bhaktivedanta turned to a traditional form of Hindu religiosity, which he embraced as an alternative to British colonial modernism. Yet just as electricity fascinated Abhay Charan De as a child, the elder swami continued to wrestle with the problem of science, never able to completely ignore what he had repeatedly dismissed as irrelevant. In India, he wrote of the scientific discovery of antimatter as both vindication and demonstration of Vedic truths. In America he simultaneously reached out to scientists as well as belittled, even threatened, them with "kicks to the head." Throughout, A. C. Bhaktivedanta insisted on the superiority of ISKCON's religiously based science over the materialistic Western alternative and looked to his religion's views of the universe as a replacement for those of the West.

Following the death of A. C. Bhaktivedanta Swami Prabhupada in 1977, the Hare Krishna movement fragmented into a variety of sub-movements. Several of the swami's leading disciples created their own splinter groups, and even among the Hare Krishna members who remained within their International Society, competing views proliferated on topic of leadership, the nature of the guru, institutional governance, the eternality of salvation, among others. Even into the twenty-first century, several institutional forms of Krishna Consciousness compete alongside ISKCON for the mantle of leading Gaudiya Vaishnavism in the West. The immigration to the West of large numbers of Indian Vaishnava practitioners, who of course have their own perspective on how best to practice their religious tradition, further complicates the picture. While the International Society for Krishna Consciousness continued past Bhaktivedanta's death, the loss of the charismatic swami who founded the movement splintered Krishna Consciousness.[59]

On the issue of science, some of the sub-movements adopted more moderate positions, encouraging dialog with scientists and even rapprochement, while others increased their Manichean rhetoric against science. The Bhaktivedanta Institute itself, the institutional home for the treatment of science and religion issues, splintered into four branches separated by geography, ethnic background of its leaders, and ideological approaches. While the Alachua, Florida, branch led by Anglo-American converts took a more stridently anti-science position, Satsvarupa Dasa's Denver-based Bhaktivedanta Institute moderated its approach and attempted to reach out to scientists and emphasize commonalities. The Mumbai branch, run entirely by Indian-born Vaishnavites, transformed the Institute into a think tank on consciousness studies, and the American convert-led Los Angeles group dedicated itself to publishing material opposing Darwinism. Though the Bhaktivedanta Institute, like ISKCON, divided institutionally, all continued to follow Bhaktivedanta's intellectual tradition but with different points of emphasis. One commonality remained: even into the twenty-first century, the leaders and members of the International Society for Krishna Consciousness looked to their movement's own view of science, an ideology predicated in the ancient Indian texts known as the Vedas, as a *replacement* for modern science.

Part III

Science and Heaven's Gate

Remember, we're not talking about a spiritual kingdom—no clouds, no harps—even though we are talking about in the heavens. But the Heavens are no more spiritual than when you go out at night and look at the Heavenly bodies and see them. They are literally there. They are physical.
  —Marshall Herff Applewhite, *Planet About to Be Recycled*
  (1996)

Introduction

"The telescope must be defective," the Heaven's Gate member told the clerk, "and we want a refund." So tells a oft-repeated Internet rumor that circulated after the mass suicides in 1997 that claimed the lives of the thirty-nine members of Heaven's Gate. The story claimed that a few weeks before the suicides that effectively ended the group's existence, several members of the movement had purchased a high-powered telescope so that they could search the heavens for the UFO that they hoped would transport them away from Earth. But being unable to find the UFO, they returned the telescope a few days later. When the manager asked what was wrong with the device, the Heaven's Gate members reported the telescope as clearly defective, since they couldn't find the UFO. Though this tale cannot be substantiated, it does reveal a central tenet of the group known as Heaven's Gate: that the absolute truths of the universe are provable and they could prove them. Even God, the members of the group insisted, possessed a physical form that a suitably powerful-enough telescope might eventually locate. The story also reveals, however, the underlying religious nature of the group—faith ultimately trumped proof. The telescope did not reveal a UFO, but the members of Heaven's Gate did not change their beliefs that a UFO would whisk them away into the heavens. They returned the telescope. Like most urban legends, it reveals an underlying truth, even though the details are probably fictitious.[1]

"Our message is not now, nor has it ever been, religious or spiritual," declared the individual calling herself Anlody, a few months before the mass suicide.[2] The message was not religious, Anlody insisted, although her own statement containing those words also discussed the human soul, the "Chief of Chiefs," Lucifer, the Tree of Life, and eternal salvation. In the mind of Anlody and her fellow members of Heaven's Gate, the eternal fate of her soul did not qualify as a religious or spiritual concern. In a parallel development, Anlody's compatriot and leader, who called himself Do (pronounced "doe") declared of his movement, "[t]his is as scientific—this is as true as true could be."[3] Yet, the "scientific truth" that Do discussed in the video in which those words appeared included extrasensory perception, spirits, biblical prophecy, extraterrestrials, and the nature of Jesus' resurrection. Such is the irony of a group that fits most scholars' assumptions about a religion, but itself demonstrated only a tepid ambivalence toward the category of religion.[4]

Within Heaven's Gate, science and religion coexisted as unequal binary opposites. Science, the movement's members insisted, represented truth, rationalism, reasonability, and the reliance on evidence. Religion, by contrast, possessed falsehood, emotionalism, no sensibility, and reliance on faith. The former category surpassed the latter in every regard, they argued, and therefore the adherents of Heaven's Gate positioned their movement as a science. Yet in term of content, function, and the groups with which it competed, Heaven's Gate certainly qualified as a religion. For example, their worldview centered on salvation, creation and the Creator, the nature of the soul, and the Bible. The group adapted religious practices from the New Age religious subculture, such as diet regimentation, meditation, and channeling. And in their own words, they reached out to "ministers, evangelists, and [New Age] awareness centers."[5] The actions of the members of Heaven's Gate implied that it was a religion, but that they really wanted to be more like a science.

Heaven's Gate belonged to a category of new religions generally called "UFO cults" or "UFO religions." Such groups often adopt a particular treatment of science and its relation to religion that Heaven's Gate typified: the valuation of science and scientific concepts and the subsequent appropriation of science into their religious worldviews. Christopher Partridge, in his essay on "Understanding UFO Religions and Abduction Spiritualities," wrote that UFO religions and spiritualities "are distinctive in that, to one degree or another, they claim to offer a 'scientific' belief system."[6] Partridge correctly indicated that UFO-centric groups ranging from the Aetherius Society (founded 1954) to the Raelian Church (founded 1973) make this claim, and though he did not specifically mention Heaven's Gate in this context, its leaders and members also claimed to offer a scientific belief system. Brenda Denzler has explained this phenomenon similarly, in her study of self-declared contactees (people who claim to have contacted extraterrestrials) and ufologists (people who study UFO phenomenon). Denzler explained that "God-talk [among the contactees] was often conducted using the rhetoric of science rather than religion and sought to touch base not with the verities of revealed Truth, but with the verities of empirically derived truth."[7] The contactee groups that Denzler considered shared with other UFO groups a fixation with the scientific, the material, and the empirical.

One manner in which UFO religions demonstrate their scientific nature is through offering materialistic reinterpretations of what religions traditionally have understood as supernatural topics. The Raelian Church, for example, recast the idea of resurrection as genetic cloning, and around the turn of the millennium made the pursuit of cloning technology a cornerstone of their movement's mission.[8] The movement called Unarius identified angels as extraterrestrial space beings who communicated with humans using telepathic abilities, and looked to these aliens as fonts of knowledge, guides, and messengers from the heavens.[9] Both examples demonstrate that UFO religions offer materialistic explanations for religious topics, resurrection, and angels respectively.

By "materialistic" I do not mean the lusting after wealth or goods, but a treatment of all knowledge and knowable things as comprised of physical, tangible matter, as described by the sciences of physics, chemistry, and related fields. A closely allied concept, "naturalism," treats all knowledge as derived from the physical, tangible universe that human beings can access through their five senses. Naturalism holds that the physical laws of science can describe all things without recourse to divine beings, miracles, or unseeing and unknowable events. Both terms (as I use them) are methods of knowing, or epistemologies. What I call materialistic interpretation, Partridge calls physicalism. He wrote, "[w]hilst much of UFO religion contains typically religious themes, including the belief in God, salvation, reincarnation, karma and so on, we have seen that it is also 'physicalist.' That is to say, whilst the components of a religious worldview may be there, they are often reinterpreted in terms of physical phenomenon."[10] John Saliba, referring specifically to Christian UFO religions, concurred: "they remove the supernatural: the miraculous (supernaturally produced) events in the Bible become activities of superhuman beings from other planets, who possess superior technological and psychic powers."[11] Heaven's Gate's founders and members exhibited precisely this type of reinterpretation. Christ became an extraterrestrial, the Bible a set of instructions from outer space, resurrection a biological process, and eventually they transformed even the Christian concept of grace into a tag or tracking device. Especially in the first decade of Heaven's Gate's history, the production of a materialistic religious worldview dominated the group's founders.

Unlike the Unification Church or the Hare Krishna movement, Heaven's Gate did not explicitly consider the definition or meaning of science vis-à-vis religion until very late in its history and development. Unlike those groups, which posited themselves relative to science by either seeking to guide or replace it, Heaven's Gate attempted to absorb the best of science into itself. For that reason, the group said little about science until its final years, but throughout its history it tried to "be scientific" by offering naturalistic, materialistic explanations of religious concepts. Its founders and leaders incorporated methodological naturalism and materialism into their religion. Stripping supernaturalism from religion and replacing it with materialistic explanations, Heaven's Gate demonstrated how a religious group could seek to *absorb* science into religion.

5

Science and the Foundation of Heaven's Gate

The Origins of Heaven's Gate: "The Two"

Heaven's Gate grew from the nexus of two founders: Bonnie Lu Nettles (1928–85) and Marshall Herff Applewhite (1932–97). A native of Houston, Nettles was a registered nurse, mother of four children, and partner in a failing marriage. A junior high school classmate of Nettles described her as not particularly religious, although she was raised Baptist, attending church "just because the gang [of friends and family] did."[1] She had dropped out of Christian circles by the time she became an adult. In the years preceding her first meeting with Applewhite, she wrote occasional newspaper columns on astrology and spoke of receiving assistance in her astrology from spiritual beings. She belonged to the Houston branch of the Theosophical Society in America and expressed an interest in the writings of H. P. Blavatsky, one of the founders of that movement.[2] The secondary scholarship on Nettles shows her as inhabiting a New Age subculture of disincarnated spirits, ascended masters, telepathic powers, and hidden and revealed gnosis. As the sociologist Robert W. Balch, who studied and traveled with the group in its early years, wrote, "Bonnie was deeply committed to metaphysics as a way of life. Hers was a magical reality of signs, omens, spirits, ascended masters, and higher levels of reality."[3] A fascination with spirits and the spiritual would carry over into Heaven's Gate, though Nettles and her co-founder would eventually treat the idea of the "spiritual"—as opposed to religious or scientific—with reticence and even suspicion.

Known as Herff to his friends, Heaven's Gate's co-founder Marshall Herff Applewhite possessed a more conventionally Christian background. A Texan by birth, his father served as a popular and successful Presbyterian preacher, having founded and led several churches in the state. After college the younger Applewhite enrolled at Virginia's Union Theological Seminary, a Presbyterian divinity school, but left after two years to study music.[4] He earned a masters degree in music and voice from the University of Colorado but never strayed far from a religiously oriented vocation. Applewhite directed the choir at Houston's St. Mark's Episcopal Church and the Fine Arts program at the Catholic University of St. Thomas, but seemed not to identify strongly with any particular denomination in his adult life.[5]

Though Applewhite and Nettles brought different religious backgrounds to what would become Heaven's Gate, they did share a common social and cultural background. Unlike the founders of the Unification Church and ISKCON, foreigners who brought new doctrines to America, Bonnie and Herff were native-born Americans who transformed American religious traditions—the New Age and Protestant Christianity—into something new. Unlike the young college students who joined the Unification Church or the dropouts who followed Bhaktivedanta, the two founders of Heaven's Gate were middle-class adult Americans. However, like the counterculture, Applewhite and Nettles rejected white middle-class American norms. Although they gave up on American culture, they did not seek to import an Asian alternative, as did the Hare Krishnas. Heaven's Gate accepted the scientific and ideological foundation of the West (naturalism and science) but turned against normative American values such as the family, work-ethic, education, and recreation.

Nettles and Applewhite met in the spring of 1972 at the Houston hospital where Nettles worked when both were in their mid-forties and in the throes of significant life changes.[6] Nettles was separated and soon to be divorced; Applewhite, a divorcee with two children, had floundering through sexual relationships with both men and women. Rejecting the aspect of their lives that they had found most unsettling—their marriages and sexual relationships— Nettles and Applewhite formed an intense spiritual, though by all accounts platonic, relationship. While reductionist readings of Heaven's Gate portrayed Applewhite's and Nettles' muddled sexuality as prime causes for the eventual emergence of the extreme sexual asceticism that characterized the movement, the worldview of Heaven's Gate demonstrated a complexity that complicates such analyses.[7] There is little doubt that the co-founders' rejection of their sexual natures strongly influenced the new religion, but other factors did as well.

Shortly after their initial meeting, Applewhite and Nettles came to understand one another as spiritual partners destined to teach about religious and spiritual topics. To this end, they founded a small religious enterprise, called the Christian Arts Center, in borrowed space from a local church. The two hoped to use the Christian Arts Center to teach "classes in metaphysics, theosophy, [and] astrology," they explained.[8] Balch added that they also intended to offer courses in mysticism, healing, comparative religion, and the performing arts, and hoped to "promote the study of music, arts, and religion" broadly.[9] Their grand vision failed to achieve success, and the Christian Arts Center closed after encountering animosity among the local Christian community and financial instability. Applewhite and Nettles's second venture, Know Place, reproduced the same pattern, though with a more explicitly theosophical or occult angle than their earlier attempt. The Know Place also failed to achieve financial success, and the two closed it in January 1973.[10]

A three-year period of wandering and religious formulation ensued (1973–75), during which Nettles and Applewhite traveled throughout the United States and ruminated on what religious message they hoped to bring to the world. They explored numerous religious options, which included meditating on St. Francis of Assisi, how their contemporary society might respond to the Second Coming of Jesus, and the nature of reincarnation and disincarnate spirits.[11] In their own words, Nettles and Applewhite explained that they "studied the Bible more thoroughly than we had before in our separate studies. We studied the secret doctrine of Madame Blavatsky, which is theosophical material. We studied everything we could get our hands on that had to do with any sort of awareness—spiritual awareness, scientific awareness, religious awareness. Our thirst was absolutely unquenchable."[12] The two did not specify what sort of "scientific awareness" they sought, or even what such an awareness entailed, but their inclusion of science alongside religion and spirituality harbingered the place of science in their later thought.

When they emerged from their errand into the wilderness later that year, the two had transformed themselves into "the Two," or sometimes the "UFO Two," as they called themselves. (They later rechristened themselves as Guinea [Nettles] and Pig [Applewhite], Bo [Applewhite] and Peep [Nettles], and finally Ti [Nettles] and Do [Applewhite].)[13] The Two proclaimed a specific message of salvation that combined Christian millennialism, New Age self-improvement, and the religious dimensions of extraterrestrials and unidentified flying objects (UFOs). Throughout the autumn of 1975, the Two distributed the statements to those who attended their meetings and mailed them more widely to individuals and groups associated with New Age institutions (health food stores, yoga groups, independent bookshops, etc.). The first of these dense single-spaced typewritten statements, a one-page document labeled "Your Opportunity: Statement #1" carried the title "Human Individual Metamorphosis," and described the Two's goal, namely the physical transformation of a human being into a perfected extraterrestrial creature. The second, "Clarification: Human Kingdom—Visible and Invisible," detailed the nature of spirits, souls, and the means by which individuals spiritually evolve toward an extraterrestrial goal. The third, "The Only Significant Resurrection," reiterated the first two statements with explicit comparisons to the Christian concept of bodily resurrection. They signed each statement "HIM," short for Human Individual Metamorphosis, the name they had chosen for their teachings. Overall, the three statements aimed to demonstrate an understanding of individual bodily transformation into an extraterrestrial being as equivalent to personal evolution, resurrection, and eternal salvation. A close analysis of their gospel as described in the three statements reveals a rephrasing of religious concepts in the language of ufology and materialistic naturalism, as well as an underlying distrust of religious approaches that relied upon supernatural rather that naturalistic language and approaches. Though it would take years before the Two developed a more formal approach to how religion ought to absorb science, their earliest statements implied their tremendous valuation of the materialistic naturalism that roots science and scientific language.

The Two's first statement, "Human Individual Metamorphosis," began with an assumption that their own HIM process and teachings agreed with the foundation of other religions, but also a disparaging dismissal of those competing religions: "What religions have sought to understand since the beginning of their origin is what is above the human level of existence. Most have taught that if an individual lives a 'good life' adoring some savior that he will inherit some 'heaven' after his death. If only it were that simple." The heavily sardonic "some savior" and "some 'heaven,'" as well as the offsetting of "good life" within quotes revealed the authors' thinly veiled disagreement with what they regarded as the "simple" Christian teachings.[14] Years later, Heaven's Gate would utilize much the same language and explicitly note that its own approach differed because it was scientific, but the first (surviving) written material authored by Applewhite and Nettles already indicated a disparaging view of at least the Christian religion.

The HIM statement continued, laying out the basic religious message of the Two: there existed a "next evolutionary kingdom," "next kingdom," or "next level" to which a human could physically journey and join, provided that he or she "completely overcomes all the aspects and influences of the human level." The statement itself did not indicate what this process entailed, but in their subsequent teachings, the Two specified the need to reject emotional and sexual attachments to other human beings as a primary objective. Nettles and Applewhite employed a biological metaphor to explain their teachings, that of the caterpillar's metamorphosis within the chrysalis into a butterfly. Just as if a caterpillar "rises above all caterpillar ways, converts all his energies to the pursuit of becoming literally another creature who circulates in another world, he becomes a butterfly," so too could human beings transform themselves into extraterrestrial creatures.[15] Nearly every source produced in the early years of the group that would come to call itself Human Individual Metamorphosis and later Heaven's Gate repeated this metaphor and approach: the process of overcoming one's humanity and transforming into an alien creature paralleled that of a caterpillar-to-butterfly metamorphosis, alongside the recognition of some shared attributes.[16]

The chrysalis metaphor offered Nettles and Applewhite a natural and materialistic explanation of the process that they also maintained operated on a purely material and biological level, rather than a spiritual or supernatural one. The HIM statement made this clear, declaring of those who successfully completed the overcoming process that "[w]hen the metamorphosis is complete their 'perennial' and cyclical nature is ended for their 'new' body has overcome decay, disease and death. It has converted over chemically, biologically, and in vibration to the 'new' creature."[17] That the conversion included a change in "vibration" particularly situates Nettles and Applewhite's material within the New Age, which frequently utilizes the concept of vibrations to describe a person or object's characteristics.[18] Yet the reference to chemical and biological transformation also reveals the Two's materialistic assumptions. Whatever else, the salvific process that Applewhite and Nettles offered was physical and natural, "chemical" and "biological," and not merely spiritual, symbolic, or supernatural.

Following the transformation, Nettles and Applewhite explained, the newly transformed creatures would join the Two, who would also metamorphose, and journey into the heavens aboard a UFO. Rather than a spiritual transformation of the soul that might occur after death, or a resurrection of the flesh in a far-distant future time, or even a reincarnation into a new body, Bo and Peep promised of their process that it acted immediately and physically, without the need to disembody or die in order to achieve entrance into the heavens. The Two's vision of a material form of salvation, that is a chemical and biological one, explained their dismissal of "some heaven" and "some savior" that opened the statement: Human Individual Metamorphosis's heaven existed in the physical skies, its salvation an embodied physical one achieved through metamorphosis of a living human being into a living extraterrestrial. Again, though the Two did not explicitly discuss science, they implied support for its materialistic and naturalistic foundations. They also distanced themselves from the this-Earthly focus of much of middle-class America, situating themselves as a movement opposed to such terrestrial concerns.

This message nevertheless encapsulated a particular religious approach, a particular form of Christian millennialism known as dispensationalism. Dispensationalists cull biblical books—particularly the books of Daniel and Revelation—for a millennial timetable, encapsulating the history of the world into distinct epochs called dispensations. For dispensationalists, a "rapture of the true church," during which faithful Christians physically rise into midair, rendezvous with Christ, and enter the heavens, inaugurates the seventh dispensation.[19] Nettles and Applewhite accepted the idea of "the Rapture," but transformed the traditional view into a technological and material event. Rather than meeting Christ midair, their followers would aerially rendezvous with UFOs, one of which would hold the extraterrestrial whom human Christians remember as Jesus of Nazareth. The UFOs, now bearing the human beings who had overcame their humanity through the Two's process, would ascend into the literal heavens, forever leaving behind the Earth.

Nettles and Applewhite insisted that the material and biological transformation of the physical body represented the sole way that an individual could enter heaven, and that the being known as Jesus of Nazareth demonstrated that reality. After the crucifixion, the "Human Individual Metamorphosis" statement explained, Christ "did not leave His body in the grave. He converted it *into* His body of that next kingdom. This is the only way the next kingdom is entered permanently. Each human has that full potential."[20] In order to demonstrate that potential, the authors explained, Christ stayed on Earth in order to continue teaching his disciples, to show them his next-level body and "demonstrated a few of its new attributes, i.e., appearing and disappearing (changing His vibrations) before their eyes while letting some of His friends touch His 'new' body." Like the first-century Gospel writers and early Church Fathers, the Two labored to convince their readers that Christ resurrected in physical form, not merely in spiritual or symbolic outward appearance. Unlike those early believers, however, the two founders of Human Individual Metamorphosis/Heaven's Gate insisted that Christ had indeed transformed himself into a new body, an extraterrestrial next-level body, in order to show his disciples what they too might possess. Having completed his mission, the Two explained, "Jesus left them in a cloud of light (what humans refer to as UFOs) and moves and returns in the same manner."[21] The parenthetical equation of the UFO and the cloud of light paralleled both the earlier parenthetical reference to "appearing and disappearing (changing His vibrations)" and another in the first statement, "His [Christ's] transfiguration (metamorphic completion)," an apparent reference to the Transfiguration event described in the Gospels.[22] The three parentheticals revealed the Two's approach of translating traditionally religious concepts into more materialistic, physical, and even scientific language. Salvation became a chemical and biological process of transforming *Homo sapiens* into extraterrestrials. Heaven itself, they insisted, existed in the physical heavens reachable through mundane space travel.

The Two extended this materialization approach in their own self-understanding of their mission. They proclaimed that like Jesus, they too would be killed, resurrect themselves using biological and chemical means, and ascend into heaven, thereby demonstrating the reality of their claims. The Two called this "the demonstration." The demonstration that the founders of HIM espoused represented in fact a materialistic recasting of an end-time prophecy from the eleventh chapter of the New Testament's book of Revelation, a fact to which both leaders and members of the group attested.[23] The biblical text describes two witnesses who prophesy, are martyred, lie dead for three-and-a-half days, are resurrected, and ascend to heaven in a cloud (Rev. 11:3–12). Like the Two's treatment of Christ's resurrection and their followers' promised transformations, they insisted that the special case of the resurrection of the two witnesses represented a demonstration of the metamorphic possibilities of the human body. Recasting the Revelation prophecy in material terms, they insisted that the Bible's description of resurrection and the ascension to heaven "in a cloud" represented a coded or symbolic description of a totally material process and departure from the planet onboard the UFO. Heaven's Gate would later reject a literal reading of the demonstration—an interpretation no doubt predicated on the fact that it did not happen as predicted—but a materialistic rereading of Revelation and other biblical texts continued as a central part of their teachings.

The two founders of HIM did not explicitly declare their approach a science in their first three statements; instead, they built the foundation for this position in their materialism and insistence on the biological and chemical nature of their promised metamorphosis, frequently employing two terms, "biology" and "chemistry," which most readers would easily identify as scientific. The repeated description of the metamorphic process as biological and chemical, as well as the use of the terms "metamorphosis" and "transformation" rather than reincarnation, rebirth, or salvation, all indicate their materialistic approach to what most people would consider a clearly religious topic: eternal salvation and entrance into heaven. Though Heaven's Gate would later imply a fundamental break between religion and science, the Two's materials in the mid-1970s indicate their understanding of a continuum between the two, if not an outright overlap. For example, a brief one-page update, titled "What's Up?" and disseminated in July 1975, began with the same sort of assumed commonalities between religion and science that they also revealed in their first statement. "At this particular time," it began, "fictional writers, religious scholars, spiritual leaders, fundamentalist preachers, scientists, and illustrators are expressing their interpretations of what is 'happening.' Something is unique about this time span which seems to have more urgency than the various interpretations can explain, . . . and people are interpreting that change according to their comprehension." Everyone from scientists to fundamentalists tried to understand the world around them, Applewhite and Nettles maintained, and though only some of these individuals experienced the "accelerated awareness" that led to the truth, scientists and religionists alike tried to explain the "severe change taking place."[24]

Nettles and Applewhite's approach of translating religious concepts into scientific language had analogues in wider religious culture. Like the Unification Church and ISKCON, the movement that eventually became Heaven's Gate offered a more radical perspective on wider religious perspectives. In the case of Nettles and Applewhite, the two paralleled a growing interest among Americans in the New Age. The amorphous nature of the New Age makes surveying its size difficult, but as James R. Lewis and Gordon Melton write, the New Age is not "a marginal phenomenon: by the [nineteen-] eighties, it had become an integral part of a new, truly pluralistic 'mainstream.'"[25] Within the New Age community, which developed at precisely the moment that Heaven's Gate also emerged, the use of scientific language predominated. New Age practitioners discussed religion using terms such as energies, holographs, and vibratory levels, all concepts drawn from the study of physics. In addition to Fritjof Capra's aforementioned *Tao of Physics*, which helped cement the movement, Michael Talbot's *The Holographic Universe* offers a representative example. The widely read Talbot transposed the religious positions of monism and pantheism into the language of quantum physics, relatively, and holographic theory. The popularity of such approaches led James R. Lewis to state that "a desire to be 'modern' and use scientific language'" functioned as one of six central defining characteristics of the New Age movement.[26] In predicating their movement on this approach, Nettles and Applewhite represented a far wider American religious mind-set.

Human Individual Metamorphosis and the
Anti-Religious Turn

Nettles and Applewhite continued to travel around the country until spring 1975, when they encountered their first major success in gaining converts to their process. Speaking to a meeting of a Los Angeles area New Age group on April 9, 1975, the Two—then going under the names Guinea (Nettles) and Pig (Applewhite)—convinced twenty-four of the about fifty people attending the meeting to abandon their previous lives and connections and strive to overcome their human condition.[27] Even though all but one of these converts subsequently left, the experience provided enough momentum to make the Two leaders of a small, new religious group.[28] The Two achieved another major success on September 14, 1975, when according to newspaper accounts, they attracted more than two hundred people to a meeting held at a resort hotel in the coastal community of Waldport, Oregon. The Two's open meeting in Waldport convinced approximately twenty individuals to join HIM and seek to overcome their humanity. National headlines followed a month later, when newspapers recounted parents who left their children and homeowners who signed over property deeds in order to follow the Two on what attendees at the Waldport meeting said was a trip to a "higher level."[29]

During this new phase of the group's history, the Two, who now called themselves Bo (Applewhite) and Peep (Nettles)—as they would for the remainder of the decade and into the 1980s as well—made a concerted effort to portray themselves as something akin to but different than other religions. Three of the main sources from this time—a letter that they mailed to prospective candidates in fall 1975, and two extended interviews they granted in early 1976—all indicated an increasing uneasiness of the Two toward the category of religion. Implicitly, they contrasted religion with science, emphasizing the superiority of the latter because of its materialistic and naturalistic foundations. In a partial transcript of their Waldport meeting Bo and Peep explicitly contrasted their own process with that of religion. "Now if you think from what is being said that you have come to hear something that is religious or [a] sermon, it is not," they insisted. "It is the truth that was brought before and during the time between seasons[;] the world made the truth 'religion.'" Bo and Peep distinguished the truth from religion, arguing that only "between seasons," (that is, between visits by extraterrestrial-influenced teachers such as themselves) human beings reduced the truth into religions. Bo and Peep insisted that their message fell into the former category, that of truth rather than religion. Calling their message "just as true as the price tags on your groceries and just as basic," they insisted that the overcoming process they taught resulted in a "literal, actual, biological and chemical response." Again, the Two utilized the language of science to position their message, but added to it what must have surely seemed a banal comparison to grocery-store price tags. Both, however, indicated a naturalistic perspective. Human Individual Metamorphosis postulated literal, actual, scientific views. Religion, Bo and Peep implied, did not.[30]

A letter that Bo and Peep provided to prospective members of HIM demonstrated one of the earliest examples of this anti-religious, or what one might term an anti-spiritual or anti-supernatural, position. Most likely written after the Waldport meeting, and definitely prior to October 1975, the letter employed somewhat different vocabulary but described the same basic position as the three earlier statements.[31] It assumed that the readers already possessed some knowledge of what it called "the process," and provided specific details to potential adherents, or "prospective candidates," as it addressed them. Such individuals should provide the Two with a phone number, and next gather together camping gear for the trip, including "a tent, a warm sleeping bag, a stove, at least two changes of winter clothing and two for warmer weather, eating and cooking utensils." They should also bring a car and whatever money they could, Bo and Peep instructed. The letter stated that the prospective candidate would join a partner to help each other overcome their human attachments, and that other questions would be answered by fellow candidates as they arose. Beyond such minutia, Bo and Peep also used the letter to describe the nature of the process itself, taking care to distinguish it from other types of pursuit. "This is not a spiritual trip," they wrote. "To reach the Next Kingdom above human, your body must literally be converted over biologically and chemically. This metamorphic process happens automatically as you will yourself to overcome your humanness." Again in the letter, they reiterated, "[t]his is no spiritual, philosophical, or theoretical path to the top of the mountain. It is a realty; in fact, it is the only way off the top of the mountain. All roads leading to the top were good because they got you there."[32] Together, these explanations contrasted the spiritual (and in the latter case, the philosophical and theoretical as well) with the literal, biological, chemical, and real. Using the language of science (again, chemistry and biology), Bo and Peep declared that they taught a literal, real, process, as opposed to a spiritual one.

The Two's insistence of the distinction between their own method and what they regarded as spiritual approaches particularly stands out because so many of their followers came from self-declared spiritual quests and a subculture of spirituality. Based on firsthand interviews and participant-observation, Robert Balch and David Taylor described Bo and Peep's followers as "[n]early all [being] longtime seekers of truth whose previous religious and spiritual trips included yoga, Scientology, Divine Light, astrology, Transcendental Meditation, Edgar Cayce, and many others."[33] Similarly, James Phelan, who interviewed at least a half-dozen current and former members of the group in 1976 for a *New York Times* article, described their "one common denominator" as spiritual seekers. "Many have tried Scientology, yoga, Zen, offbeat cults, hallucinogens, hypnosis, tarot cards and astrology. Almost all believe in psychic phenomenon."[34] Mirroring the pseudonymous Sheila Larson, the spiritual seeker who in Robert Bellah's *Habits of the Heart* study declared her self-created religion "Sheilaism," one representative follower of Bo and Peep who had joined the group at the Los Angeles New Age group meeting declared, "I used to sort of have my own religion, which was sort of a conglomeration of everything. I was into yoga, meditation and I read different things, I studied metaphysics, I just tried to be, you know, nice in my own way."[35] All these individuals identified with the idea of spirituality and the spiritual quest. Why then did Bo and Peep insist that their own project was something else?

The Two might have declared their process "not a spiritual trip" in order to differentiate themselves from their fellow competitors in America's spiritual marketplace, though that seems an odd manner in which to appeal to spiritual seekers. Bo and Peep's reasoning became clearer in light of an interview they granted UFO researcher Brad Steiger on January 7, 1976. Bo and Peep, the interview revealed, considered religion and spiritual pursuits dogmatic and fantastical, prone to irrationalism and illogical claims. In other words, religion was not scientific enough. When Steiger asked the Two what constituted the central message of their mission, the Two responded by stressing the *real* nature of their message. In doing so, they again contrasted their own position to religion: "We say, . . . 'Try to make them aware of the next level of existence so that they'll know that it actually exists, that Jesus is not a fantasy floating on a cloud someplace. God is not floating on a cloud someplace. It's as real as what you are right now. It's *more* real.'"[36] The published transcript of the interview contains very few words printed in italics, indicating that the Two must have strongly stressed the concept of their message's reality. Their dismissive tone toward those who took a less corporeal view of the heavens, who did not believe that Jesus and God possessed physical bodies in the physical heavens of outer space, also revealed their antagonism toward religion, particularly the Christianity of the majority of Americans. They repeated this hostile tone elsewhere in the interview. For example, when Steiger asked if the UFOs they postulated were physical vehicles, they explained that the flying saucers are "actual means of transportation that serve as protection and an expedient function of travel. Members of the next level do not flap around on wings, and they are not spirits that can just travel with a swift process of the mind."[37] Next-level aliens, Bo and Peep insisted, possessed physical bodies and were therefore real, unlike more spiritual conceptualizations that other religions might possess. The Two equated reality and materialism, and implied that the spiritual, which empiricism could not verify, represented falsehood. For the Two, science offered a rhetorical opportunity to distance themselves from the suspect category of religion.

When Steiger asked the Two their opinion of the "orthodox churches" and "orthodox churchmen," Bo and Peep reiterated a point that they had made at the Waldport meeting, namely that religion arose as the invention of human beings during times when the Earth was out of contact with the next level. Combining that sentiment with language that mirrored Protestant theological critiques of the rise of early Roman Catholicism, the Presbyterian-raised Applewhite and Baptist-born Nettles declared that religion relied on dogmatism and ritual, rather than truth:

> When Jesus brought the truth, he did not bring it as a religion. The *world* made it a religion after he left. The world couldn't really do any better during that season of darkness after Jesus left than to make his teachings dogmatic religions and to practice rituals that made them feel like they were coming closer to God. But when the season is here to expose the truth, it's time to get out of those practices and put into realistic action what it takes to get to the next level—in the same way that Jesus demonstrated.[38]

Dogmatism and ritual characterized religion, Bo and Peep declared, as compared to the "truth" brought by the extraterrestrial Jesus (as they understood him) and themselves. Given their equation of religion with such characteristics, the Two's dismissal of their message as "not spiritual" makes somewhat more sense. It combined their materialistic assumptions with a very Protestant suspicion of ritual and institution.

Nevertheless, Bo and Peep preached a fundamentally religious message, and they fixated on religious concepts. In response to an audience question, they had willingly accepted even during the Waldport meeting that "the Bible is the most significant history book that exists on this planet," despite the influence of its human compilers on the text.[39] Religion was not a complete "delusion," the Two admitted, because it described the activities of previous next-level visitors and generally taught that "this next level is reached only by individuals who have become weaned of Earth-type lusts, and have become creatures that Earthlings would call completely good."[40] Though they hastened to insist that Christ's transfiguration and resurrection represented "a *natural* process" (again, the stress stands out in the published transcript), Bo and Peep insisted to the UFO investigator Steiger that Christianity had some value. Several times they cited the New Testament in response to apparently nonreligious questions, for example their reference to the parable of the vineyard owner when asked if latecomers to their overcoming process could receive the same benefits as earlier converts.[41] When asked what abilities next level extraterrestrials possess, Bo and Peep responded that "[j]ust as Jesus had the capacity to change his molecular structure and to walk through walls after his resurrection, one's capacities become almost limitless."[42] Despite their avowal of materialism and naturalism, the Two continued to use religious language and ideas, particularly those drawn from the New Age and Protestant Christian traditions. Nor could Bo and Peep deny that their message originated in their earlier religious quests and their reading of religious texts.

Religion, Science, and Faith

The German Physicist Max Planck, one of the founders of quantum physics, wrote that "over the entrance to the gates of the temple of science are written the words: Ye must have faith."[43] Fittingly, Bo and Peep insisted that their materialistic religion also required faith. They had absorbed the scientific approaches of naturalism and empiricism into their religious system, but the Two could not separate themselves from the idea of faith. In particular, they stressed that potential followers and candidates for their technological rapture must have complete faith in the process of overcoming humanity through biological metamorphosis. Bo and Peep's embracing of this position developed over several years and coincided with another important change within the group, a transition from a highly individualistic approach to a more hierarchal one stressing the religious authority of the Two. Both shifts indicate the complex nature of the Two's movement, which despite claiming the tools and rhetoric of science, upheld a fundamentally religious message of personal faith, transformation, rapture, and salvation. It also reveals a transition within the movement from a position more in keeping with that of science, namely that the overcoming process required an individual's accurate reproduction of experimental methods, to one more in keeping with what

Americans consider religious, i.e., necessitating both faith and the guidance of a religious leader.

The Two's earliest written sources minimized both the value of faith and that of relying on outside support. In addition to frequent mentions of the biological and chemical nature of the process of bodily transformation, the first statement, "Human Individual Metamorphosis," explicitly called Bo and Peep's message "the formula," phrasing that implied an almost automatic nature to the overcoming process. While their statement did recognize the need for belief, it stressed achievement over motivation or intention. "Those who can believe this process and *do* it will be 'lifted up' and 'saved' from death—literally," they promised, stressing that the process required action or *doing*.[44] Their third statement, "The Only Significant Resurrection," made similar claims as to both the importance of action and the automatic nature of the process for those who completed it. "Each individual who can endure to the end of his lessons will come into his indestructible body just as the caterpillar comes into the body of a butterfly." Like the chrysalis, the Two's process required effort toward material transformation, not faith.[45] Caterpillars became butterflies whether they believed they would or not, just as (theoretically) materialistic scientists could achieve an experimental effect whether or not they had faith in whatever results the procedure promised to produce.

Bo and Peep's statements also insisted that their process required individual effort only and not the active guidance of other human beings. The Two's third statement declared that the "chemical conversion" integral to the overcoming process was a "'selfish' time-span" during which a human being concentrated solely on overcoming the human condition and beginning their metamorphic process. Therefore potential students must prepared themselves to both reject companionship with others and be rejected by those around them.[46] Bo and Peep's followers understood this explicitly. One reported, "[t]his isn't a group metamorphosis and the organization isn't going to heaven."[47] Further, even the Two were not necessary. In their interview with Brad Steiger, Bo and Peep explained that if anyone "truly seeks to enter the kingdom of Heaven, the option is his and he will do it if he chooses to. Such people do not do it through us. They do it through the information we are sharing."[48] Even the name of the group, Human *Individual* Metamorphosis demonstrated this highly individualistic approach. Achieving the transformation into an extraterrestrial and journeying with Bo and Peep into the heavens required neither faith nor guidance, the Two insisted. Though not identical, this approach harkens to the image of the lone scientist perfecting the experiment and seeking truth.

Shortly after the Two composed their three statements, several current and former members of the group stressed not only the value of belief or faith within the process but also challenged the materialism that apparently dominated the movement. One former member of the movement, a twenty-year-old spiritual seeker who left HIM in September 1975 after several months in the group, provided a summary of the Two's teachings to George Williamson, a *San Francisco Chronicle* reporter. Williamson summarized the young apostate as saying that "[t]he center of HIM theology asserts that converts must develop 100 percent faith in capacities to The Two's capacities to die and then resurrect. After the promised event, full believers supposedly will then be rewarded with a UFO dispatched to carry them to a higher plane of existence." The allusion to a technological demonstration and rapture matched the Two's own statements, but the concept of "one hundred percent faith" had not appeared in any of the previously published or disseminated materials produced by the group or its members.[49] Nor did the other published accounts and interviews with current or former members of the group published near this time mention a need for faith.[50]

Yet this apostate was not alone in his understanding of the value of faith. Several months earlier in July 1975, another young member named Peggy wrote a letter to her parents that repeated the same position of the necessity of belief. Peggy's short letter covered the basics of the movement, with the first paragraph explaining that she sought entrance into the "next evolutionary kingdom—which has been called the Kingdom of Heaven," and the second paragraph describing both the process and the demonstration. She provided few details and offered nothing different from the Two's own positions in their work. The young woman's third paragraph turned to the notion of how one enacted the process, and whether her parents, who had never met Bo and Peep, might follow in the footsteps of their daughter: "You may be interested in doing this yourself—either now or at the end of the next age. (2000 years.) The only thing necessary to do it is simply to believe it possible and natural, want to do it, and get in touch with your heavenly father—i.e., the one who is already a members of the next kingdom and will guide you (though invisible) through the process. And that's it."[51] Peggy's summary of HIM's teachings matched that of the group's leaders, and therefore her assessment of the nature of the process would also seem accurate. Bo and Peep's naturalized materialistic religion did indeed seem to require belief, or faith, as well as the support of a guide. Here the image of the objective experimental scientist breaks down, at least if one assumes the standard Western, naturalistic, empiricist, scientific worldview.

It is interesting that only two members, rather than the leaders of HIM, discussed the notion of faith with outsiders, though certainly many other members did not mention the concept of faith in their interviews. Such discrepancies might owe to differences in how adherents understood the message that the Two preached, but it probably also indicates that Bo and Peep vacillated on this issue during the summer and autumn of 1975, since their followers understood the topic of faith differently during this time. HIM's leaders would eventually reach a consensus, first shared with interviewer James Phelan in early 1976, and that consensus continued into the group's later history. The Two stressed to Phelan that potential passengers on the UFO, or those who wished to take part in their technological rapture, must possess faith. Phelan summarized that the Two insisted on "unquestioning faith," and that "[t]o qualify for the voyage, they say, one must believe in them without 'any of those little tricks,' as they refer to miracles." Regarding the demonstration, the interviewer noted, "they point out [that it] will be staged not to convince their followers but to confound the scoffers."[52] At this point, although the Two appeared to settle this issue in their conversation with Phelan, they would periodically return to the question of faith, which would haunt the movement even in its final days. Faith presented a problem for Heaven's Gate. Did its leaders emulate religion and demand some level of faith, or declare themselves objective empiricists, like science? Ultimately, the leaders of Heaven's Gate opted for the former.

Shortly after Bo and Peep's interview with James Phelan, the Two also enacted another shift in their movement's worldview, namely the transition from an extremely individualistic approach to the overcoming process to one that insisted on the value of guides and teachers. This shift also marked a transition away from purely individualistic empiricism reminiscent of science toward the more authoritative model of knowledge associated with religion. The young follower Peggy's description of invisible aids to the individual's process of human metamorphosis hinted at the basis of that transformation, the Two's long-standing acceptance of the idea of spiritual guides. Nettles, even before she met Applewhite, claimed to have a spiritual guide, a deceased monk named Brother Francis, who spoke to her from the spirit world and helped her prepare astrological charts.[53] The positive view of spirit guides carried over into HIM, which despite minimizing the value of human help, extolled the significance of next-level guides. The second statement, "Clarification: Human Kingdom—Visible and Invisible" focused on the issue of spirit guides, warning that many would lead astray potential followers of the overcoming process, but that some, those of the next level or the "Heavenly Father" could direct a person by providing tests and opportunities to overcome their humanity.[54] Similarly, the Two wrote in their letter to prospective candidates that "[i]f you recognize this as Truth; [sic] you have only to ask with all your might (out loud or in your head) for your Father(s) in the Next Kingdom to give you whatever tests are necessary for your overcoming."[55] That is, next level aids could assist Bo and Peep's followers through offering tests to encourage them to overcome their humanity. While at first the Two minimized the potential value of any other helpers beyond these invisible spirit guides, during the later 1970s they taught that HIM's adherents, and therefore anyone who wished to accompany them on their technological rapture, needed to assistance of the Two themselves.

Unfortunately no documents survive from this period, but Robert Balch, who studied the group ethnographically during the 1970s and later interviewed former members, offered both evidence of the transition as well as an explanation for it. Balch noted that "when disputes arose, each individual could justify his or her opinion by claiming to have received guidance directly from a member of the next kingdom," leading to conflicts within the group as well as between the leaders and their followers.[56] Such anti-nomianism endangered the group's stability, and its leaders stepped in to prevent complete chaos. "The Two solved the problem by eliminating any possibility of individual revelation," wrote Balch. "They explained that all information from the next level was channeled through a 'chain of mind'" that linked the next kingdom to individual members through Bo and Peep. The Two, he summarized, "became necessary intermediaries between members and the next level."[57] Balch reports that following this new revelation, commitment levels increased and defection rates dropped.[58]

These two transitions, from rejecting the idea of faith to embracing it, and from emphasizing extreme individualism to the value of the movement's two leaders, demonstrate an important transition in the early days of the group that would become Heaven's Gate. Though the movement's materialism and naturalism carried through into the 1980s and 1990s, Bo and Peep's early emphasis on a purely individualistic and empirical approach to religion could not sustain a religious group. This approach, again reminiscent of that lone scientist studying the world in search of truth, required their followers to rely solely on their own senses, intuition, and whatever contact they felt with invisible next-level guides. It permitted if not encouraged anti-nomianism and discouraged the ability to maintain a community. Individualistic empiricism proved too costly for the movement, and Bo and Peep curtailed it. Further, since the demonstration did not occur—the "delay of the parousia" problem that first-century Christians also faced—the Two could not rely upon an empirically verifiable illustration of the truth of their religious message. Belief, faith, and the requirement of heeding the words of religious leaders replaced the pure materialistic individualistic naturalism of HIM's early days.

"A Focusing": Religion, Science, and Prayer

Despite the introduction of concepts of faith and religious leadership, Human Individual Metamorphosis did not leave behind the naturalistic approach to religion that characterized the group. The movement would disappear from popular notice between 1976 and 1988, and unfortunately very few primary sources exist from this period.[59] One of the few sources, a short booklet titled *Preparing for Service*, survived through the efforts of a former member of the group. Describing it as "written by [Bo and Peep]" and also a "little booklet some class members compiled from things [Bo and Peep] had said or written," the text offers a glimpse of how the Two's followers, who by then referred to themselves as a "class" interpreted and recorded the message of their teachers.[60] Most of the text contains a series of aphorisms, ranging from the banal (e.g., "Forget your fears. Realize that your condition is of your own making. There is no power that can keep you down but yourself.") to restatements of the fundamental positions of the movement ("Help me have no human ways. No thoughts of self, No [*sic*] faults to see. Only the ways of space.").[61] The majority of the adages conveyed the message that the readers could control their bodies, subjugate it to their minds, and cleave to a next-level consciousness. Given Bo and Peep's earlier material, the statements in *Preparing for Service* demonstrated a continuity of thought. Salvation or resurrection, the members of the movement continued to believe in 1985, meant a physical metamorphosis of the body through a process of rejecting human influences and seeking to follow the guidance of extraterrestrial teachers. The process remained entirely materialistic and natural.

The booklet ended with a long prayer or meditation exercise titled "A Focusing," which, to use its own words, encouraged a reader to focus inward on the process of bodily transformation. The prayer provides a rare glimpse of how the members of the movement that became Heaven's Gate (it is unclear what name the group used at the time they produced the booklet[62]) put into practice their approach of absorbing science into religion. Though clearly a prayer or meditation, it mixed language of science and religion, fixating on the development of something akin to a "next-level gland," which the reader of the prayer hoped to develop. The "Focusing" meditation reveals how the adherents of Heaven's Gate applied their materialistic understanding of a personal metamorphosis to the traditionally religious notion of prayer.

Composed of twenty-five short verses, the booklet indicated pauses before many of them and showed several marked off by parentheses, which might have indicated instructions to read those verses silently. This created a set of natural divisions within the meditation: a four-verse opening, a central section of ten verses preceded by what the instructions referred to as "especially long pauses," four transitional verses marked off by parentheses, and a six-verse conclusion. Taken as a whole, the meditation developed a theme of personal transformation through bodily control and material metamorphosis, using language drawn from both scientific and religious repertoires.

The reflection began with a short section that combined the rhetoric of the spiritual seeker with that of science and religion: "I would like to know more than I now know. / I would like to have more control over my vehicle— it's [sic] chemistry—its thoughts—its responses—its desires—than I now have. / I would like to rise above the things that distract me and bind me to this world." The prayer's opening line situated the meditation as one centered on knowledge, using words with which most people would no doubt concur, namely the desire "to know more than I now know."[63] This mantra, one that a scholar or scientist might also take to heart, set the tone for the remainder of the prayer. Members of Heaven's Gate did not worship beings of the next level, nor did they ask their invisible guides for succor or support. They did not thank their Creator for giving them a body or mind or soul, nor make any particular requests. Instead they stated their desire for knowledge. The second verse shifted the prayer toward what would become its theme—the aspiration to master the body. As members of many other world religions, particularly mendicants and monastics, seek the mastery of the body, so the members of Heaven's Gate almost uniquely stated their desire to control not only the whirlwind of the mind but also the chemical makeup of their bodies.[64] And in keeping with the early statements of the movement's leaders, the members of Heaven's Gate continued to seek a bodily metamorphosis.

The nucleus of the prayer focused on a physical "spot" on the body, what the meditation compared to a gland, drawing the attention of the reader to the spot and emphasizing its value in the process of bodily transformation. "There is a spot in the middle of my head. / I am now concentrating-focusing on that spot. (It is about the size of my eyeball, it is like a gland that has been asleep, inactive, waiting for me to concentrate on it.) / I am, right now, going to feel it become active and alive. / I am focusing on it, I can feel it now in its location. / All of my energy is being directed toward this Next Level gland. / As this spot accepts all of my energy it is helping my chemistry change. / I can feel the power of that energy there. / I can feel the calm of that power. / I can feel my chemistry in control. / I feel no frustration or anxiety. / I feel only that calm, powerful energy."[65] That the center of the Focusing prayer treated a gland and the control of bodily chemistry reveals the continued place of the materialistic understanding of transformation within Heaven's Gate, or the absorption of scientific concepts into its religion. The "spot in the middle of the head" might also have alluded to the Hindu concept of the seventh *chakra*, the energy center positioned either between the eyes or on the crown of head from which some Hindus believe a *yogi* can project their consciousness, as we saw in the case of Gaudiya Vaishnavism and the International Society for Krishna Consciousness. During the 1970s and 1980s the Hindu concept of chakras had become very popular in the New Age movement, and it is quite possible that the Focusing prayer alluded to a belief in the chakra, though the only explicit mention of the chakra concept among Heaven's Gate material is a dismissal of the value of the system in a member's written statement in 1997.[66]

Regardless of whether the cranial gland represented a reference to a chakra, the central portion of the Focusing prayer clearly considered the presence of this spot highly valuable and important in the overcoming and transformative process. The spot itself represented a "next-level gland" and therefore a tangible and material representation of the physical heavens to which members of Heaven's Gate wished to journey. By activating the gland—medical language that itself reveals the naturalistic assumptions of the group—the reader of the prayer hoped to become calm and remove frustration and anxiety, all of which represented a step in overcoming. Even more importantly, energizing the gland led to the physical metamorphosis itself, or as the prayer declares, "helping [the] chemistry change."

The prayer continued with four verses marked off by parenthesis. Unfortunately the booklet did not indicate the meaning of this typographical offsetting. Possibly readers of the prayer spoke these verses silently, or perhaps the parentheses marked them as optional. They continued the same theme of the earlier section, reiterating the value of the spot in the overcoming process and therefore what the prayer's reader hoped to be a bodily metamorphosis: "(As this spot becomes more alive it will help me sustain this calm.) / (It will eliminate distraction from my goal.) / (It will keep me clear.) / (I will know more.)" The prayer concluded with a spoken declaration of intent and entreaty for the physical process of metamorphosis to continue:

As I recognize higher control and knowledge I will adopt it quickly, discarding my weaknesses.

My potential for growth is limitless.

I am rapidly changing.

Growth has been offered to me and I am choosing to become it.

I feel and hear that spot coming more to life!

Change! Vehicle, Change! Chemistry.

I am going to hold onto this until I sit and become even more![67]

Repeating the themes with which the prayer began, it concluded with a call for transformation and mastery of the body, or "vehicle," as the movement had come to call the physical form. The prayer's conclusion brought into focus the materialistic and naturalistic approach of the group. Human beings possessed a "weakness" that one could overcome through control and knowledge. Successful command over the physical body and its needs resulted in both growth and rapid change, the metamorphosis that earlier sources proclaimed and that gave the group its name, Human Individual Metamorphosis.

The final two verses also reveal a movement at the point of transition. Twelve years after the members of Heaven's Gate wrote the Focusing prayer, they would commit mass suicide, leaving behind the bodies that they had labored for so long to transform. They hoped through that act to propel their spirit forms into the heavens, where they would assume next-level bodies prepared for them. During that decade-long period, Heaven's Gate shifted from a purely materialistic understanding of the metamorphosis to a more symbolic one, while simultaneously extending the group's materialism in new directions. The body became merely a "vehicle," a shell that conveyed the spirit or soul from one incarnation to another, rather than a caterpillar awaiting its transition into a new perfected state, and the "metamorphosis" of 1975 became a "shedding of the vehicle" of 1997. The penultimate verse of the "A Focusing" meditation, composed approximately halfway between the movement's beginning and its end, encapsulated both the earlier and later positions regarding transformation and salvation. Calling the body a "vehicle," it hinted at the easiness with which the members of the group would later shed their bodies, like a person upgrading from one automobile to another. Yet in the same verse, the readers of the prayer invoked a hoped-for change in chemistry, a reference to the group's original view of material metamorphosis. When Heaven's Gate again appeared in the national limelight in 1988, the group itself had transformed.

6

Science and the End
of Heaven's Gate

*From Human Individual Metamorphosis
to Heaven's Gate*

In March 1997, police in the posh San Diego suburb of Rancho Santa Fe, California, burst into a sprawling mansion in a luxurious gated community to discover thirty-nine decomposing bodies.[1] In ritual precision, the members of the group had orchestrated a mass suicide, the ultimate terminus of a new religious movement founded two decades earlier. A media circus ensued, each new story describing an even more bizarre "religious cult." Dubbed "Heaven's Gate," the name of the group's webpage, the movement was none other than Human Individual Metamorphosis, still led by Marshall Herff Applewhite in its last earthly days and holding the final allegiance of members who had joined in Los Angeles, Waldport, and other meetings from HIM's early days.

Heaven's Gate had transformed in the twenty years since Nettles and Applewhite founded it. Bonnie Lu Nettles had died in 1985, leaving Applewhite the sole leader of the religious group in its final decade. Applewhite, who renamed himself Do (pronounced "doe") and his deceased co-founder "Ti" ("tea"), had introduced several new doctrines.[2] Do né Bo had intensified the apocalypticism of the movement, embracing a catastrophic view of the end-times. After Nettles's death, he had upgraded Ti née Peep from equal to superior, and declared her the chief next-level administrator of the planet Earth, at times implying that she was the entity that the ancient Hebrews addressed as God. He stressed government cover-ups of UFO sightings and conspiracies to hide imprisoned extraterrestrials, revealing an increasing tension with American wider society and suspicion of American governance. Most crucially, Do transformed the group's understanding of salvation, eschewing the materialistic naturalism of HIM's early days and adopting a more spiritual concept of the transmigration of the soul. Overall, Heaven's Gate demonstrated a twofold approach in its final years: on the one hand, they extended thoroughly materialistic scientific-sounded explanations of several religious concepts; on the other hand they retreated from several of HIM's naturalistic approaches. These latter departures represented exceptions that proved the rule of materialistic reinterpretation. Heaven's Gate continued to absorb science into religion though appropriation of science's basic methodological assumptions, materialism and naturalism.

A Movement in Transition: the '88 Update

The movement did not make national headlines again until after the mass suicides in 1997. However, Heaven's Gate did attempt to broadcast its views several times before that time through a flurry of videos, advertisements, books, and websites, peaking around 1993 and then again in 1997. Even before this, the movement produced a short booklet titled '88 Update, which they disseminated to New Age centers and ufologists.[3] Written by Do in 1988, the booklet described the group's origins and history, provided some background of the "UFO Two" (as Do called himself and his partner), and told the story of how Human Individual Metamorphosis had continued to grow after its disappearance from the limelight. The group made no attempt to recruit through the booklet and included no contact information. They did, however, include a permission statement to duplicate the material and a request that readers who "want to help us" disseminate it "far and wide."[4] Overall, the text gave the impression of taking part in a conversation with both ufologists and religionists, with frequent mentions of particular UFO researchers and UFO sightings alongside biblical quotes and a footnote written especially for "religious scholars."[5] A three-page list of recommended readings included a medley of religion, ufology, and paranormal selections, ranging from the Bible, the Dead Sea Scrolls, and the Nag Hammadi Library to UFO crashes in Roswell, government conspiracies to coverup extraterrestrial life, and accounts of close encounters with space aliens.[6]

The '88 Update both extended and curtailed Heaven's Gate's materialistic and naturalistic approach to religion. The extensions followed the patterns that the Two had set a decade earlier, namely the movement's view of Christ and of the physical nature of heaven and the heavens. The '88 Update focused on the group's basic doctrine, invoking just such materialistic understandings. Referring to his movement in the third person, Do wrote that "they felt that they really had no choice but to tell the world what the real Kingdom of Heaven was—a physical evolutionary level, instead of some mystical cloud-and-harp, spiritual existence. . . . They knew that Jesus had come or been sent to share exactly the same truth with 'those who had the eyes to see,' but that His body might have been a Next Level hybrid by means of artificial insemination, offering Him more Next Level capabilities."[7] Here the update echoed the Two's earliest printed declaration, the "Human Individual Metamorphosis" statement, which the *'88 Update* later quoted in its entirety. Do equated heaven with the heavens, and like the first statement's disparaging dismissal of those who put their faith in "some savior" and "some 'heaven,'" the update booklet contrasted the physicalist approach of Heaven's Gate with belief in "some mystical cloud-and-harp, spiritual existence." The addition of the term "evolutionary" further cemented Heaven's Gate's attempt to employ scientific rhetoric in distinction to the normally religious language used to describe heaven.

The *'88 Update*'s depiction of Christ extended the materialistic approach of earlier Heaven's Gate sources. Earlier, especially in their conversation with ufologists Brad Steiger and Hayden Hewes, the Two had described Jesus as leaving behind a body to incarnate on Earth, completing a metabolic transformation through the Transfiguration, repairing himself after the Crucifixion, and returning to the literal heavens in a UFO that humans referred to as a cloud of light. Now, Do offered that Christ was a "hybrid" created by means of artificial insemination. This characterization, no doubt even more offensive to many Christians than the earlier material, further indicated the group's materialistic view of Christ: Jesus might be a human-extraterrestrial hybrid produced by artificial insemination. Such a position both described and defined Christ using purely naturalistic, scientific language, and ascribed his nature to a technological act, that of artificial insemination.

One way to understand this statement is through changes in the wider UFO subculture, which Heaven's Gate reflected through an explicitly religious lens. By the late 1980s that subculture had developed a fixation with human-alien hybrids and the possibility of both extraterrestrial as well as government experiments in genetically engineering such beings. Regardless of possible influences, Do's musing on the subject indicated a continuation of the group's materialistic rereadings of religion. Christians have argued over the nature of Christ's essence since the first century, with some schools claiming him as a sort of "hybrid" between human and God, and others as purely divine (Docetism) or purely human (Adoptionism).[8] Do and Heaven's Gate took the "hybrid" side of this debate, the same that the orthodox church also accepted. In other words, the movement had translated into the language of science what many Christians accepted on a religious level—that Christ was both human and divine at the same time. By accepting other ufologists' suspicions about government experiments and cover-ups, Do and Heaven's Gate also reiterated their rejection of wider American society, a theme that the movement had developed since its earliest days of emphasizing an immediate exodus from Earth.

Do also turned to the wider question of the physical beings who dwelt in the heavens. As far back as the first three statements, the group had equated the extraterrestrials who lived in the next level with the members of God's kingdom, and the update continued this perspective.[9] Unlike the vague allusions to membership in a kingdom of heaven in those earlier HIM materials, the update began to provide specifics of the next-level entities. These specifics linked Heaven's Gate vision of the material and physical life of heaven with the same process of overcoming human attachments that they had upheld since their earliest days. Just as human beings needed to overcome sexuality and attraction to other humans, the next-level aliens possessed no reproductive systems, eschewing biological reproduction as beneath them. Do explained, "there are apparently no active reproductive organs in the physical bodies of members of the Next Level, though the bodies of some of the younger (less advanced) members of the Next Level, if examined, might show signs of internal remnants of reproductive organs long since all but atrophied."[10] Repeating one of Heaven's Gate's themes, namely the denial of gender and sexuality, Do dismissed those who upheld the idea of gender in heaven. Yet he emphasized that life in the heavens was a physical, natural reality, and not a spiritual state or supernatural existence.

Again, the manner in which Do depicted the physical nature of the next-level alien beings probably developed from evolutions in the UFO subculture, which by the 1980s included discussions of government labs performing experiments on captured extraterrestrials and direct encounters between human beings and alien creatures.[11] Do and the other members of Heaven's Gate accepted these accounts, explicitly stating in the '88 Update that governments "have retrieved 'crashed' spacecrafts, live 'EBE's' (extraterrestrials), and numerous bodies, autopsies of which have revealed characteristics mentioned previously (even though investigators interpret these occurrences incorrectly)."[12] Accepting what many other ufologists also believed, that the government performed medical experiments on captured aliens, Do interpreted this belief in light of Heaven's Gate's position that the heavens represented heaven. Unless one "interpreted these occurrences incorrectly," one would come to the same conclusions, he insisted: next-level extraterrestrials possessed bodies, but not reproductive organs.

For the first time, Heaven's Gate offered an explanation of how the next level produced additional members. In keeping with their overall naturalism, Do offered a strikingly materialistic view of the operation of heaven. "Our understanding is that Next Level bodies (the normal bodies for that Kingdom level, in the same way that human bodies are the norm for the human kingdom) are grown as plants from a vine. . . . There seem to be actual grafting processes used and genetic binding from Older Members. 'I am the vine, ye are the branches'—could that mean something more than previously thought?"[13] This passage combined a direct quote from the King James Bible (John 15:5) with the idea of "genetic binding" between different members of heaven, revealing a specific manner in which Heaven's Gate absorbed science into religion. The overall religious concept remained, i.e., a heaven where the members of Heaven's Gate hoped to travel, but the specifics used the language and concepts of science. The "Older Members" of heaven used genetic technology to grow new heavenly beings on physical vines.

Cognitive Dissonance and the Retreat from Materialism

While the '88 Update generally enhanced materialistic views of religious topics, it also retreated from two central concepts that the Two had labored to portray in a purely naturalistic and materialistic manner: the demonstration and the metamorphosis. Unlike the naturalizing approach to describing the occupants of heaven, the booklet employed a supernatural and symbolic approach to re-explain these two concepts. The demonstration, it declared bluntly, no longer represented the physical death of the Two's bodies and subsequent biological repair, but a symbolic death by the news media.[14] Instead of demonstrating the truth of the process and the possibility of physical, chemical, bodily metamorphosis, the leader and members of Heaven's Gate now believed that the demonstration provided a symbolic example of how the Two could soldier on, despite adversity, and continue to lead the group. Unlike other acts of reinterpretation within the group that transformed spiritual concepts to physical ones, this one proceeded on the opposite track, from a naturalistic understanding to a symbolic one.

The best explanation for this reversal is also the simplest: the demonstration as predicted did not occur, and the Two needed to respond to this unexpected reality. Rather than jettison the concept altogether, they moved to a more symbolic reading, one that allowed them and the members of their movement to confirm the preexisting belief in the demonstration as well as their experience of its failure to occur as expected. In doing so, the Two minimized what Leon Festinger termed "cognitive dissonance." In his flawed but valuable study (1956) of a group he called the "Seekers," a small UFO religion, Festinger utilized the concept of dissonance in order to explain how the Seekers responded to a similar failed prophecy. The predicted events in the two groups are quite similar—for the Seekers, the UFO that they sought did not land—and for Heaven's Gate, the Two did not undergo martyrdom and subsequent rapture aboard a UFO. The result was also the same: cognitive dissonance. "The fact that the predicted events did not occur is dissonant with continuing to believe both the prediction and the remainder of the ideology of which the prediction was the central item," wrote Festinger.[15] In the case of the Seekers, the disappointed believers attempted to reduce the dissonance by proselytizing, Festinger argues. In the case of Heaven's Gate, Ti and Do reversed their normal naturalizing hermeneutics and provided for their followers a new symbolic reading of the demonstration, thereby satisfying Festinger's requirement that the group minimize dissonance in order to survive.[16]

The cognitive dissonance model also explains the other interpretive shift in Heaven's Gate's '88 Update, their view of the metamorphic process itself. Just several years earlier, the movement had encapsulated its materialistic approach to the metamorphosis in the meditative prayer, "A Focusing," which evoked a chemical change in the body and the slow biological transformation from human being into next-level alien. The update bluntly rejected this earlier position, which had served as the heart of the group's approach to salvation since the Two's very first statements.[17]

The leader of Heaven's Gate now explained that the group's members did not hope for a biological transformation into next-level beings, but believed themselves *already* next-level extraterrestrials who only currently inhabited human "vehicles" for some sort of task or purpose. The '88 Update did not expand on the ramifications of this transition, though later sources would do so. It did however muddy the waters that previously had offered so naturalistic an approach to salvation. Instead of converting human bodies into biologically alien creatures and then flying away aboard UFOs, the members of Heaven's Gate now believed that their consciousnesses would transfer out of their human bodies and into new next-level ones. The notion of the transmigration of mind and consciousness replaced that of a physical, material transformation, and of physical, material transportation aboard a flying saucer.

Do both claimed and limited materialistic naturalism in explaining the process by which he and his followers incarnated on Earth. "They were briefed as a crew aboard a spacecraft about how they would incarnate into human vehicles in order to do a task," he wrote in the update. "Some left their bodies behind in 'cold storage,' or the Next Level's wardrobe, for the duration of this task. Others were in 'spirit,' having not yet earned Next Level bodies since having left the human kingdom."[18] While the conceptualization of physical next-level bodies in the heavens reinforced the traditionally physicalist approach that the Two had assumed, Do's depiction of next-level creatures existing "in 'spirit'" actually directly contrasted his earlier rejection of this view, as he declared numerous times that next-level space aliens had physical bodies and did *not* exist in spirit forms. A decade later, the belief in the transmigration of consciousness instead of bodily metamorphosis would permit the adherents of the movement to accept the destruction of their human bodies, i.e., suicide, as a viable method of freeing their minds to journey to the next level. In 1988, it stood as a reversal of one of the group's long-standing central tenets.

The best explanation for this transformation and reversal lies in the death of Bonnie Lu Nettles, Applewhite's co-founder and co-leader of the movement. Her 1985 death of liver cancer shocked and reshaped the group. Since the earliest days of Heaven's Gate, Ti and Do had taught that a UFO would descend to Earth and, in a technological reenactment of Revelation's prophecy of the rapture of the faithful, in fact bodily save the select few true believers. Yet no extraterrestrials appeared to whisk away Nettles before her body succumbed to cancer, nor did the saucers land to claim her physical body. This was likely a moment of *massive cognitive dissonance* in the movement, though no available documents survive to prove this conjecture. Heaven's Gate survived because Do introduced the supernatural or symbolic reading of the metamorphosis into the movement's theology. Language referring to the body as a "vehicle" proliferated in the *'88 Update*, and by 1992 the body had become merely a "container."[19] In the booklet, Do explained that "a member of the Next Level wears a body like a suit of clothes."[20] By introducing this symbolic reading of the metamorphosis and replacing the earlier biological, chemical, physical one, Do transformed Nettle's death into Ti's soul's departure for the literal heavens, thereby overcoming the cognitive dissonance that her death entailed. The recasting of both the demonstration and the metamorphosis in symbolic and supernatural terms, rather than naturalistic and physical ones, stand out from other transformations in the movement. But they are the exceptions that proved the rule of naturalization. Both served to heal cognitive dissonance and prevent the complete dissolution of the movement. Overall, the *'88 Update* revealed a continuation of Heaven's Gate's absorption of naturalism, with the exception of the notions of demonstration and transformation.

Beyond Human: Physical Beings in the Material Heavens

Heaven's Gate disappeared again after the *'88 Update*, making no effort to proselytize or communicate with the outside world, until late December 1991, when the group produced a series of satellite television broadcasts called *Beyond Human—The Last Call*. Shortly thereafter, Do and his followers transferred *Beyond Human* to videocassette, and in the coming years (1993–94) traveled across the country in small groups to hold public meetings and present their videotaped teachings.[21] To prepare the way for their evangelization, Heaven's Gate—now using the name "Total Overcomers Anonymous" (TOA)—purchased a one-third page advertisement in *USA Today* on May 27, 1993, later reprinted in about two dozen alternative newspapers throughout the nation. The group's new name emphasized the continued focus on *overcoming* the human condition, thereby replacing the earlier moniker Human Individual Metamorphosis, with its now-problematic concentration on physical metamorphosis. They titled the advertisement "'UFO Cult' Resurfaces with Final Offer," and used it to declare their movement's fundamental religious positions. Together with the *Beyond Human* broadcasts, this advertisement and several posters that TOA utilized during this period offered a comprehensive picture of the movement's religious approach during the early 1990s. Heaven's Gate's period as TOA demonstrated the same basic pattern that characterized the movement in the previous decade: an attempt to convey a materialistic, physicalist, tangible vision of heaven and its inhabitants.

If the *'88 Update* provided a glimpse of how Do and his followers had both limited and extended the naturalizing impulse of Human Individual Metamorphosis, then the twelve-part video and satellite series *Beyond Human* offered a scenic vista. Over the course of thirteen and a half hours, Do and his students provided a relatively complete look at their movement's ideological position. The video series continued the overall attitude of the preceding years, representing a naturalized approach to religious topics that emphasized the physical nature of religious concepts. Much of what Do presented in *Beyond Human* followed in direct line from his and Ti's earliest materials, for example the insistence on the material physical nature of the next-level heavens and the beings who lived there. Do added further explanations of the tangible physical reality of Christianity's major theological actors, Christ, God the Father, and Lucifer. Like the *'88 Update* booklet, the *Beyond Human* video and satellite series eschewed the earlier concept of physical metamorphosis, envisioning the process of salvation as the transmigration of the soul or consciousness. The series continued the *'88 Update*'s symbolic reading of bodily transformation and extended it, explicitly embracing a view of the soul as completely independent of the body.[22]

The real, physical nature of the next level remained a core tenet of Do and TOA's materialistic approach to religion. The movement literally inscribed this position onto the dust jackets of the *Beyond Human* series, which began with a summary and exhortation: "This series of tapes explains simply, clearly, and understandably how we get to 'Heaven.' *Don't stop! Read on!* It explains how Heaven is not where we go after we die 'if we are good,' but is a physical Kingdom Level above the human kingdom." The jacket repeated this theme twice more, repeating the phrase "the literal physical Heavens."[23] If a viewer decided to watch the video they encountered the same claim in its opening minute: heaven was a real, physical, tangible place: "the Kingdom of Heaven—the *physical* Kingdom of Heaven, not a spiritual Kingdom of Heaven." Retreating a moment, perhaps remembering that viewers had no background on his Total Overcomers Anonymous movement, he added, "[n]ot that it isn't spiritual, but it is not etheric [*sic*]. It is not only spiritual, which represents the character of the soul, but it is a physical kingdom as well."[24] This restatement of what had remained a key notion, combined with an almost apologetic defense of his dismissal of the idea of the "spiritual," immediately situated Do and TOA as a religion unlike other religions, one that insisted on materialism and naturalism over the spirit and the supernatural.

The series focused on what had long occupied the center of Heaven's Gate theology: the bodily transformation into an extraterrestrial being. Although Do, along with Ti, had declared the reality of the next-level beings sixteen years earlier, in *Beyond Human* Do provided explicit details about the material and bodily nature of such beings. Do explained that these space aliens—a peaceful, enlightened, rational, and organized race—occupied themselves with managing the affairs of the universe. Functioning on a level far surpassing humanity's limited mental, biological, and moral resources, the next-level aliens were selfless and group-minded, living solely for the purpose of functioning within an immense celestial bureaucracy. Immune to the ravages of time, genderless, needing no sustenance, and nearly immortal, none of the normal tethers of human life limited them. The next-level aliens functioned as materialistic equivalents to the traditional Jewish-Christian-Muslim notion of angels.

Like the early material produced by HIM, which extolled the possibility of metamorphosing into such a creature, Do promised in *Beyond Human* that one could become a next-level alien through mastering oneself and overcoming one's humanity, which could result in the transference of consciousness from a human vehicle (or body) to a perfected next-level one. That new form presented numerous advantages: "[y]ou take on a vehicle that is imperishable and incorruptible. . . . Not only does the soul have life, but you can wear a vehicle that, for all intents and purposes, doesn't need to decay. It doesn't have any age, it doesn't come from a baby, it doesn't get old and need to be changed out for another one. There's no loss of consciousness."[25] Next level aliens represented the ideal form of biological life: perfect, eternal, and incorruptible. As Total Overcomers Anonymous's final poster declared, the next level "is a genderless (sexless), non-mammalian (though certainly non-reptilian), crew-minded, service-oriented world that finds greed, lust, and self-serving pursuits abhorrent."[26] This poster rejected what Do and Heaven's Gate considered the mainstays of American culture—greed, lust, and a self-serving attitude—as well as competing religious views of the heavens. Rather than envision a heaven of angels-on-wings and the souls of the saints, Do foresaw one of eternal biological, that is material and natural, beings. Yet, like the Christian view of heaven, Do and his TOA movement offered the chance for immortality in the heavens, albeit in a purely *material* form.

The topic of Christ dominated conversations during several of the twelve *Beyond Human* sessions and many of the later posters, often because TOA's leader compared his own mission, as he understood it, to that of Christ. When Do spoke of Jesus, he repeated the same claim that he and Ti had made during the days of Human Individual Metamorphosis: both before and after Christ's incarnation he possessed a physical body in the next level, and during the Incarnation itself he possessed a physical body on Earth. Such a position, of course, does not differ from that of many Christians, though the question of whether Christ possessed a physical body before the Incarnation has divided theologians for millennia. Do considered the topic directly. "Did not Jesus take a human vehicle (body)? . . . Of course, He had had a vehicle before He took that human vehicle."[27] A poster put this another way, "[t]wo thousand years ago, an Older Member in the real Kingdom of Heaven, left behind His Next Level (non-mammalian) body and incarnated into a 'picked' and 'prepped' human body at approx. its 29th year."[28] Total Overcomers Anonymous taught that Christ, like God the Father and the other next-level beings, was a fundamentally physical, biological creature, a next-level alien who took a temporary body on Earth before returning to his own in the heavens.

Just as did the '88 Update, the Beyond Human series de-emphasized the role of Christ's bodily metamorphosis, what had been a staple of Ti and Do's message during the mid-1970s when they were still only the Two. The interpretation introduced in the '88 Update represented a denaturalizing or "re-supernaturalizing" of the movement's view of Christ. The video series not only amplified the particular view of the update but also engaged in a simultaneous materialistic rereading by limiting the role and value of the ultimate supernatural element in the Christ story, the Resurrection itself. Here Do thoroughly naturalized Jesus, and like the Deists two centuries earlier, treated Christ as a teacher and holy man but denigrated both the view of him as God as well as the possibility of the miracle of resurrection. That is, while Do and TOA simultaneously downplayed the naturalistic and materialistic elements that the Two had first mentioned (the Resurrection and to a lesser extent the Transfiguration), they emphasized the naturalistic and physicalist nature of Jesus himself. This also fits the pattern of the '88 Update and other later Heaven's Gate material.

Qualifying his critique by claiming that he could not know if Jesus' Resurrection represented a bona fide miracle, a staged event, or a later invention, Do attacked a supernataralist reading of the concept as unnecessary for the understanding on Christ's message. "I heard a pretty prominent television minister not long ago say if Jesus did not resurrect, literally, physically, actually *resurrect* from an honest-to-goodness *dead* state from in the tomb, after having been on the cross, if that *miracle* of resurrection from the dead did not occur, then *everything* in Christianity is a farce. That appalls me. I can't identify with that kind of thinking at all."[29] The Resurrection itself, Do added, didn't matter "a hill of beans," since the words and message of Christ mattered far more than any demonstration that Jesus might have performed. Here, Beyond Human materialized and naturalized the story of Christ while simultaneously implying an almost scientific open-mindedness. It did not matter, Do indicated, whether one accepted the Resurrection; what mattered was what one learned from it. [30]

Science, Religion, and Faith

For the first time in the history of the group that became Heaven's Gate, the *Beyond Human* series included a *specific* discussion of science and its relation to religion, rather than merely evidence of the absorption of scientific approaches into religion. In the video series, Do attempted to both seize the mantle of science as well as limit what he considered the main scientific critique of religion, namely that the latter relies upon faith. Do continued to insist that his own movement represented a naturalistic materialistic way of looking at the world; he rejected the pure empiricism that he believed science recommends, doing so in a way strikingly similar to that of ISKCON's A. C. Bhaktivedanta Swami. Like the Hare Krishna leader, Do lamented that scientists claimed to know the truth but have historically changed their minds about major theories. Do specifically mentioned astronomy as an example. "Scientists frequently in this human world say, 'I will believe what I see. I have to see it to believe it. I can't accept this religious concept of believing something on faith or just because it's some legendary concept or religious concept. I believe what I see.' And yet, how many times have the astronomers rewritten their history books because they thought they had seen things that meant so and so were the facts and only to later find out that what they had seen didn't mean that, it meant something else. And then later to only understand that even that was off, and have to continually rewrite their books, even though they are the ones that say, 'I believe what I see.' You don't know what you see when you see it. We can all misjudge what we see," declared Do during the seventh *Beyond Human* session.[31] Unlike Bhaktivedanta, who rejected the notion of accurate senses, Do doubted empiricism because he doubted people could accurately process what they saw. The difference between Do and Bhaktivedanta derived from the Heaven's Gate's leader's materialistic naturalism, a position that ISKCON explicitly rejected. Do believed that the world and the heavens could be accurately observed, but he doubted that observation provided enough data to allow a cogent theory. He insisted that science's empiricism lacked the crucial ability to accept data on faith, knowledge that the next level provided directly through its representatives.

In other words, despite Do and TOA's avowal of naturalism, they could not accept the inductive approach to knowledge that scientific empiricism claimed. They valued the deductions of belief over empirical demonstrations of truth. For that reason, Do moved in *Beyond Human* from the question of empiricism to the notion of faith. Faith, he defined, "is evidence of things unseen," and the faith that he and his movement put in the next level overwhelmed any sort of counter evidence.[32] "[A] good example of that," he added, "would be: as we are fed information concerning the workings of the Kingdom of Heaven and the workings of overcoming, the more that picture grows and grows and grows, and begins to just amaze us and astound us, because these intricate pieces of the puzzle begin to fit together in that picture, and soon that picture is so magnificent, so beyond anything we could have dreamed of, that it is evidence of things unseen. Therefore, it is proof to us. . . . So, the basis of faith works."[33] Heaven's Gate, like many other religions, looked to deduction, direct revelation, and religious authority to determine truth, rather than the empirical process of gathering data in order to construct a hypothesis. While accepting the foundation of science—materialistic naturalism—Heaven's Gate maintained its reliance of the methods of religion rather than those of science. Empiricism could not replace scripture and the teachings of the movement's leader.

The philosopher of science Tom Sorell has defined scientism as "the belief that science, especially natural science, is much the most valuable part of human learning—much the most valuable because it is much the most authoritative, or serious, or beneficial."[34] Though Heaven's Gate naturalized its religious ideology, it was not a form of scientism. In *Beyond Human*, Do made clear that science and scientific approaches did not provide "the most valuable" way of understanding the world. Do linked science to empiricism and the denial of faith, two epistemological approaches that he and other members of the group clearly rejected. They clearly valued science and scientific language—for example talking of the mind as a computer and their communication with the next level as type of radio signal exchange. Do and the other members of Heaven's Gate insisted that the next level could communicate directly with them, bypassing the normal senses and thereby disqualifying pure empiricism as the best approach to understanding the world and heavens.[35] In other words, if science conflicted with its own ideology, Do indicated in *Beyond Human*, TOA could dismiss it.

Despite his caution toward science, Do reserved his harshest words for religion, and in fact the satellite and video series and the subsequent advertisements spent far more time and space criticizing religion than they did science. "I don't want to start condemning religions," Do declared during the fourth *Beyond Human* session, "but, you know, there's something we have to return to here, and that is that our Father's Truth is not a religion. It's simply the facts. Simply the way it is—it's the facts. Once we even begin to label it 'religion' we are already, at that point, a significant degree away from the facts, the Truth."[36] Do might not have wanted to condemn religions, but that is precisely what he did, condemning religion as a category as well as individual religions. All the while, however, he continued to admit that TOA itself was a religion. This irony—the leader of a new religion who condemned the concept of religion—reveals the tremendous value that Do ascribed to scientific methods of thought, and the suspicion he held for any epistemology not rooted in empiricism and rationalism.

Religious language, Do declared several times during the video series, was less objective, less true, and less accurate than other language.[37] He did not provide an explanation for why religious language possessed such attributes, but he did remark on how religion naturally "tainted" the truth due to "the passage of time and because of the lack of closeness of the Next Level."[38] Religion itself, rather than any particular form of religion, seemed to bear the blame for this tainting. The *USA Today* advertisement declared that "[y]ou cannot *preserve* the Truth in your religions. It is with you only as long as a *Truth bearer* is with you."[39] Several of the posters made similar claims.[40] Some of Do's vehemence might have originated in his position as the founder and leader and an alternative religious movement in competition with other religions. Certainly that would have explained his opposition to his competitors. Indeed Do did challenge particular religions, primarily Christianity, Judaism, and the New Age, on several occasions. Ultimately Do, and later several members of the Heaven's Gate movement, explicitly attacked religion as a category and form of knowledge.

In one of the most explicitly anti-religious sections of *Beyond Human*, Do explained that his group's criticism of religion originated in their view of religion as possessing fantastical, illusionary views of the world and heavens. This revelation occurred during an exchange with one of his students in the closing minutes of the final *Beyond Human* session:

STUDENT: How do these items [i.e., teachings] relate to overcoming: religion?

DO: Well, because of what so-called religions are, at times we feel like we don't want to associate with that term because we want to say the Truth that we have is real. It's not a religion because religions have become fantasy and illusion, and they have adjusted all their thinking so that they don't have to do anything about changing.[41]

Religion itself is something that must be overcome, Do answers. TOA's leader believed that he represented the truth, which was real, whereas religions represented fantasy and illusion. Like his rejection of pure scientific empiricism, Do linked his criticism on religion to his belief that the next level provided direct, accurate information directly to him and his movement. While Do clearly indicated his rejection of the category of religion in *Beyond Human*, he did not provide a clear explanation for it. Here Do unwittingly repeated a critique of religion promulgated by modernist critics of religion, namely that religion was less concerned with truth than it is wish fulfillment. Although we cannot know if Do had previously read Sigmund Freud's *Future of an Illusion*, in calling religion a fantasy and illusion, Do accepts the Freudian complaint that religions operate as delusions rather than accurate assessments of the world.

Do did not explain why he rejected religion: his students did. Shortly before the March 1997 suicides that ended Heaven's Gate, its leader and members collected the various materials they had produced over the years into an anthologized collection, which they titled *How and When "Heaven's Gate" (The Door to the Physical Kingdom Level Above Human) May Be Entered*, (abbreviated hereafter as HGA [Heaven's Gate anthology]), published electronically before the suicides and printed posthumously. The book represented the group's final attempt to communicate its teachings with outsiders, and for the first time included a series of short theological treatments written by members of the group other than its leaders. Using their religious names within the group, all of which ended with the suffix "ody"—which signified their status as inchoate members of the Next Level—individuals such as Anlody, Jwnody, Qstody, and Stmody offered twenty-three assessments of their movement's religious positions. Several themes predominated in these "Statements by Students," as the HGA called them. Nearly all of the authors stressed the physical nature of the next level and the physical biological disposition of next-level aliens. Many denigrated specific religions and religion generally. Several different voices emerged from those individual statements that nevertheless agreed on one basic concept: Heaven's Gate offered a naturalistic, materialistic message of how a person could enter the physical heavens, whereas other religions, or perhaps religion more broadly, did not. Although many of these views repeated what Do had earlier discussed in *Beyond Human* or the *'88 Update*, the students also offered their own explanations of Heaven's Gate ideology. The HGA anthology not only offered the theological positions of the members of the movement, but as one of the final sources that the group produced, it provided the last word on Heaven's Gate's religious understandings.

Of the themes that the Heaven's Gate members repeated most frequently, they commented on the physical nature of heaven and of the next-level entities who lived there, as well as the physical makeup of Satan and the Luciferian space aliens. Here they repeated but amplified their leader, Do. Many of the group's members wrote what easily might have been the words of their leaders two decades earlier, for example the Heaven's Gate member calling herself Jnnody, a woman who had first met the Two in Waldport, Oregon, in 1975, and joined the movement shortly thereafter. Jnnody wrote that the "'Kingdom of God,' the 'Evolutionary Level Above Human,' the 'Next Level,' and the 'Kingdom of Heaven' . . . is a many-membered Kingdom, a physical level of existence in deepest space (outside of man's concept of time) *beyond* this human level—advanced physically, technologically, behaviorally, ethically, genetically, and in the wisdom and knowledge of service in the Creator's world."[42] Jnnody's coreligionist Smmody, another longtime member who joined in 1976, similarly declared that "[t]he true Kingdom of God (the Next Level) is a real place—a reachable place."[43] Even the name of the anthology itself, which declared open the door to the "Physical Kingdom Level Above Human" repeated this central claim that the next level was a physical, material, tangible place. Other adherents of the group who contributed to the volume offered explanations of the biological nature of the next-level aliens and their opposites, the Luciferian extraterrestrials.[44]

Several of the Heaven's Gate members contrasted their physicalist approach with the spiritual or supernaturalist perspective of other religions, or of religion more broadly. Many linked the theme of the material nature of the heavens with their dismissal of religion. A member writing under the name Chkody lamented that "[w]ith all the misinformation about the Next Level put out by religions, it is not surprising that individuals have a hard time grasping that the Next Level exists in the literal Heavens and is more physical and more real than the human world."[45] Chkody considered this concept so important that the HGA printed the entire sentence in boldface. Religion, Chkody explained, confused people because it denied the physical nature of the heavens, or in Do's words from around the same period, offered "clouds and harps" instead of the reality of physical biological bodies.[46]

Chkody, whose birth name and life circumstances remain unknown, offered several additional criticisms of religion in her contribution to the HGA, "The Hidden Facts of Ti and Do." Opening with a dismissal of "antiquated religion" and "New Age spiritualism," she rejected the religions as offering only "misinformation."[47] Religions failed, Chkody explained, because they reduced the truth to belief systems and rituals, rather than accepting the pure truth that the next level periodically provided the Earth. Chkody's criticism occupied an unstable region between rejecting religion generally and all of the world's religions specifically. On the one hand, she stated that the malevolent Luciferian space aliens had influenced all known religions and infused them with misinformation meant to control the hapless human inhabitants of the planet, which although uncharitable to religions, spared the category of religion itself. On the other hand, Chkody declared, emphasizing the point, that "*[o]nce a movement becomes a religion, it's already lost the practical 'truth' it had to offer. It's plain facts—that is what truth is. Once it is even called a religion, it is corrupted.*"[48] Such a blanket dismissal of religion implied a rejection of the entire class "religion" as irredeemable. What Chkody wanted was *the truth*, not beliefs or rituals. She wanted the method of overcoming her humanity, not rites of adoration. Here Chkody offered a critique of religion that encapsulated and mirrored a Protestant critique of Catholic ritualism as well as a modernist rejection of the category of religion itself.

Other members of Heaven's Gate presented differing objections to religion. Jwnody, another longtime member who had joined the movement in 1975 and contributed several statements to the Heaven's Gate anthology, tailored one of her pieces as an all-out assault on religion, "Religions are Humans' #1 Killers of Souls." Jwnody laid out several positions in this statement, but most centrally she argued that Luciferian agents used religion to control humanity. "Sadly," Jwnody wrote, "it has become quite evident that *all* of Earth's religions are a product of extensive psychological manipulation and tampering by these space-alien races."[49] In addition to this explicit point against "*all* of Earth's religions," Jwnody also implied a distrust of the category of religion itself. In fact, she used "religious" as a synonym for "false," indicating an underlying rejection of the concept of religion as well as each of the specific religions. Combining a restatement of one of Heaven's Gate's fundamental positions with a rejection of religion, Jwnody wrote that "[t]he Kingdom of Heaven is not an etheric [*sic*] or spiritual place, but a many-membered physical Kingdom that exists in deep space. . . . [And] the one who was Jesus was a member of this Kingdom who was sent to take you out of your ignorance—a man from the only real, potential future, not some religious, mythical icon."[50] These two sentences paralleled the concepts of real and physical, contrasting them with those of religious, spiritual, and "etheric" (by which she probably meant "ethereal"). In making this parallel, she implied that "the religious" opposed "the real." Her compatriot the nearly identically named Jnnody repeated this position almost verbatim, "Jesus was not a religious man. He was a man from the only real potential future—in another world, an evolutionarily advanced level of existence—the Next Level."[51]

Jwnody and Jnnody made a very clear connotation: others believed in a *religious* or *mythical* Christ, whereas they followed a *real* Christ. Both indicated though their rhetoric an opposition between religion and reality, the religious and the real.

Jwnody and Jnnody's statements, and others like them from their fellow adherents of Heaven's Gate, indicated the overall view of religion within the movement. Religion, they believed, equaled false knowledge. This explains Anlody's odd declaration in her statement that their "message is not now, nor has it ever been, religious or spiritual."[52] Anlody, whose membership dated to 1976, went on to discuss God, heaven, the soul, and Lucifer in her brief statement "Investments," despite her explicit denial of any religious element to her message. On her movement's apocalyptic expectations of the oncoming "end of the age," she flatly declared "[w]e've been saying the planet was due to be recycled at the end of the age. That is not religious beliefs."[53] The naturalistic language—"recycling" to mean the apocalypse, for example—provided a way out for Anlody and her compatriots to deny the religious nature of their message, even though she did use religious language in bluntly criticizing those who "stop[ed] having a need for God or Heaven."[54] The members of the Heaven's Gate treated the concept of religion independent of the implicit religious nature of their own message. They could criticize the category while still using its notions, such as God, the soul, and salvation.

One cannot easily rectify the uneasy relation between Heaven's Gate's dismissal of religion and the actual content of their religious system. The best explanation is that Heaven's Gate, while itself a religion, encapsulated an atheistic critique of religion, which they then deployed against the very category in which their movement belonged. Though certainly not a majority opinion, a large number of Americans agreed with Heaven's Gate that religion represented a false form of knowledge, mere sloppy thinking that transformed myths into absolute truths. Such a position found many proponents among both professional scientists and ufologists. The astronomer Carl Sagan, whose *Demon-Haunted World* thundered against both UFO sightings and miraculous healings, represented such a position, as did many leading members of the ufology community, such as Frank Edwards, whom Brenda Denzler quoted as denigrating religion as an "irrational and rigid belief system."[55] Heaven's Gate appropriated this view when it absorbed scientific naturalism within itself. Such a position emerged in the smug refutations of Heaven's Gate members Yrsody, who said that religious people "walk righteously down a dead-end street," and Qstody, who called the "distracted, self-satisfied slaves" of religion "programmed puppets worshipping false myths, rituals, futile belief systems and counterfeit fantasy gods."[56] Without explanation, such depictions of religion existed alongside the author's descriptions of what most would consider self-evidently religious topics.

Knocking on Heaven's Gate

For more than twenty years, Heaven's Gate had adopted a materialistic, naturalistic ideological approach, recasting religious concepts in the language of science. Christianity's major theological figures had become tangible biological entities, prayer and revelation became radio wave communication, and heaven itself a distant corporeal location in the sky. One concept, however, had troubled the movement since its origin: the notion of the self and the soul. Ti and Do, then merely the Two, accepted an extremely materialistic reading of the self as the physical body as well as a conceptualization of the reincarnation of the soul and disincarnate spirits. After Nettles's death in 1985, Do had moved to a less materialistic view of the soul that treated the body as merely a container or "vehicle." The *Beyond Human* video series in 1992 added to that approach the idea of the deposit, the tag, a physical marker that Do at times equated to the soul. Some of the last materials produced by Heaven's Gate—the statements by students and final two videos that Do produced—made explicit the equation of the soul and the deposit, providing a purely materialistic explanation for the soul. They also continued to accept the notion of the transmigration of the soul, and this belief made possible their decision to commit a mass suicide. The soul, though physical, could transfer between one container and another; it possessed both physical and nonphysical elements, just as Heaven's Gate was both a religion and not one.

Nearly every one of the "Statements by Students" in the Heaven's Gate anthology included mention of deposits, and in each of these cases the authors described the deposits as the basis of the soul. Many took explicitly physicalist approaches to the soul, others used materialistic metaphors to explain the soul but refrained for overtly declaring it a tangible object. Lvvody, a member of whom nothing is known save his or her name within the group, wrote that the next-level administrators "make a 'deposit' that contains a soul with a very small amount of Next Level information—it's like a tiny Next Level fetus. The program in that deposit contains a '*chip*' of recognition."[57] Lvvody identified this deposit as akin to a tiny fetus but does not elaborate on its physical nature. Lvvody's compatriot Drrody took the same approach, something between a metaphoric and materialistic treatment of the deposit. "A Next Level deposit is like a computer chip or a piece of hardware that functions in two ways," he wrote. "First, it acts as a homing device to guide one to the opportunity to connect with Teachers, or Representatives, sent from our Kingdom. . . . Second, it provides a container for housing Next Level Mind or information."[58] Apart from describing the deposit's function, neither Lvvody or Drrody commented on its true nature. The deposit, however, clearly functioned within Heaven's Gate thought as a technological analog to the human soul. Without having to use spiritual language or rely to a nonmaterial concept such as the spirit, the deposit allowed the members of Heaven's Gate to simultaneously uphold physicalism as well as the religious concept of the soul.

Others, such as Jwnody, who forcefully attacked religion in her "Religions are Humans' #1 Killers of Souls," used her "'Away Team' From Deep Space Surfaces Before Departure" to defend a explicitly naturalistic understanding of the deposit. Much of her statement used the vernacular of the *Star Trek* science fiction series to explain Heaven's Gate's religious perspectives, and clearly she valued the scientific-sounding language of that television series. Calling Heaven's Gate an "away team," *Star Trek's* term for a group of crewmembers who leave their spaceship to visit a planet, she called the human condition a "gestation circumstance" that prepared individual souls for birth into the next level.[59] On the nature of the deposit she used just as naturalistic language. "The 'soul,'" she declared, "is a physical container residing within the body that can house living mind (or Next Level information), without which no life can be present."[60] Like Drrody, Jwnody envisioned the deposit as both soul and information storage vessel, but unlike her coreligionist, Jwnody declared the soul "a physical container."

Truly physical or not, Jwnody, Drrody, Lvvody, and all of their fellow members of Heaven's Gate simultaneously upheld the notion that the self could be transferred between bodies. Lvvody declared that "'I'—the identity—am the soul—containing Next Level mind, [and] this borrowed human body I am wearing is not me."[61] Wknody just as tellingly wrote that "[w]hen *we* speak of life, we are referring to the mind, and in our case, the soul, for that is what we identify as."[62] The denigration of the physical human body, despite an avowal of the physical nature of the soul, permitted the movement to entertain the possibility of committing suicide in order to free the self of its material confines, allowing it to transit into the heavens. The death of Ti a decade earlier reinforced for the group that the soul might indeed journey to the next level without waiting for a UFO, and for reasons that scholars continue to debate, by 1996 Heaven's Gate considered actively encouraging the process. In all likelihood the movement's experience of wide-scale rejection by potential converts, the failing health of Do, apocalyptic pessimism toward the human world, and rumors in the UFO community of a flying saucer trailing the Hale-Bopp comet combined to instigate the decision to perform a mass suicide, or "exit," as the members themselves called it. The final source that Heaven's Gate produced, a self-styled "Exit Press Release" posted onto their Internet website, employed the same materialistic language with which the movement began: "RANCHO SANTO FE, CA—By the time you receive this, we'll be gone—several dozen of us. We came from the Level Above Human in distant space and we have now exited the bodies that we were wearing for our earthly task, to return to the world from whence we came — task completed. The distant space we refer to is what your religious literature would call the Kingdom of Heaven or the Kingdom of God." The press release continued for several paragraphs, explaining the basic beliefs of the group. "The Kingdom of God, the Level Above Human, is a physical world, where they inhabit physical bodies," it declared, mirroring the words of the Two's first statement. The release concluded with a quote from the book of Revelation, "Blessed are the dead who die in the Lord" (Rev 14:13).[63]

Thus, Heaven's Gate ended on the same note with which it began, the transformation of religious concepts and ideas into the language and terminology of materialism and naturalism. Death had become an "exit," their suicides a "graduation," the invitation to join them a "boarding pass," and the opening to heaven that they sought a "window."[64] Though the movement never explained why it chose the name Heaven's Gate for itself, the materialistic nature of the appellation provided a fitting closure on the movement that throughout its history attempted to absorb the materialistic, naturalistic underpinnings of science into religion.

Conclusion

This book has aimed to demonstrate that the three new religions considered—the Unification Church, ISKCON, and Heaven's Gate—offered three distinct methods of understanding the nature of science and its relation to religion. In each case, the group's approach to science existed in concert with wider religious perspectives. Yet far more than mere accretions onto broader belief systems, each group's position on science functioned as a central component in its worldview. For Unificationists, guiding science and shepherding it toward its eventual millennial union with religion represented a core part of the movement's self-understanding. Similarly, the Hare Krishna movement's rejection of Western science and espousal of an Indian alternative functioned alongside ISKCON's wider rejection of Western social norms and postcolonial identity. Finally, the leaders of Heaven's Gate not only placed science at the center of its theological system but self-consciously declared their movement to be a science. In each case, science served a central role in the group's self-understanding and identity.

Despite the distinct religious and cultural locations of each of the groups, the three responded to a common set of historical circumstances: the postwar burgeoning of American science and the social response to that growth, both within the scientific community as well as from countercultural critics. The American scientific establishment peaked during this decade in which the new religions thrived, and like other American social commentators, the leaders and members of the NRMs (New Religious Movements) responded to that development. The three movements sometimes offered criticism of science and its growth, but they also recognized the remarkable cultural legitimacy afforded by the cloak of science during the mid- to late-twentieth century.

In addition, the three groups offered representative but radical positions, which often paralleled broader understandings of science present in both religious and secular subcultures. That new religions were representative hardly surprises: they responded to the same tensions as other American social movements and religions, and came to some of the same conclusions. However, NRMs also offered more radical solutions as compared to North America's more established religions. For example, of America's religions, only Unificationism sponsored a multidecade series of science conferences meant to guide the scientific establishment. Nor did the more established religions declare themselves sciences, as did Heaven's Gate. New religions upheld such radical positions because they, unfettered by mainstream institutional and theological constraints, creatively developed new understandings of science in keeping with their broader agendas. Further, the new religions offered such solutions because they possessed comprehensive worldviews that envisioned the complete transformation of the world, culture, and the individual. Science, as one of the defining characteristics of modern society, required a response from all religions, both new and old. But new religions offered the most extreme positions. In this regard, they functioned as bellwethers that revealed currents that similarly affecting other religions. By examining new religions, one can see trends that more slowly influenced American's other religions as well.

In proffering three distinct approaches to understanding science, the three new religions considered in this book offer the basis of a typology of how other new religions—and possibly older religions—might also respond to science. Though not quite ideal types in the Weberian sense of the term, the three new religions nevertheless serve as useful models for the construction of such a typology. Each group distilled a particular perspective on science and religion into a easily recognizable symbolic relationship between the two: guide/replace/absorb. The sociologist Susan Palmer noted a similar pattern in how new religions defined gender roles and the relationship between the sexes, with each NRM offering a single, well-defined alternative to the multiple messages present in wider culture. Regarding those new religions, Palmer wrote that "[t]his clarity and simplicity is often achieved by emphasizing one role and de-emphasizing, or rejecting, other roles."[1] Palmer's study of sexual identity in new religions concluded with an assessment of how the clarity of gender roles offered by the NRMs functioned within a broader typology of the ideology of gender in new religious movements. Similarly, in his study of Victorian Buddhists in America, Thomas A. Tweed developed a typology of new Buddhistic movements in America, looking to the movements' underlying ideologies as well as the reasons that potential converts found them attractive.[2] Subsequent scholars have found both of these typologies helpful. Recognizing the value that such typologies offer, I conclude with a similar typology of how new religions construct understandings of science and its relation to religion.

The typology presented here includes three poles: religion ought to *guide* science toward a particular set of goals; religion ought to *replace* science with an alternative system; and religion ought to *absorb* the methodologies, epistemologies, or approaches of science. The Unification Church represented the first approach. They aimed to *guide* science and the American scientific establishment. They positioned science as a sphere separate from religion, yet at the same time attempted to direct science's ethical boundaries, methods, and even research goals. The Hare Krishnas embodied the second position. ISKCON sought to *replace* Western science with an alternative scientific-religious system rooted in their own Hindu religious tradition. The science of ancient Indian religious texts, they insisted, offered a more accurate and socially healthy paradigm than that of the contemporary American scientific establishment. Heaven's Gate represented the third position. Its leaders and members attempted to *absorb* or incorporate science and scientific elements into their religious system. They looked to methodological materialism and naturalism as the ideal epistemology, and declared their movement the truest form of science.

For a typology to offer any traction, it must offer explanatory power. Building on the three new religions considered here, several factors might explain why a movement adopts one of these three approaches. Though one might hypothesize numerous variables that lead to a new religion's position, I focus on two. Recognizing that many new religions emerged from the twentieth-century colonial context, a group's understanding of science reflects how it positions itself relative to its former colonial power and the broader Euro-American Western world. Second, I look to a movement's understanding of the nature of the human self. Highly dualistic movements that postulate the mind or soul as completely distinct from the body understand science in a characteristic way as compared to movements that reject the reality of the material world and body (or, in rarer cases, accept only the material world).

Of the two variables, the first offers perhaps the best predictor for how new religions respond to science. Within my study, both the International Society for Krishna Consciousness and the Unification Church emerged from colonial circumstances and looked to science as a powerful symbol for the West. Swami Bhaktivedanta's experience as a youth in British-controlled India impacted the eventual direction of the Hare Krishna movement. Bhaktivedanta rejected both British culture and science, stressing instead the value of indigenous Indian alternatives. The swami and those who joined his movement looked to ancient Hindu civilization and its sacred text, the Vedas, as the source for their religious world. Science, so deeply embedded as a core component of Western culture, came to represent all that the Hare Krishnas thought wrong with Western, including American, society. ISK-CON therefore adopted the position of seeking to replace Western science with a Vedic alternative. The Unification Church also emerged from a colonial context, yet it came to the radically different perspective of supporting the Western scientific establishment and guiding it toward what the movement considered its foreordained goal. Reverend Moon also witnessed his country forcibly modernized, with native Korean religion and culture devalued and replaced by imported systems. But crucially, rather than Western colonialists controlling Korea, Japanese ones did. Though Japanese authorities did introduce normative Western science to Japan—with Moon himself having studied science in Japan—Moon understood modern science as born out of Europe and America, and therefore it avoided the taint of symbolizing the oppression of the colonial experience. In fact, Moon looked to Western science as an alternative legitimizing force, since he viewed it as developing alongside the Enlightenment and Protestant Christianity, which he held in high esteem. Unificationists therefore looked positively rather than negatively upon Western science. In both cases, science functioned as a powerful symbol of the modern West, and a group's position on science revealed its overall approach to modern Western culture, history, and religion. By contrast to the other two groups, Heaven's Gate emerged out of Texas, and though it offered strong criticisms of American society, the movement did not associate modern Western norms with an imposed cultural system. Absent of a colonial background, the founders of Heaven's Gate treated science as most other Americans did, an assumed epistemological foundation for Western culture. In a radical move, the group even absorbed that epistemology. Considered synoptically, the three new religions imply that science operates as a symbol of the modern West, and a movement's understanding of science develops out of its overall approach to the modern Western world.

While the colonial background of a new religion certainly has a powerful impact on how a group relates to Western science, not all NRMs emerge from such a context, and even those that do need not define themselves by that experience. This is why a second variable, that of mind-body dualism, also serves as an indicator as to how a movement might fall within the guide/replace/absorb typology. Religious groups that uphold mind-body dualism envision the human essence as divided between the material body and nonmaterial mind or soul. As the philosopher Charles Taliaferro writes, "[a] dualist holds that a human person is constituted by a body *and* what may be called a mind or soul or consciousness."[3] Those movements that reject classical philosophical dualism argue that human life is either entirely physical (materialism), or completely spiritual and nonmaterial (idealism).[4] Most religious groups that reject mind-body dualism declare the seat of the human essence to be the nonmaterial soul but still accept the reality of the human body, with the repercussion that the material is accepted but devalued. Philosophers call such a rejection of dualism "Cartesian dualism, since it follows René Descartes in admitting the reality of the physical world but subjugating it to the spiritual. The Hare Krishna movement upholds such a position, though it did so because of an analogous Hindu philosophical position derived from Vedic sources that envision the world as illusion, or *maya*. In chapters three and four, the founders and leaders of ISKCON declared that human beings existed as spiritual beings, and that any true understanding of the human condition must center on the nonmaterial. Cartesian dualism's subjugation of the physical carries over into the movement's perspective on the physical world and the physical sciences. The Hare Krishna movement's leaders declared that the best appraisals of the world must draw on Vedic insights into the nonmaterial realm rather than flawed material observations of a flawed world. Bhaktivedanta hammered against Western scientists because they assumed an empirical and materialistic approach to their studies. In rejecting Western science, the Hare Krishna movement followed its devaluation of the physical born of its Cartesian dualism.

Heaven's Gate similarly also rejected classic dualism, but it represented the opposite perspective, that of materialism. That movement's precise formulation changed over time, yet throughout the group's history it prioritized the physical and the embodied. Applewhite and Nettles first insisted on physical transit to the literal heavens, and ironically even the suicides that ended the movement represented a desire to physically depart the Earth and enter the next level, employing new material bodies prepared for the journey. Heaven's Gate's absorption of scientific rhetoric and epistemologies—within limits, as I argue in chapter six—emerged from the materialistic tendencies born of their rejection of dualism and upholding of materialism. That is, Heaven's Gate's strong materialism resulted in a propensity toward absorbing the approaches and assumptions of science.

Of the three groups considered in this book, only the Unification Church truly accepted classical dualism, declaring that a human was both a physical and spiritual being. This position derived from the movement's Daoist sensibilities of the complementary balance between opposites, notably the spiritual and material. Native Korean belief in a fully developed spirit world that existed alongside the physical world further solidified this position. This theological dualism led the movement to adopt an explicit position of mind-body dualism, declaring that the human being existed both in the material realm as body and brain and in the spiritual realm as mind and soul. Such a position directly led the movement to support science because it valued the material alongside the spiritual. Unificationists sought to guide science because they believed it could solve problems of health, energy, and international relations, just as they looked to their own movement to solve the spiritual problems of the world. Ultimately, Unificationism envisioned science as a twin of religion. As a religious movement, the Unification Church naturally looked to the spiritual as director of the material. Therefore the movement understood itself as a guide to science.

All religious movements take some position on the nature of dualism, and if the three cases considered here are any indication, this position has a powerful effect on a group's understanding of science. Movements that accept mind-body dualism recognize both the spiritual and material aspects of human nature, and therefore value both the pursuit of the spiritual as well as study of the material world. This translates into a tendency toward upholding a conciliatory but not capitulatory approach to science. Groups that deny the material nature of the human identity or adopt some form of Cartesian dualism are unlikely to positively value the overall material world. Such movements would likely reject the Western science model, so rooted in empiricism and materialism, and seek its replacement with some other alternative more in keeping with their nonmaterial perspective. Those rare religions that uphold purely materialistic worldviews envision human beings as fundamentally physical beings. These types of groups naturally value the material world and its study, and would likely adopt the approaches meant to study the physical and material, namely science.

While one might find other variables at work that indicate how a group might fall on the guide/replace/absorb typology, some characteristics seem to have little effect. Millennialism, for example, does not appear to influence a group's perspectives on science. Most new religions exhibit some form of millennialism, and certainly a movement's perspectives on the ultimate purpose and end of human society has a powerful impact on their view of science. Millennialism, however, demonstrates such diversity that as a variable it cannot predict how a movement understands science. Catherine Wessinger's distinction between catastrophic and progressive millennialism helps to distinguish different forms of millennialism, but this distinction still provides little traction. Catastrophic millennial movements expect an immanent seismic end to the world as it presently exists. Absent other factors, such movements are unlikely to look to science as offering much long-term potential, nor to dedicate significant energy to developing an ideology of science and its relation to religion. As such, catastrophic millennialism itself cannot influence how a group understands science, and other factors become far more important. Heaven's Gate, an almost prototypical catastrophic millennial movement, took an interest in science only because of the strict materialism born of its rejection of dualism. By contrast, progressive millennial movements look to themselves as harbingers of a utopian new world. How they understand science depends on their particular vision for that new world. The Unification Church and ISKCON clearly function as a progressive millennial movements, and as such offer distinct visions for the world that they wish to transform. These two movements offer radically different hopes for a transformed society. The Hare Krishnas look to an idealized ancient India featuring a restored Vedic scientific model, whereas Unificationism hopes to usher in a new modern world born of the fusion of East and West. These two visions lead to radically different views of normative modern science, with ISKCON rejecting the current models in favor of Vedic alternatives, and Unificationism looking to contemporary science as an ally to be guided toward the realization of the millennium. In both cases, the group's position on science emerged directly from its millennial vision and was central to the group's mission, but in neither case did millennialism itself shape the movement's understanding of science.

Having considered two possible variables—and discounted another—it is clear that the guide/replace/absorb typology offers scholars of new religions a fresh way to understand the ideologies and worldview of NRMs. The typology also represents a relatively new approach to the study of new religious movements that I hope other scholars will consider: the serious study of the intellectual positions of NRMs. With some notable exceptions—most notably Mary Farrell Bednarowski's *New Religions & The Theological Imagination in America*—monographic studies of new religions tend not to focus on the content of the religious messages proffered by such groups, but instead consider sociological issues. While this approach to new religions offers valuable insights to the field of NRM studies, I hope that other students of new religions similarly will look to their theologies as fertile ground for exploration.

NRMs and American Religious History

The Unification Church, Hare Krishna movement, and Heaven's Gate treated the concept of science and the relation of science to religion and the wider society during the late twentieth century. The Unification Church hoped to *guide* science toward a divinely mandated goal while ISKCON sought to *replace* Western science with a Hindu alternative, and Heaven's Gate attempted to *absorb* the methodology, epistemology, and legitimacy of science. Each of these approaches challenged the status quo of American science and religion, as well as of the American scientific and religious establishments. Taken as a whole, they form a typology (replace/absorb/guide) of how religious groups—new, old, alternative, or mainstream—could respond to the tremendous growth of power and prestige of science in late twentieth-century America. The new religions served as harbingers of a dawning conversation on the relation of science to religion, as well as prisms that refracted that wider conversation through their particular theological approaches. The book shows that religious groups had several methods of creatively responding to science, and that the often-assumed conflict-based model of "science vs. religion" must be replaced by a more nuanced understanding of how religions operate in our modern scientific world.

Viewed synoptically, the manner in which the three new religious movements responded to the power, prestige, and place of science in America demonstrates the multiple ways that religious groups can incorporate creative tension with science into their broader intellectual positions. The three groups emerged from different cultural and historical circumstances, ranging from Bengal to Korea to east Texas, and took differing views of science and religion. Yet each insisted that religion could respond to science with neither warfare nor surrender. This book opened with a montage of events occurring in 1972. That year witnessed numerous scientific breakthroughs and global political events. It saw the Unification Church's first International Conference of the Unity of Science, the publication of Swami Bhaktivedanta's *Easy Journey to Other Planets*, and the birth of Heaven's Gate. Also in 1972 Sydney Ahlstrom, one of the generation's most influential historians of American religion, published his magisterial *Religious History of the American People*. Ahlstrom's text has shaped the study of American religious history and, as fellow historian Catherine Albanese has noted, no subsequent book has attempted to treat American religious history with the same "sweep and narrative scope."[5] Ahlstrom's text is a classic. Yet in the book's more than one thousand pages, Sydney Ahlstrom discusses science only twice, once when he considers New Thought, and again in his treatment of the fundamentalist-modernist controversy. The time has come to focus more attention on how individuals and groups throughout American religious history have related to science. New religious movements, by virtue of their desire to offer transformative solutions to the problems of the modern world and their freedom to innovate beyond the confines of tradition, represent the cutting edge of the American religious response to science. The NRMs considered in this book acted as prisms, refracting wider concerns through their specific theological lenses. American religious historians more broadly need to look to these new religions as trendsetters that reveal the continuing religious response to the tremendous power and prestige of science in the modern world.

Notes

NOTES TO INTRODUCTION

1. For a treatment of the creation of recombinant DNA (rDNA), see Susan Wright, "Recombinant DNA Technology and Its Social Transformation, 1972–1982 " *Osiris* 2 (1986). On the history of the computer language C, Dennis M. Ritchie, "The Development of the C Language," in *History of Programming Languages*, ed. Thomas J. Bergin Jr. and Richard G. Gibson Jr. (New York: ACM Press, 1996). (Appropriately, it is easiest to access that paper digitally using the Internet, at http://cm.bell-labs.com/cm/cs/who/dmr/chist.html.) For details on the Fermi National Accelerator Laboratory, see Daniel J. Kevles, *The Physicists: The History of a Scientific Community in Modern America* (Cambridge, MA: Harvard University Press, 1995), 420–23; Catherine Lee Westfall, "The First 'Truly National Laboratory': The Birth of Fermilab" (PhD diss., Michigan State University, 1988).

2. William Sims Bainbridge, *The Endtime Family: Children of God* (Albany: State University of New York Press, 2002), 43.

3. Thomas S. Kuhn, *The Structure of Scientific Revolutions* (Chicago: University of Chicago Press, 1962).

4. Michel Foucault, *Birth of the Clinic: An Archaeology of Medical Perception*, trans. A. M. Sheridan Smith (New York: Pantheon Books, 1973). First published in French as *Naissance de la Clinique*, 1963.

5. Bruno Latour and Steve Woolgar, *Laboratory Life: The Social Construction of Scientific Facts* (Beverly Hills, CA: Sage Publications, 1979).

6. Several schools of thought predominate in the debate over the constructed nature of science. On the constructivist end of the spectrum, the "strong programme," or Edinburgh school, treats science and scientific knowledge as wholly produced by social networks. Continental thinkers such as Bruno Latour have produced similar work under the title "actor-network theory." Those who prefer a softer constructivist approach often follow the lead of the late Thomas Kuhn in considering science as practiced within social networks but not necessarily bound to them. For more on the various schools of thought, see Jan Golinski, *Making Natural Knowledge: Constructivism and the History of Science* (Cambridge: Cambridge Unviersity Press, 1998); Andrew Ross, *Science Wars* (Durham, NC: Duke University Press, 1996).

7. Luis W. Alvarez et. al., "Amicus Curiae Brief of 72 Nobel Laureates, 17 State Academies of Science, and 7 Other Scientific Organizations, in Support of Appellees, Submitted to the Supreme Court of the United States, October Term, 1986, as Edwin W. Edwards, in His Official Capacity as Governor of Louisiana, et al., Appellants V. Don Aguillard et al., Appellees," 1986. Note that the Supreme Court handed down its decision in 1987, the year after it accepted the amicus curiae brief.

8. Ibid.

9. Most scholars credit the physicist and government scientist Alvin Weinberg with coining the term (see his collected essays on the subject). Alvin Martin Weinberg, *Reflections on Big Science* (Cambridge, MA: M.I.T. Press, 1967).

10. Paul Boyer, *By the Bomb's Early Light: American Thought at the Dawn of the Atomic Age* (Chapel Hill: University of North Carolina Press, 1994).

11. Heinz Haber, *The Walt Disney Story of Our Friend the Atom* (New York: Dell Publishing Group, 1956), 127.

12. Herbert N. Foerstel, *Secret Science: Federal Control of American Science and Technology* (Westport, CT: Praeger, 1993); Greta Jones, *Science, Politics and the Cold War* (New York: Routledge, 1988); Stuart W. Leslie, *The Cold War and American Science: The Military-Industrial Academic Complex at MIT and Stanford* (New York: Columbia University Press, 1993).

13. Here I use the term "establishment" in the colloquial sense. Although critics attacked the churches as part of the establishment, America's religious institutions were not established in the formal, legal sense of being state-churches.

14. Kurt Vonnegut Jr., *Cat's Cradle* (New York: Holt, Rinehart and Winston, 1963).

15. E. F. Schumacher wrote, "[i]n the excitement over the unfolding of his scientific and technological powers, modern man has built a system of production that ravishes nature and a type of society that mutilates man." His *Small is Beautiful* called for a reclamation of anthropocentrism over technology. E. F. Schumacher, *Small Is Beautiful: A Study of Economics as If People Mattered* (London: Blond and Briggs, 1973), 275.

16. See Robert Booth Fowler, *The Greening of Protestant Thought* (Chapel Hill: University of North Carolina Press, 1995).

17. Ronald L. Numbers, *The Creationists: From Scientific Creationists to Intelligent Design*, rev. ed. (Cambridge, MA: Harvard University Press, 2006), 373–98.

18. John William Draper, *History of the Conflict between Religion and Science* (New York: D. Appleton & Company, 1874); Andrew Dickson White, *A History of the Warfare of Science with Theology in Christendom* (New York: D. Appleton & Company, 1896).

19. Norman F. Furniss, *The Fundamentalist Controversy, 1918–1931* (New Haven, CT: Yale University Press, 1954); Edward A. White, *Science and Religion in American Thought* (Stanford, CA: Stanford University Press, 1952).

20. Richard Hofstadter, *Anti-Intellectualism in American Life* (New York: Knopf, 1963).

21. David C. Lindberg and Ronald L. Numbers, *When Science & Christianity Meet* (Chicago: University of Chicago Press, 2003); David N. Livingstone, D. G. Hart, and Mark A. Noll, eds., *Evangelicals and Science in Historical Perspective* (New York: Oxford University Press, 1999).

22. David N. Livingstone, "Situating Evangelical Responses to Evolution," in *Evangelicals and Science*.

23. Peter Burke, *What is Cultural History?* (Cambridge: Polity Press, 2004), 3.

NOTES TO PART I INTRODUCTION

1. International Conference on the Unity of the Sciences (hereafter ICUS in notes), *The Re-Evaluation of Existing Values and the Search for Absolute Values: Proceedings of the Seventh International Conference on the Unity of the Sciences, November 24–26, 1978, Boston, Massachusetts*, 2 vols. (New York: International Cultural Foundation Press, 1979), 13–15.

2. Brian Gruber, "World Scientists Launch Assault on Global Problems," *World Student Times*, 12 December 1978; Alan MacRobert, "Moon Science Conference: Walking into 1984," *The Real Paper*, 9 December 1978. The exact cost of the Boston conference has not been publicized, but the *Boston Globe* provided estimates in its coverage. Robert Cooke, "Moon Conference: Demonstration That Jargon Is Universal," *Boston Sunday Globe*, 26 November 1978, 32.

3. International Cultural Foundation, *What ICUS Is* (Booklet, 1978), New Religious Movements Organizations: Vertical Files Collection, GTU 99-8-1, The Graduate Theological Union Archives, Berkeley, CA, 3.

4. Ibid., 16.

5. Ted Agres, "Science & Values: Turning Point?" *Industrial Research* 18, no. 1 (1976): 24.

6. Richard Bevilacqua and Earl Marchand, "Moon Eludes Pickets at Boston Conference," *Boston Herald American*, 25 November 1978, 1. See also Howie Carr, "Anti-Moonies to Picket His Science Conclave," *Boston Herald American*, 23 November 1978; Robert Cooke, "Foes Ask a Boycott on Moon Meeting," *Boston Globe*, 23 November 1978.

7. Allen Tate Wood, "Statement by Mr. Allen Tate Wood, Former Member and Official of the Moon Organization, 22 November 1978," (Typewritten Note, 1978) Cult Awareness Network (CAN) Collection, ARC Mss 19, Department of Special Collections, University Libraries, University of California, Santa Barbara.

8. For more on Jonestown, see David Chidester, *Salvation and Suicide: An Interpretation of Jim Jones, the Peoples Temple, and Jonestown* (Bloomington: Indiana University Press, 1988).

9. On the media response to Jonestown and treatment of "cults," see ibid., 24–45; Sean McCloud, *Making the American Religious Fringe: Exotics, Subversives, and Journalists, 1955–1993* (Chapel Hill: University of North Carolina Press, 2004), 127–59.

10. Sir John Eccles, "Letter to Participants, October 15, 1976," (personal correspondence, 1976) Warder [Michael] Collection, ARC Mss 31, Department of Special Collections, University Libraries, University of California, Santa Barbara.

11. Robert Cooke, "Scientists Defend Role at Moon Parley," *Boston Globe*, 25 November 1978, 3.

12. There is some debate over whether the Unification Church is in fact Christian. The Unification Church envisions itself as Christian, but the majority of other Christian groups reject it as such. Historically, Unificationism emerged from a Christian context, and for that reason I refer to it as Christian, though recognizing that it may not satisfy some theological definitions.

NOTES TO CHAPTER 1

1. Moon's original name was Yong Myung Moon, which he changed in the 1950s.

2. Bruce Cumings, "The Origins and Development of the Northeastern Asian Political Economy: Industrial Sectors, Product Cycles, and Political Consequences," *International Organization* (Winter 1984):14.

3. Bruce Cumings, *Korea's Place in the Sun: A Modern History* (New York: Norton, 1997), 166–70. A more detailed economical analysis is Sang-Chul Suh, *Growth and Structural Changes in the Korean Economy, 1910–1940* (Cambridge, MA: Council on East Asian Studies of Harvard University, 1978). See also the recent anthology by Gi-Wook Shin and

Michael Robinson, eds., *Colonial Modernity in Korea* (Cambridge, MA: Harvard University Asia Center, 1999).

4. Adrian Buzo, *The Making of Modern Korea* (London: Routledge, 2002), 30.

5. Michael Breen, *Sun Myung Moon: The Early Years, 1920–53* (Hurstpierpoint, West Sussex: Refuge Books, 1997), 19.

6. Ibid., 29.

7. There are several differing accounts of this charge, varying both in terms of the specific date of the revelation as well as the content. No doubt much of the confusion owes to the accepted fact that Moon did not share his experience until years later. See ibid., 30–31; Jonathan Gullery, ed., *The Path of a Pioneer: The Early Days of Reverend Sun Myung Moon and the Unification Church* (New York: HSA Publications, 1986), xii.

8. Breen, *Sun Myung Moon: The Early Years, 1920–53*, 31.

9. Ibid., 41.

10. Gullery, *Path of a Pioneer*, xii–xiii.

11. Eileen Barker, *The Making of a Moonie: Choice or Brainwashing?* (Oxford: Basil Blackwell Publishing Ltd, 1984), 39.

12. Breen, *Sun Myung Moon: The Early Years, 1920–53*, 73.

13. Ibid., 98–100.

14. Massimo Introvigne, *The Unification Church* (Salt Lake City: Signature Books, 2000), 10.

15. Sun Myung Moon, "Let Us Become the Citizens Who Take Possession of the Kingdom of Heaven (2 June 1957)," in *Sermons of the Reverend Sun Myung Moon*, vol. 2 (New York: HSA, 1994), 188.

16. The Unification Church's own publications generally utilize the Revised Standard Version (RSV) translation of the Bible, which I have followed here.

17. Moon, "The Path, Its Purpose and Its Value (29 September 1957)," in *Sermons of the Reverend Sun Myung Moon*, vol. 3 (New York: HSA, 1995), 48–49.

18. Ibid., 54.

19. General Board of the National Council of Churches of Christ in the United States of America, "Christian Concern and Responsibility for Economic Life in a Rapidly Changing Technological Society," February 24, 1966.

20. Moon, "Let Us Establish the Glorious Original Homeland (6 October 1957)," in *Sermons of the Reverend Sun Myung Moon*, vol. 3 (New York: HSA, 1995), 75.

21. Moon, "Where Is the Refuge in Which Heaven Can Dwell? (12 January 1958)," in *Sermons of the Reverend Sun Myung Moon*, vol. 3 (New York: HSA, 1995), 189.

22. Moon, "Let Us Establish the Glorious Original Homeland (6 October 1957)," 75.

23. Ibid., 76.

24. Paul S. Boyer, *When Time Shall Be No More: Prophecy Belief in Modern American Culture* (Cambridge: Belknap Press of Harvard University Press, 1992), 67–68.

25. Walter Rauschenbusch, *Christianity and the Social Crisis* (New York: Hodder, 1907), 345.

26. Catherine Lowman Wessinger, *How the Millennium Comes Violently: From Jonestown to Heaven's Gate* (New York: Seven Bridges Press, 2000), 16–17.

27. Moon, "Our Position," (sermon, 2 January 1979, trans. Bo Hi Pak, 1979).

28. Moon, "Let Us Establish the Glorious Original Homeland (6 October 1957)," 77.

29. Moon, "Where Is the Refuge in Which Heaven Can Dwell? (12 January 1958)," 193.

30. Moon, "What Is God Going to Do with Exiled Humanity? (30 March 1958)," in *Sermons of the Reverend Sun Myung Moon,* vol. 4 (New York: HSA, 1995), 100.

31. Moon, "The Path, Its Purpose and Its Value (29 September, 1957)," 53.

32. I have omitted an organizational history of the early Unificationist movement. Those interested should consult Michael L. Mickler, *40 Years in America: An Intimate History of the Unification Movement, 1959–1999* (New York: HSA Publications, 2000); and Mickler, *A History of the Unification Church in America, 1959–1974: Emergence of a National Movement* (New York: Garland, 1993).

33. Mickler, *40 Years in America,* 29. See also Mickler, *History of the Unification Church,* 103.

34. Young Oon Kim, "The Divine Principles, by Young Oon Kim [1st ed., 1960]," http://www.tparents.org/Library/Unification/Books/DP60/ (accessed 13 July 2006), preface. See also Young Oon Kim, *The Divine Principles* (San Francisco: HSA, 1963).

35. See David Sang Chul Kim, *Individual Preparation for His Coming Kingdom* (Portland, OR: United Chapel of Portland, 1968) and the pamphlet series by Sang Ik Choi, *Principles of Education: Purpose of Mankind, Principles of Education: Theory of Happiness, Principles of Education: Theory of the Ideal Man, Principles of Education: Theory of the Origin of Crimes,* and *Principles of Education: Theory of Universal Value* (San Francisco: Re-Education Center, 1969–70).

36. See chap. 6 in Mickler, *History of the Unification Church,* "A National Movement Emerges: 1972–74" ; see also chap. 2 in "The Transplantation of the Unificationist Movement" in David G. Bromley and Anson D. Shupe, Jr., *Moonies in America: Cult, Church, and Crusade* (Beverly Hills: Sage Publications, 1979); and chap. 3 in "The Unification Church: An Historical Background" in Barker, *Making of a Moonie.*

37. Unificationists look to Sun Myung Moon as the author of *Divine Principle,* with Dr. Won Pok Choi as translator. I have followed the lead of the church in referring to Moon as the author, aware that the translator shaped the resulting English-language text. Unificationists, of course, consider the Principle a divine revelation but accept that Moon shaped the revelation and wrote the actual text of the *Divine Principle.*

38. Moon, *Divine Principle* (New York: The HSA, 1973), 35.

39. Ibid., 34.

40. Song Hang-Nyong, "A Short History of Taoism in Korea," *Korea Journal* 26, no. 5 (1986): 14.

41. Isabelle Robinet, *Taoism: Growth of a Religion,* trans. Phyllis Brooks (Stanford, CA: Stanford University Press, 1997), 7.

42. Ibid., 10.

43. Moon, *Divine Principle,* 26–27. Moon uses the term "Tao," following the older Wade-Giles transliteration method. Scholars now use the pinyin method, rendering the word as "Dao." The terms are equivalent.

44. Fritjof Capra, *The Tao of Physics: An Exploration of the Parallels between Modern Physics and Eastern Mysticism* (Berkeley, CA: Shambhala, 1975), 12.

45. Ibid., 25.

46. Moon, *Divine Principle,* 58.

47. Ibid., 7.

48. James R. Lewis, *Legitimating New Religions* (New Brunswick, NJ: Rutgers University Press, 2003), 14.

49. Ibid., 3.

50. For example, Moon explains that "[b]ecause of the fall, however, mankind has not been able to realize this world. Instead, man has brought about a world of sin and has fallen into ignorance." Ibid., 13.

51. Ibid.

52. Ibid., 431–32.

53. Ibid., 108.

54. Ibid., 4.

55. See Auguste Comte, *The Catechism of Positive Religions*, trans. Richard Congreve, 1st English ed. (London: Kegan Paul, Trench, Trübner, & Co. Ltd, 1891); Gertrud Lenzer, ed., *Auguste Comte and Positivism* (New Brunswick, NJ: Transaction Publishers, 1998).

56. Moon, *Divine Principle*, 432.

57. Ibid., 3–4.

58. Stephen Jay Gould, *Rock of Ages: Science and Religion in the Fullness of Life* (New York: Ballantine Books, 1999), 4.

59. Moon, *Divine Principle*, 5.

60. Ibid., 8–9.

61. The classic treatment of the Reformers' view of the passing of the age of miracles is that of Max Weber, *The Protestant Ethic and the Spirit of Capitalism*, trans. Talcott Parsons (New York: Scribner, 1958). For a fine treatment of the lingering influence of the early Protestant view of the age of miracles as having passed, see Marcel Gauchet, *The Disenchantment of the World: A Political History of Religion*, trans. Oscar Burge (Princeton: Princeton University Press, 1997); Robert Bruce Mullin, *Miracles and the Modern Religious Imagination* (New Haven: Yale University Press, 1996).

62. Moon, *Divine Principle*, 9.

63. Ibid., 131.

64. Ibid., 8.

65. Ibid.

66. Ibid., 4.

67. Ibid., 8.

NOTES TO CHAPTER 2

1. Catherine Lowman Wessinger, *How the Millennium Comes Violently: From Jonestown to Heaven's Gate* (New York: Seven Bridges Press, 2000), 16–17.

2. Bromley and Shupe, *Moonies in America*, 26. Bromley and Shupe envision their concept of the "world-transformative" religious movement as a corrective to Roy Wallis's tripartite schema of world-affirming, world-rejecting, and world-accommodating new religions. Wallis himself identified the Unification Church as a world-rejecting movement, a view with which I, along with Bromley and Shupe, disagree. Wallis does not provide a succinct definition of world-rejecting, so it is difficult to refute his assessment. Yet he does provide some characteristics of such movements, for the example that they prescribe clear moral demands, possess clear conceptions of God as personal yet distinct from humankind, view the prevailing social order negatively, and require service to a guru, messiah, or prophet. The Unification Church does share many of these attributes, but these factors hardly indicate that any such movement would deny the world. One

could easily imagine many religions, mainstream Christianity among them, possessing these traits, making the category so wide that the world-rejecters in fact comprise the majority of the world. Roy Wallis, *The Elementary Forms of the New Religious Life* (London: Routledge & Kegan Paul, 1984).

3. The Collegiate Association for the Research of Principles (CARP) provided an example of such unethical behavior. In 1977 CARP attempted to establish a wing at University of Texas–Arlington. Its organizer misrepresented himself as a student, obfuscated his organization's ties to the Unification Church, and broke several campus rules related to employing outside personal in gathering petitions to allow the group to form. The petitions themselves skimmed the surface of ethical conduct, represented CARP as merely an "Oriental Religion." When a university administrator contacted a random set of the one hundred thirty signers, he found that none of them was aware of CARP's affiliation with Unificationism. Linda Neighbors, "'The Moonies Are Coming, the Moonies Are Coming!'" (term paper, 1977 [?]) Center for the Study of New Religious Movements Collection, GTU 91–9–03, The Graduate Theological Union Archives, Berkeley, CA, 5. Neighbors does not provide the number of students contacted by the administrator.

4. Sraffan Berg, "Big Bang Theory Makes a Commotion," *World Student Times*, 12 December 1978, 6.

5. Nate Windman, "An Introduction to the Divine Principle: What the Moonies Believe," *World Student Times*, October 1980, 11.

6. R. Laurence Moore, *Selling God: American Religion in the Marketplace of Culture* (New York: Oxford University Press, 1994), 241.

7. *The Freedom Leadership Foundation*, (pamphlet, ca. 1976) New Religious Movements Organizations: Vertical Files Collection, GTU 99–8–1, The Graduate Theological Union Archives, Berkeley, CA, 4–5.

8. The best source on the history of the Unification Theological Seminary is Susan Diane Schroeder's dissertation, "The Unification Theological Seminary: An Historical Study." Although I have also seen sources that indicate forty-six students in the opening class, Schroeder's detailed history of the seminary lists the attendance as fifty, providing names, nationalities, and undergraduate majors of the attendees. Attendance numbers for the following decades fluctuated between a low of thirty-eight in 1984 to fifty-four in 1987. Susan Diane Schroeder, "The Unification Theological Seminary: An Historical Study" (EdD diss., Columbia University, 1993), 319. In terms of faculty, the seminary opened with five faculty and six administrators, alongside one part-time instructor. Ibid., 148.

9. Unification Theological Seminary, "UTS Course Catalog," (1977/1978) American Religions Manuscript Collection, ARC Mss 1, Department of Special Collections, University Libraries, University of California, Santa Barbara, 11.

10. Kurt Johnson, "The Scientific Basis of Divine Principle: Religion and Society 590," (Coursepack, 1981) Unification Theological Seminary Special Access Collection; Schroeder, "The Unification Theological Seminary," 438.

11. Unification Theological Seminary, "UTS Course Catalog," (1979/1980) American Religions Manuscript Collection, ARC Mss 1, Department of Special Collections, University Libraries, University of California, Santa Barbara, 57.

12. Johnson, "The Scientific Basis of Divine Principle," i.

13. Ibid., 1.

14. Ibid.

15. Ibid., 4.

16. Ibid., 5.

17. Ibid., 6.

18. For quantum physics, see ibid., 17–19. On molecular biology, ibid., 21–23. On evolutionary biology, ibid., 37–38. On political science, ibid., 72–73.

19. Ibid., 38.

20. An excellent description of the history and development of the IRAS is James Gilbert, *Redeeming Culture: American Religion in an Age of Science* (Chicago, University of Chicago Press, 1997), 273–95.

21. Edward Haskell, ed., *Full Circle: The Moral Force of Unified Science* (New York: Gordon and Breach, 1972), 174.

22. Ibid., 219.

23. International Conference on the Unity of the Sciences (hereafter ICUS), *Science and Absolute Values: Proceedings of the Third International Conference on the Unity of the Sciences, November 21–24, 1974, London, United Kingdom*, 2 vols. (Tarrytown, NY: International Cultural Foundation, 1974), xxvii–xxxii; International Cultural Foundation, "What ICUS Is," 4. Please refer to table 2.2, chap. 2, for ICUS conference dates.

24. Andrew F. Blake, "'Messiah' Sponsors World Science Meet," *Boston Sunday Globe*, 17 November 1974, 62.

25. For excellent insider details of the management of the conference, see Kenneth Mellanby, "Attending a Moon Conference," *Nature* 258, no. 5536 (1975). For another take on the same fourth ICUS conference that Mellanby discussed, see Cy A. Adler, "A Moon Shines on Science," *New Engineer*, March 1976. Numerous private correspondences also demonstrate the scientists' view that the Unificationists held little sway over the proceedings: Eccles, "Letter to Participants, October 15, 1976."; Daniel Lerner, "Letter to Dr. Morris Zelditch, January 13, 1977" (personal correspondence, 1977) Warder [Michael] Collection, ARC Mss 31, Department of Special Collections, University Libraries, University of California, Santa Barbara; Alan C. Nixon, "Unpublished Letter to Editor of *Science*, January 4, 1977" (personal correspondence, 1977) Warder [Michael] Collection, ARC Mss 31, Department of Special Collections, University Libraries, University of California, Santa Barbara. Also see media accounts, such as Cooke, "Scientists Defend Role at Moon Parley"; Linda Loyd, "Rev. Moon Addresses Conference's 1st Session," *Philadelphia Inquirer*, 27 November 1982; Linda Loyd, "Science Meeting Told of Religion, Moon Style," *Philadelphia Inquirer*, 29 November 1982; Richard Miller, "Scientists Exchange Ideas, Hear Rev. Moon's Critics," *Daily Californian,* 1977; "Professors Praise Science Meeting Sponsored by Unification Church," *New York Times*, 28 November 1977; "Rev. Moon's Boycotters Are Jealous or Ignorant, Savants Attending Say," *Sacramento Bee*, 26 November 1977.

26. For example, ICUS chair Morton Kaplan, the University of Chicago sociologist who chaired the ninth through twelfth ICUSs (1980–83), reported occasional conflicts with Moon over the lack of "any relationship at all between the program and the title." Loyd, "Rev. Moon Addresses Conference's 1st Session," 1.

27. ICUS, *ICUS III Proceedings* [1974], 372.

28. ICUS, *Absolute Values and the New Cultural Revolution: Commemorative Volume of the Twelfth International Conference on the Unity of the Sciences, Chicago, Illinois, 1983* (New York: ICUS Books, 1984).

29. ICUS, *The Search for Absolute Values and the Creation of the New World: Proceedings of the Tenth International Conference on the Unity of the Sciences, November 9–13, 1981, Seoul, Korea*, 2 vols. (New York: International Cultural Foundation Press, 1982), 10.

30. Moon, *Proposal for International Highway*, (pamphlet, 1981) American Religions Collection, Vertical Files Collection, Department of Special Collections, University Libraries, University of California, Santa Barbara, n.p. Compare to ICUS, *ICUS X Proceedings* (1981), 16–17.

31. Morton A. Kaplan, "Letter to Dr. J. Gordon Melton, December 15, 1982," (personal correspondence, 1982) American Religions Collection, Vertical Files Collection, Department of Special Collections, University Libraries, University of California, Santa Barbara.

32. International Cultural Foundation, "Statement of Purpose of ICUS XVI," (Leaflet, 1987) American Religions Collection, Vertical Files Collection, Department of Special Collections, University Libraries, University of California, Santa Barbara, 4.

33. ICUS, *ICUS VI Proceedings* (1977), 9.

34. ICUS, *The Centrality of Science and Absolute Values: Proceedings of the Fourth International Conference on the Unity of the Sciences, November 27–30, 1975, New York*, 2 vols. (Tarrytown, NY: International Cultural Foundation, 1975), 10.

35. ICUS, *The Responsibility of the Academic Community in the Search for Absolute Values: Proceedings of the Eighth International Conference on the Unity of the Sciences, November 22–25, Los Angeles, California*, 2 vols. (New York: International Cultural Foundation Press, 1980), 11.

36. ICUS, *ICUS IV Proceedings* (1974), 7. Cf. Moon's speech to the International Conference on Unified Science, wherein he declared that science primarily aims to create a "happy, ideal society." Sun Myung Moon, *Science and Absolute Values: Twenty Addresses* (Lexington, KY: International Conference on the Unity of the Sciences, 1997), 26.

37. ICUS, *ICUS VIII Proceedings* (1979), 9.

38. ICUS, *Absolute Values and the Creation of the New World: Proceedings of the Eleventh International Conference on the Unity of the Sciences, November 25–28, 1982*, 2 vols. (New York: International Cultural Foundation Press, 1983), 13.

39. Ibid., 16.

40. Fowler, *Greening of Protestant Thought*.

41. ICUS, *Modern Science and Moral Values: Proceedings of the Second International Conference on the Unity of the Sciences, Tokyo, November 18–21, 1973* (Tokyo: International Cultural Foundation, 1973), 571–72.

42. Of pollution, Moon explained "[i]f we had created the climate of science centered on human dignity the formidable problem of pollution would have been prevented," ibid., 572. Moon might also have been alluding to infrastructure chaos, since his November 1973 speech to the second ICUS fell just two months after the beginning of an OPEC oil embargo of the United States and many other Western nations to punish them for support of Israel, leading to gas shortages and massive inflation. Since the Unification Church held the second ICUS in Tokyo, Japan, Moon's address might also have alluded to the host nation's lingering effects of the nuclear attacks of World War II.

43. Ibid., 573.

44. ICUS, *ICUS III Proceedings* (1974), 7.

45. ICUS, *ICUS IV Proceedings* (1975), 9.

46. "Attitudes toward Science and Technology, 1976," survey by Opinion Research Corporation, 13 September–30 September 1976 (retrieved 10 August 2006 from Lexus Nexus Academic Database).

47. For more on the influence of Kubrick and Clark's *2001: A Space Odyssey* (M-G-M, 1968) on the American counterculture, see the introduction and P. Barton Palmer's first chapter, "2001: The Critical Reception and the Generation Gap," in *Stanley Kubrick's 2001: A Space Odyssey: New Essays*, ed. Robert Kolker (New York: Oxford University Press, 2006).

48. Schumacher, *Small Is Beautiful*, 149.

49. Ibid., 275.

50. For example, a 1968 survey found that 20 percent of Americans "strongly agreed" that science had caused the world to change too fast. Two years later, a similar study discovered that 10 percent of its respondents felt that scientific progress had made life worse. A 1974 NSF-funded study found that only 4 percent felt that science had done more harm than good, but a large proportion (31 percent) thought that science had done as much harm as good. Louis Harris and Associates, "Harris Survey," January 1971 (retrieved 10 August 2006 from Lexus Nexus Academic Database); National Opinion Research Center, "SRS Amalgam Survey," April 1968 (retrieved 10 August 2006 from Lexus Nexus Academic Database); Opinion Research Corporation, "Attitudes toward Science and Technology, 1972," 13 May–28 May 1972 (retrieved 10 August 2006 from Lexus Nexus Academic Database). For similar results, see Gallup Organization Institute for International Social Research, "Hopes and Fears," 1 October 1964 (retrieved 10 August 2006 from Lexus Nexus Academic Database).

51. The 1971 Harris Survey found that approximately three-quarters (76 percent) of Americans felt that science had surpassed our ability of managing human problems and the "human side" of life, and about the same percentage (72 percent) agreed with the statement that "science is making people so dependent on gadgets and machines, people don't know what nature is anymore." Louis Harris and Associates, "Harris Survey," January 1971.

52. ICUS, *ICUS II Proceedings* (1973), ix.

53. ICUS, *ICUS IV Proceedings* (1975), 12.

54. Ibid., 1305.

55. ICUS, *ICUS XI Proceedings* (1982), 22.

56. ICUS, *ICUS XIII Proceedings* (1982), 35–38.

57. For a detailed history of the cult wars, see Benjamin Zablocki and Thomas Robbins, eds., *Misunderstanding Cults: Searching for Objectivity in a Controversial Field* (Toronto: University of Toronto Press, 2001).

58. K. H. Barney, quoted in Carr, "Anti-Moonies to Picket His Science Conclave," 23.

59. Cooke, "Foes Ask a Boycott on Moon Meeting," 3.

60. The woman is identified only by her surname, Greene, as quoted in Miller, "Scientists Exchange Ideas, Hear Rev. Moon's Critics," 12.

61. Surveys show a consistent approval of science and respect for scientists. For example, a June 1958 survey found science only slightly behind medicine and ahead of all other fields in degree of prestige, when measured by how likely parents were to support their children entering the field. Roper Organization, "Public Opinion Poll," June 1958 (retrieved 10 August 2006 from Lexus Nexus Academic Database). A similar survey in

1974 found nearly identical results when directly querying respondents' "own personal opinion of the prestige or general standing that such a job has," with science ranking just below medicine but above all other fields. 61 percent ranking scientists as excellent, and 28 percent as good. Opinion Research Corporation, "Attitudes toward Science and Technology, 1974," 19 July–10 August 1974 (retrieved 10 August 2006 from Lexus Nexus Academic Database). See also Opinion Research Corporation, "Attitudes toward Science and Technology, 1972," 13 May–28 May 1972; Gallup Organization Institute for International Social Research, "Hopes and Fears," 1 October 1964; Gallup Organization, "America's Mood in the Mid-Sixties," February 1965 (retrieved 10 August 2006 from Lexus Nexus Academic Database); Louis Harris and Associates, "Harris Survey," 8 October–16 October 1977 (retrieved 10 August 2006 from Lexus Nexus Academic Database); Opinion Research Corporation, "Attitudes toward Science and Technology, 1976," 13 September–30 September 1976 (retrieved 10 August 2006 from Lexus Nexus Academic Database).

62. C. H., "Moon's Annual Science Meeting Is Becoming a Tradition," *Science* 194, no. 4271 (1976): 1254.

63. Toronto *Globe and Mail*, reprinted in "Professors Praise Science Meeting Sponsored by Unification Church," 10.

64. "Moon's Credibility Game," *Christian Century*, 24 September 1975, 813.

65. Allen Tate Wood, quoted in Carr, "Anti-Moonies to Picket His Science Conclave," 23.

NOTES TO PART II INTRODUCTION

1. Bhaktivedanta arrived in Boston, passed through customs and immigration, spent two days there, and then continued on the ship to its final destination of New York City, where he began his mission in earnest. See Satsvarupa Dasa Goswami, *Planting the Seed, New York City 1965–1966*, vol. 2, *Srila Prabhupada-Lilamrta: A Biography of His Divine Grace A. C. Bhaktivedanta Swami Prabhupada* (Los Angeles: Bhaktivedanta Book Trust, 1980), 4–7.

2. See Goswami, *A Lifetime in Preparation, India 1986–1965*, vol. 1, *Srila Prabhupada-Lilamrta*, 287. For more on Bhaktivedanta's journey to America, see Goswami, *Planting the Seed*, 1–5.

3. Goswami, *Lifetime in Preparation*, 173.

4. Jerry Erber, "New Indian Religion Sends You Higher Than LSD!: Secrets of Krishna Consciousness " *National Insider*, 23 April 1967, 11.

5. Ginsberg, as quoted in James R. Sikes, "Swami's Flock Chants in Park to Find Ecstasy," *New York Times*, 9 October 1966, 24.

NOTES TO CHAPTER 3

1. Hinduism had indeed spread to America earlier. Swami Vivekananda and Paramahansa Yogananda had each brought their teachings to this country, yet neither practiced devotional Hinduism, as Bhaktivedanta did. Hence the Vedanta Society and the Self Realization Fellowship predated ISKCON, but the Hare Krishnas represented the first transplant of devotionalism, the most popular form of Hindu religiosity in India.

2. Few sources describe Abhay Charan De's childhood. Most of the early materials produced on ISKCON focused on sociological concerns and understood the Hare Krishna

movement as one among many other new religious cults, hence the inattention to the Indian background to this Hindu sectarian group. While I concur that ISKCON is a new religious movement, its rootedness in the Indian colonial experience requires more scholarly attention. For details on Abhay's early life, see E. Burke Rochford, Jr., "Hare Krishna in America: Growth, Decline, and Accommodation," in *America's Alternative Religions*, ed. Timothy Miller (Albany: State University of New York Press, 1995), 10–11; Goswami, *Lifetime in Preparation*, 2–7.

3. Goswami, *Lifetime in Preparation*, 13–14.

4. Thomas J. Hopkins, "The Social and Religious Background for Transmission of Gaudiya Vaisnavism to the West," in *Krishna Consciousness in the West*, ed. David G. Bromley and Larry D. Shinn (Lewisburg: Bucknell University Press, 1989), 49.

5. Goswami, *Lifetime in Preparation*, 26.

6. Dalhousie, as quoted in Stanley A. Wolpert, *A New History of India* (New York: Oxford University Press, 2004), 226. For more on the Indian rail system, see Claude Markovits, *A History of Modern India, 1480–1950*, trans. Nisha George and Maggy Hendry (London: Anthem, 2002), 415–16; Wolpert, *New History of India*, 225–29.

7. Markovits, *History of Modern India, 1480–1950*, 439.

8. Ibid., 426–39.

9. Goswami, *Lifetime in Preparation*, 16.

10. For additional biographical data, see Hopkins, "The Social and Religious Background," 49–50; Kim Knott, *My Sweet Lord: The Hare Krishna Movement* (Toronto: University of Toronto Press, 2001), 27–29; Larry D. Shinn, *The Dark Lord: Cult Images and the Hare Krishnas in America* (Philadelphia: Westminster Press, 1987), 34–39; Federico Squarcini and Eugenio Fizzotti, *Hare Krishna*, ed. Massimo Introvigne, *Studies in Contemporary Religion* (Salt Lake City: Signature Books, 2004), 3–7.

11. Goswami, *Lifetime in Preparation*, 34–35.

12. Graham M. Schweig, "Krishna, the Intimate Deity," in *The Hare Krishna Movement: The Postcharismatic Fate of a Religious Transplant*, ed. Edwin Bryant and Maria Ekstrand (New York: Columbia University Press, 2004), 17.

13. Edward C. Dimock and Tony Kevin Stewart, *Caitanya Caritamrta of Krsnadasa Kaviraja: A Translation and Commentary by Edward C. Dimock, Jr.* (Cambridge, MA: Harvard University Press, 1999), 5.

14. The best work on Chaitanya is Dimock's introduction to his translation of the sixteenth-century hagiography, *Chaitanya Charitamrta*, 3–146. See also the studies of Majumdar and Chakravarti: Asoke Kumar Majumdar, *Caitanya, His Life and Doctrine: A Study in Vaisnavism* (Mumbai: Bharatiya Vidya Bhavan, 1969); and Chakravarti Ramakanta, *Vaisnavism in Bengal, 1486–1900* (Calcutta: Sanskrit Pustak Bhandar, 1985).

15. The best histories on the Brahmo Samaj are David Kopf, *The Brahmo Samaj and the Shaping of the Modern Indian Mind* (Princeton: Princeton University Press, 1979); and M. C. Kotnala, *Raja Ram Mohun Roy and Indian Awakening* (New Delhi: Gitanjali Prakashan, 1975).

16. For details on Vivekananda and Ramakrishna, see Shamita Basu, *Religious Revivalism as Nationalist Discourse: Swami Vivekananda and New Hinduism in Nineteenth Century Bengal* (New York: Oxford University Press, 2002); Carl T. Jackson, *Vedanta for the West: The Ramakrishna Movement in the United States* (Bloomington: Indiana University Press, 1994); Amiya P. Sen, *Swami Vivekananda* (New York: Oxford University Press, 2000);

Narasingha P Sil, *Ramakrishna Revisted: A New Biography* (Lanham, MD: University Press of America, 1998).

17. Hopkins, "The Social and Religious Background," 47.

18. For more on the Bengali Hindu reformers, see Amiya P. Sen, *Hindu Revivalism in Bengal, 1872–1905: Some Essays in Interpretation* (Delhi: Oxford University Press, 1993).

19. Jan Brzezinski, "Charismatic Renewal and Institutionalization in the History of Gaudiya Vaishnavism and the Gaudiya Math," in Bryant and Ekstrand, *Hare Krishna Movement*, 80; Paul H. Sherbow, "Bhaktivedanta Swami's Preaching in the Context of Gaudiya Vaishnavism," in ibid., 130.

20. See also Hopkins, "The Social and Religious Background," 38–41.

21. See Brzezinski, "Charismatic Renewal and Institutionalization," 82–84.

22. A. C. Bhaktivedanta Swami Prabhupada, as quoted in Goswami, *Lifetime in Preparation*, 43.

23. Reprinted in *The Harmonist*, an Indian Gaudiya Vaishnava periodical, and subsequently in ibid., 84.

24. Letter from Swami Bhaktisiddanta Sarasvati to Abhay Charan De, December 1936, as reprinted in ibid., 93.

25. A. C. Bhaktivedanta Swami (hereafter Bhaktivedanta), "Godhead and Potentialities," *Back to Godhead*, February 1944, 5.

26. Bhaktivedanta, "Theosophy Ends in Vaishnavism," ibid., 15.

27. A representative example of such phraseology is Abhay Charan De's note on his article submission policy. He wrote: "Scientific and self-realised thoughts on spiritual knowledge, will always be welcome for publication in the 'Back to Godhead.' Unauthorized sentiments or dry philosophical speculative imaginations will not be entertained." Bhaktivedanta, "Submissions Policy," *Back to Godhead*, March 1956, 4.

28. Bhaktivedanta, "The Science of Congregational Chanting of the Name of the Lord," *Back to Godhead*, February 1944, 20

29. Bhaktivedanta, "Advertisement: Geetopanishad, by Abhay Charan De," ibid., 36.

30. Bhaktivedanta, "The Science of Congregational Chanting of the Name of the Lord," 27.

31. There are numerous examples. For example, Abhay wrote that "modern scientific and experimental thought" can never bring "real happiness to the human being," since the study of the material world was itself useless (A. C. Bhaktivedanta Swami, "Lord Shri Chaitanya, His Welfare Activities (and His Teachings)," *Back to Godhead*, April 1956, 3. Somewhat more colloquially, he declared that the "basic defect of the scientific mode of thinking, [like] any literature which is not derived from the authentic sources of Vedic literature, is considered as ordinary country news with no effect of actual knowledge. Such literatures are full of mistakes, irrelevancy, cheating, and imperfectness." Bhaktivedanta, "Lord Buddha," *Back to Godhead*, May 1956, 4. See also Bhaktivedanta, "As Essential Service," *Back to Godhead*, November 1956, 2; Bhaktivedanta, "Back to Godhead," *Back to Godhead*, June 1956, 4; Bhaktivedanta, "Progressive Ambition (and Unsatiated Lust)," *Back to Godhead*, October 1956, 2; Bhaktivedanta, "Religion Pretentious and Religion Real (Religiosity Real and Apparent)," *Back to Godhead*, June 1956, 2; Bhaktivedanta, "Shri Chaitanya Mahaprabhu (Lord Chaitanya & His Teachings)," *Back to Godhead*, June 1956, 3; Bhaktivedanta, "Sri Ishopanishad," *Back to Godhead*, April 1960, 2–4; Bhaktivedanta, "Standard Morality," *Back to Godhead*, November 1958, 3.

32. Bhaktivedanta, "All Compact in Thought," *Back to Godhead*, April 1956, 4.

33. Bhaktivedanta, "Definition of Vice & Its Scope," *Back to Godhead*, November 1956, 1–2.

34. Bhaktivedanta, "Who Is a Sadhu?," *Back to Godhead*, March 1956, 2.

35. Bhaktivedanta, "Variety of Planetary Systems," *Back to Godhead*, April 1960, 3.

36. Bhaktivedanta, "As Essential Service," 1.

37. For two other examples of the use of science as rhetorical legitimation, see Bhaktivedanta, "Sufferings on Humanity," *Back to Godhead*, May 1956, 1; Bhaktivedanta, "The S.R.C. Catastrophe," *Back to Godhead*, March 1956, 2.

38. Lewis, *Legitimating New Religions*, 89–102.

39. Technically, Abhay Charan De had changed names twice before. When he first accepted initiation into the Gaudiya Vaishnava lineage, his guru Bhaktisiddanta gave him the new name Abhay Charanaravinda De. In 1939 leaders of his sect bestowed the name of Bhaktivedanta ("master of devotional knowledge") upon him in recognition and honor of his missionary work, hence Abhay Charanaravinda Bhaktivedanta. In his final initiation, he became a monk, receiving the honorific title *swami*, therefore becoming known as A. C. Bhaktivedanta Swami. The swami's disciple often add the term "Prabhupada," a term applied in Vaishnava groups to one's spiritual master. In keeping with ISKCON standards, I have called Bhaktivedanta by his given name, Abhay Charan De, in my description of his history, activities, and publications up to his monastic initiation in 1959.

40. Bhaktivedanta, "Letter to Raja Mohendra Pratap, 13 July, 1947," in *The Bhaktivedanta Vedabase (Version 2003.1)* (Sandy Ridge, NC: The Bhaktivedanta Archives, 2003).

41. Bhaktivedanta, "Letter to Sardar Patel, 28 February, 1949," in ibid.

42. Bhaktivedanta, "Letter to Mahatma Gandhi, 12 July, 1947," in ibid.

43. Meera Nanda, *Prophets Facing Backwards: Postmodern Critiques of Science and Hindu Nationalism in India* (New Brunswick, NJ: Rutgers University Press, 2003).

44. Bhaktivedanta, "Letter to Jawaharial Nehru, 20 January, 1952" in *Bhaktivedanta Vedabase*.

45. Roszak, still alive as of my writing, has lived long enough to see some of his fears come alive. Theodore Roszak, *The Making of a Counter Culture: Reflections on the Technocratic Society and Its Youthful Opposition* (Garden City: Doubleday, 1969), 271–74.

46. Jacques Ellul, *The Technological Society*, 1st American ed. (New York: Knopf, 1964).

47. Hayagriva Das Brahmachary, "Krishna Consciousness and American Poetry, Part IV," *Back to Godhead* 1, no. 13 (1967): 19.

48. Ibid.: 20.

49. Bhaktivedanta, "From the Lectures of Swami A. C. Bhaktivedanta," *Back to Godhead* 1, no. 2 (1966): 3.

50. Ibid.

51. Bhaktivedanta, "From the Lectures of Swami A.C. Bhaktivedanta," *Back to Godhead* 1, no. 14 (1967): 5.

52. Ibid., no. 15: 10.

53. Bhaktivedanta, "A Study in Mysticism," *Back to Godhead* 1, no. 25 (1969): 14.

54. Bhaktivedanta, "Sri Ishopanisad," *Back to Godhead* 1, no. 22 (1969): 28–29.

55. See, for example, Bhaktivedanta's insistence that "[o]ur sputnik drivers are very proud of their achievements, but they do not look to the Supreme Driver of these greater, more gigantic sputniks called planets." Ibid., 29.

NOTES TO CHAPTER 4

1. Ralph Eugene Lapp, *The New Priesthood: The Scientific Elite and the Uses of Power*, 1st ed. (New York: Harper & Row, 1965).

2. The last issue of the Indian run of *Back to Godhead* was vol. 4, no. 1, published 5 September 1960. The first issue of the American run (vol. 1, no. 1) appeared 23 October 1966. Until 1974, *Back to Godhead* continued as vol. 1, with the final issue of 1974 published as no. 68. Starting in January 1975, *Back to Godhead* leaped to vol. 10, and thereafter the editors advanced the volume number each calendar year.

3. Hayagriva Das Brahmachary, "The Hare Krishna Explosion: The Birth of Krishna Consciousness in America, 1966–1969," in *Bhaktivedanta Vedabase (Version 2003.1).*

4. Rayarama also cosigned one of ISKCON's incorporation documents, the "Constitution of Association." It is unclear what became of him once he left ISKCON.

5. Hayagriva Das Brahmachary and Rayarama Das Brahmachary, "Back to Godhead," *Back to Godhead* 1, no. 1 (1966): 2.

6. Editorial, *Back to Godhead* 1, no. 2 (1966): 1.

7. Hayagriva Das Brahmachary, "Krishna: The End of Knowledge," *Back to Godhead* 1, no. 5 (1967): 13–14.

8. Hayagriva Das Brahmachary, "Doubt, Thy Name Is Bondage," *Back to Godhead* 1, no. 7 (1967): 13–14.

9. "Advertisement: Two Essays," *Back to Godhead* 1, no. 17 (1968): 1, Hayagriva Das Brahmachary, "Krishna Consciousness in American Poetry," *Back to Godhead* 1, no. 12 (1967): 15; Rayarama Das Brahmachary, "The Transmigration of the Soul," *Back to Godhead* 1, no. 8 (1967): 16; Rayarama Das Brahmachary, "The Unconditioned State," *Back to Godhead* 1, no. 3 (1966): 19.

10. Nayana Bhiran Das Brahmachary, "Parts and Parcels," *Back to Godhead* 1, no. 20 (1968): 5.

11. Roszak, *Making of a Counter Culture*, 270.

12. There are three distinct redactions of these conversations: the transcriptions of the tapes; the "Life Comes from Life" manuscript, available in the archives of the University of California at Santa Barbara; and the published book, *Life Comes From Life: Morning Walks with His Divine Grace A. C. Bhaktivedanta Prabhupada* (Los Angeles: Bhaktivedanta Book Trust, 1979). The transcripts are the most accurate, but there is none available for the conversations on 18 April, 7 May, 8 May and 11 May (what *Life Comes From Life* calls the first, sixth, seventh, and eighth morning walks). The intermediate manuscript generally matches the published book; however, it contains some material from the transcripts that editors removed before publishing. The book itself is a poor source for the original conversations between Bhaktivedanta and his followers, since its editors rearranged, sanitized, and otherwise changed nearly every conversation.

13. Bhaktivedanta, "Morning Walk—December 10, 1973, Los Angeles (731210mw.La)," in *Bhaktivedanta Vedabase (Version 2003.1).*

14. International Society for Krishna Consciousness, "Life Comes from Life," (manuscript, ca. 1977) Muster Betrayal of the Spirit Collection, ARC Mss 28, Department of Special Collections, University Libraries, University of California, Santa Barbara, 1.

15. Bhaktivedanta , *Life Comes from Life*.

16. See the morning walks of 19 April, 14 May, and 3 December 1973, the transcripts of which are available on the Bhaktivedanta Vedabase.

17. Bhaktivedanta, "Morning Walk—April 28, 1973, Los Angeles (730428mw.La)," in *Bhaktivedanta Vedabase (Version 2003.1)*.

18. "Dr. W. H. Wolf-Rottkay to Srila Prabhupada, 10/1975," (letter, 1975) J. Stillson Judah: New Religious Movements Collection, GTU 95-6-01, The Graduate Theological Union Archives, Berkeley, CA.

19. For other instances of Bhaktivedanta using similar statements, see the conversations from 1 April, 4 May, 15 May, and 7 December 1973, the transcripts of which are available on the Bhaktivedanta Vedabase.

20. Ellipsis in the original. Bhaktivedanta Swami, "Morning Walk—April 19, 1973, Los Angeles (730419mw.La)."

21. For details on the Creation Research Society as well as representative poll data, see Numbers, *Creationists*, 239–68.

22. The word "dasa" or "das" means "servant," and the first name of each of the devotees represents an ideal or demigod within Gaudiya Vaishnavism. Hence, Yogesvara Dasa means "Servant of the Lord of Yoga." Also note that the capitalization of the word is inconsistent within ISKCON.

23. For details on Yogesvara Dasa's personal life, see the webpage associated with his book on fellow ISKCON devotee George Harrison (d. 2001): Yogesvara Dasa, "Here Comes the Sun: The Author," http://www.herecomesthesunbook.com/press.author.html (accessed 7 February 2007).

24. Yogesvara Dasa, "Primal Origins," *Back to Godhead* 1, no. 67 (1974): 23.

25. Ibid.

26. The material produced by Christian Creationists provides a ready example; see John Clement Whitcomb and Henry Madison Morris, *The Genesis Flood: The Biblical Record and Its Scientific Implications* (Philadelphia: Presbyterian and Reformed Pub. Co., 1961). For a Jewish analog, see Gerald L. Schroeder, *Genesis and the Big Bang: The Discovery of Harmony between Modern Science and the Bible* (New York: Bantam Books, 1992).

27. Yogesvara Dasa, "Primal Origins," 25.

28. Bali Mardan Dasa, "Darwin's Mistake," *Back to Godhead* 10, no. 10 (1975): 10, Lapp, *New Priesthood*, 227.

29. Bali Mardan Dasa, "Darwin's Mistake," 12. For details on Christian (and some Jewish opponents of Darwinism), see Numbers, *Creationists*.

30. Bali Mardan Dasa, "Darwin's Mistake," 12.

31. Ibid., 13.

32. Pancaratna Das, telephone call to Author, 27 December 2006.

33. J. Frank Kenney and Pancaratna Das, "An Experimental Course in Krishna Consciousness," *Council on the Study of Religion Bulletin* 5, no. 5 (1974): 3.

34. Ibid., 4.

35. Ibid., 3.

36. Ibid., 4.

37. In my conversation with Pancaratna Das, he also spoke of his personal attachment to Krishna Consciousness on the "rational" and "scientific" levels and not only the "experiential." He stressed that his teaching approach derived from the movement's wider focus on science and not merely his own practices.

38. International Society for Krishna Consciousness, "The Bhaktivedanta Institute," (Brochure, 1974[?]) American Religions Collection, ARC Mss 1, Department of Special Collections, University Libraries, University of California, Santa Barbara.

39. Svarupa Damodara Dasa, *The Scientific Basis of Krsna Consciousness* (New York: Bhaktivedanta Book Trust, 1974), 58.

40. Ibid., 8–10.

41. William Paley, *Natural Theology; or Evidences of the Existence and Attributes of the Deity, Collected from the Appearances of Nature* (Trenton, NJ: Daniel Fenton, 1824), 10–11.

42. Svarupa Damodara Dasa, *Scientific Basis of Krsna Consciousness*, 12.

43. Ibid., 11.

44. Ibid., 15.

45. Ibid., 24.

46. Ibid., 27.

47. For the section on Darwinism, see ibid., 33–34. The quote on the completion and perfection of the Puranas comes from Svarupa's defense of their divine origin, Svarupa Damodara Dasa, *Scientific Basis of Krsna Consciousness*, 41. He describes the Puranas as infallible throughout the text, but most particularly in the chapter, "Sastric [Vedic] Injunctions Are the Supreme Judgement," ibid., 41–47.

48. Ibid., 36–38.

49. Ibid., 46.

50. For details of ISKCON membership, including statistical breakdowns, see E. Burke Rochford Jr., *Hare Krishna in America* (New Brunswick, NJ: Rutgers University Press, 1985), 43–85.

51. Dharmadhyaksa Dasa et al., *Spiritual Revolution*, (pamphlet, 1975) New Religious Movements Organizations: Vertical Files Collection, GTU 99-8-1, The Graduate Theological Union Archives, Berkeley, CA, 1.

52. Ibid., 3.

53. For details on the development of ecology during the 1970s, see Stephen Bocking, *Ecologists and Environmental Politics: A History of Contemporary Ecology* (New Haven: Yale University Press, 1997); Anna Bramwell, *Ecology in the 20th Century: A History* (New Haven: Yale University Press, 1989).

54. Dharmadhyaksa Dasa et al., *Spiritual Revolution*, 3.

55. Ibid. Ellipses in the original.

56. Ibid., 4.

57. Interestingly, of these four scientists, three worked in the field of general relativity, with Einstein as one of its founding fathers, Eddington a leading experimental researcher, and Jeans a popularizer. J. B. B. Haldane worked in population genetics. Though ISKCON's positive valuation of the work of Haldane might have stemmed from his a large-scale statistical analysis, which viewed individual human actions as probabilistic rather than predetermined, the brief article did not dwell on his work. Nor did it explain the relevance of relativity to Krishna Consciousness. Rather, the author incorporated these scientists as examples of scientific supporters of the Hare Krishna perspective that con-

sciousness derived from the nonmaterial soul, the "antimaterial particle" as Bhaktivedanta called it. Ibid.

58. Ibid.

59. For details of the "post-charismatic fate" of ISKCON, as many scholars have called it, see the later half of Bryant and Ekstrand compilation, *Hare Krishna Movement*, particularly chaps. 10–15. A somewhat shorter account is provided by Steven J. Gelberg, "The Call of the Lotus-Eyed Lord: The Fate of Krishna Consciousness in the West," in *When Prophets Die: The Postcharismatic Fate of New Religious Movements*, ed. Timothy Miller (Albany: State University of New York Press, 1991).

NOTES TO PART III INTRODUCTION

I have cited numerous sources in this section that are included in the Heaven's Gate anthology: Heaven's Gate, *How and When "Heaven's Gate" (the Door to the Physical Kingdom Level above Human) May Be Entered* (Mill Springs, NC: Wild Flower Press, 1997). I have abbreviated this source as "HGA" in subsequent notes.

1. Several examples of this rumor are still available on the Internet at the time of this writing. Cliff Bostock, "Heaven's Gate: Some Brief Questions and Observations from a Depth-Psychological Perspective," http://www.soulworks.net/writings/essays/site_008. html (accessed 2 February, 2007); Simpos, "Heaven's Gate Mass Suicide," http://www.stelling.nl/simpos/heavgate.htm (accessed 2 February, 2007).

2. Anlody, "Investments," in HGA, sec. A, 98–100 (originally produced 1996).

3. Heaven's Gate, "Planet About to Be Recycled—Your Only Chance to Survive—Leave with Us [Edited Transcript]," http://www.heavensgate.com/misc/vt100596.htm (accessed 13 November, 1997 [Defunct]).

4. It is certainly not my intention to enter into the debates over the definition of religion. Certainly scholars differ on how to define the concept, and I wish to note here that according to most definitions with which I am familiar, Heaven's Gate is a religion.

5. Heaven's Gate, *'88 Update*, in HGA, sec. 3, 2–19 (originally produced 1988).

6. Christopher H. Partridge, *UFO Religions* (London: Routledge, 2003), 37.

7. Brenda Denzler, *The Lure of the Edge: Scientific Passions, Religious Beliefs, and the Pursuit of UFOs* (Berkeley: University of California Press, 2001), 106–7.

8. See Susan J. Palmer, *Aliens Adored: Raël's UFO Religion* (New Brunswick, NJ: Rutgers University Press, 2004).

9. See Diana Tumminia and R. George Kirkpatrick, "Unarius: Emergent Aspects of an American Flying Saucer Group," in *The Gods Have Landed: New Religions from Other Worlds*, ed. James R. Lewis (Albany: State University of New York Press, 1995).

10. Partridge, *UFO Religions*, 21.

11. John A. Saliba, "Religious Dimensions of UFO Phenomena," in *Gods Have Landed*, 34.

NOTES TO CHAPTER 5

1. "Boisean Remembers Knowing Bonnie Lu, 'UFO Recruiter,'" *Idaho Statesman*, 2 November 1975, 12D. For more on Nettles's Christian upbringing, see Robert W. Balch and David Taylor, "Salvation in a UFO," *Psychology Today* 10, no. 5 (1976): 66; James S.

Phelan, "Looking For: The Next World," *New York Times*, 29 February 1976, 62. Unfortunately, Nettles never revealed the specific Baptist denomination to which she belonged, nor does the secondary literature indicate such specifics. However, she was most likely a Southern Baptist, statistically speaking. A 1971 study showed that 37.5 percent of all Christians living in Texas declared a religious affiliation as Southern Baptists. No other Baptist group accounted for more than 0.1 percent of Texas Christians. Douglas W. Johnson, Paul R. Picard, and Bernard Quinn, *Churches and Church Membership in the United States: An Enumeration by Region, State, and County* (Washington, DC: Glenmary Research Center, 1974), 11. The same study found that in the eight-county Houston region where Nettles grew up and resided (Brazonia, Chambers, Fort Bend, Galviston, Harris, Liberty, Montgomery, and Waller counties) the second largest Baptist group, the Baptist Missionary Alliance, represented only 2.3 percent of the size of the largest denomination, the Southern Baptist Convention. Ibid., 193–204.

2. For more on Nettles's involvement in the Theosophical Society in America, see Wessinger, *How the Millennium Comes Violently*, 232, n55.

3. Robert W. Balch, "Bo and Peep: A Case Study of the Origins of Messianic Leadership," in *Millennialism and Charisma*, ed. Roy Wallis (Belfast: The Queen's University, 1982), 34. Biographical information on Nettles is scant. These details come from the secondary literature, especially that of Robert Balch. See ibid.," 28.

4. At the time, Virginia's Union Theological Seminary (not to be confused with New York City's seminary of the same name) affiliated with the Presbyterian Church of the United States (PCUS), the southern branch of American Presbyterian. In 1983 the PCUS merged with the United Presbyterian Church of the United States of America (UPCUSA) to form the Presbyterian Church of the United States of American (PCUSA), the largest national Presbyterian denomination.

5. This biographical sketch is based on secondary materials, especially Balch, "Bo and Peep," 29. See also the sidebar "Bo and Peep" in Balch and Taylor, "Salvation in a UFO," 66. Readers interested in a more lengthy description and analysis of Nettles's and Applewhite's history should see Robert W. Balch, "Waiting for the Ships: Disillusionment and the Revitalization of Faith in Bo and Peep's UFO Cult," in *Gods Have Landed*, 141–42; Phelan, "Looking For: The Next World."

6. Applewhite's reasons for being in the hospital are unclear; he may have been either a visitor or patient at the time. Balch, for example, calls the encounter "chance," noting that Applewhite was visiting a friend recovering from an operation. Balch, "Bo and Peep," 33; Balch, "Waiting for the Ships," 143. After the mass suicides, several media outlets claimed that Applewhite had been a mental patient at the time. See Evan Thomas, "Web of Death," *Newsweek*, 7 April 1997, 31.

7. Perhaps the most obvious example of such a reductionist reading of Heaven's Gate is David Daniel, "The Beginning of the Journey," *Newsweek*, 13 April 1997, 36–37.

8. "Bo and Peep Interview with Brad Steiger, 7 January 1976," in *UFO Missionaries Extraordinary*, ed. Hayden Hewes and Brad Steiger (New York: Pocket Books, 1976), 82–83.

9. Balch, "Bo and Peep," 35.

10. See ibid., 36–37. (Some early sources indicate that Applewhite ran the Know Place and Nettles the Christian Arts Center, implying that they existed in parallel, but other sources show that the two ran both operations in serial. Victoria Hodgetts, "UFO Cult

Mystery Turns Evil," *Village Voice*, 1 December 1975, 12, Lynn Simross, "Invitation to an Unearthly Kingdom," *Los Angeles Times*, 31 October 1975, 4.)

11. Balch, "Bo and Peep," 39.

12. "Bo and Peep Interview with Brad Steiger, 7 January 1976," 84. See also Heaven's Gate, *'88 Update*, in HGA.

13. Applewhite and Nettles used a plethora of names during the first years of their evangelism. During the early days of the movement when they were experimenting with their religious identities, Nettles and Applewhite adopted the monikers Guinea and Pig. "They explained that they were being used as guinea pigs in an experiment of cosmic proportions," writes Balch in "Bo and Peep," 53. Later when the two became religious leaders and began gathering a flock, they claimed the names Bo (Nettles) and Peep (Applewhite). The '88 Update, authored by Do, explains that the two took the names because "it looks like we're gathering our lost sheep." Heaven's Gate, "'88 Update," in HGA, 7. Finally, the Two renamed themselves Ti and Do, the names of two musical notes. They never explained the reason for their final choice of names, though their use of the two highest notes on the standard Western musical scale (do, re, mi, fa, so, la, ti, do) might have represented their attempt to reach toward the "next level." That "do" wraps around to the base of the scale could also have symbolically represented his continued presence on Earth while Ti had ascended to the heavens. I am grateful to the musician and scholar Emily Mace for this suggestion.

14. Human Individual Metamorphosis (hereafter in notes HIM), "Statement #1: Human Individual Metamorphosis," 1975, American Religions Collection, ARC Mss 1, Department of Special Collections, University Libraries, University of California, Santa Barbara. The statement is also reprinted in HGA. Heaven's Gate, "First Statement of Ti and Do," in HGA, sec. 2, 3–4 (originally produced 1975).

15. HIM, "Statement #1: Human Individual Metamorphosis."

16. Around the same time that Nettles and Applewhite began their work together, Trina Paulus's *Hope For the Flowers* (published 1972) had become popular among countercultural circles. The book described two caterpillars on what might be called a spiritual quest. I am grateful for my colleague at Temple University, Dr. Lucy Bregman, for directing me to that book.

17. Ibid.

18. Very few studies consider religious themes across the New Age, hence there are no secondary sources that explore the place of the concept of "vibrations" in various New Age movements. For a specific example, see Michael F. Brown's *The Channeling Zone*, which describes channeling participants using the term to describe states of being as well as a general word to mean a characteristic quality (e.g., "bad vibrations," "peaceful vibrations," etc.). Michael F. Brown, *The Channeling Zone: American Spirituality in an Anxious Age* (Cambridge, MA: Harvard University Press, 1997).

19. See C. I. Scofield, ed., *The Scofield Reference Bible* (New York: Oxford University Press, 1901), 1349, n1 (commenting on Rev. 19:19); 1269, n1 (on 1 Thess. 4:17); and 1228, n1 (on 1 Cor. 15:52).

20. Emphasis in the original. HIM, "Statement #1: Human Individual Metamorphosis."

21. Ibid.

22. I say that the authors apparently referenced the Transfiguration because of the context of this quote: it appears after their description of the resurrection but before their declaration that Christ returned to heaven in a UFO. The Gospels however describe the Transfigu-

ration as occurring before the Resurrection, and given Applewhite's otherwise theological sophistication, I am unsure whether the Two meant the term in its theological sense.

23. See "Bo and Peep Interview with Brad Steiger, 7 January 1976," 96, Hewes and Steiger, *UFO Missionaries Extraordinary*, 16–18.

24. HIM, "What's Up?," (1975) American Religions Collection, ARC Mss 1, Department of Special Collections, University Libraries, University of California, Santa Barbara.

25. James R. Lewis and Gordon Melton, eds., *Perspectives on the New Age* (Albany: State University of New York Press, 1992), ix.

26. Lewis, "Approaches to the Study of the New Age Movement," in *Perspectives on the New Age*, 7.

27. Robert W. Balch, "The Evolution of a New Age Cult: From Total Overcomers Anonymous to Death at Heaven's Gate," in *Sects, Cults, and Spiritual Communities: A Sociological Analysis*, ed. William W. Zellner and Marc Petrowsky (Westport, CT: Praeger Publishers, 1998), 1–2. For more details on this meeting, see Balch, "The Evolution of a New Age Cult,"; Simross, "Invitation to an Unearthly Kingdom."

28. Balch, "The Evolution of a New Age Cult," 23–24.

29. See "20 Missing in Oregon after Talking of a Higher Life," *New York Times*, 7 October 1975; "Cults: Out of This World," *TIME*, 20 October 1975; James R. Gaines, "Cults: Bo-Peep's Flock," *Newsweek*, 20 October 1975; Douglas E. Kneeland, "500 Wait in Vain on Coast for 'the Two,' U.F.O. Cult Leaders," *New York Times*, 10 October 1975; Austin Scott, "Music Teacher, Nurse Led Search for 'Higher Life,'" *Washington Post*, 18 October 1975.

30. Eve Muss, "'Grave Not Path to Heaven,' Disciples Told," *Oregon Journal*, 10 October 1975.

31. For example, the prospective candidate letter most frequently used the capitalized term "Next Evolutionary Level" rather than "next level," and spoke of "the process" rather than resurrection, transformation, or metamorphosis.

32. HIM, "Prospective Candidate Letter," http://www.rkkody.com/rkk/rkkomat.htm (accessed 13 November, 1997 [Defunct]).

33. Balch and Taylor, "Salvation in a UFO," 61.

34. Phelan, "Looking For: The Next World," 64.

35. Paul McGrath, "UFO 'Lost Sheep' Tell Cult Secrets," *Chicago Sun-Times*, 16 October 1975, 1. For comparatives purposes, consider Sheila Larson's response, "My faith has carried me a long way. It's Sheilaism. Just my own little voice. . . . It's just try to love yourself and be gentle with yourself. You know, I guess, take care of each other." Robert Bellah et al., eds., *Habits of the Heart: Individualism and Commitment in American Life* (Berkeley: University of California Press, 1985), 221.

36. Emphasis in the original. Hewes and Steiger, *UFO Missionaries Extraordinary*, 88.

37. Ibid., 102–3.

38. Ibid., 100.

39. Muss, "'Grave Not Path to Heaven,' Disciples Told."

40. Hewes and Steiger, *UFO Missionaries Extraordinary*, 101.

41. Ibid., 132.

42. Ibid., 91.

43. Max Planck, *Where Is Science Going?* trans. James Murphey, English ed. (London: George Allen & Unwin Ltd., 1933), 214.

44. Emphasis in the original. HIM, "Statement #1: Human Individual Metamorphosis."

45. HIM, "Statement #3: The Only Significant Resurrection," 2.

46. Ibid.

47. As quoted in Balch and Taylor, "Salvation in a UFO," 106. Another similar statement, by two members quoted in the *Houston Chronicle*, echoed this position: "We are not a cult or group. We are individuals who share a common goal. But we each achieve that goal in very individual ways," they declared. Pat Reed, "Two Women UFO Disciples Reveal Identity; Say They Are Not Cult," *Houston Chronicle*, 26 November 1975.

48. "Bo and Peep Interview with Brad Steiger, 7 January 1976," 110.

49. George Williamson, "'It Was a Sham': Why One Convert Left the UFO Cult," *San Francisco Chronicle*, 13 October 1975, 2.

50. Contrast, for example, with the lack of any discussion of the need for faith or belief in the other published accounts that include extended interviews or comments from members of HIM: McGrath, "UFO 'Lost Sheep' Tell Cult Secrets"; Eve Muss, "No Disease Promised," *Oregon Journal*, 9 October 1975; Penson, "During the Summer of 1974 UFO Couple Visited Boise Men"; Reed, "Two Women UFO Disciples Reveal Identity; Say They Are Not Cult"; Simross, "Invitation to an Unearthly Kingdom."

51. Hodgetts, "UFO Cult Mystery Turns Evil," 13.

52. Phelan, "Looking For: The Next World," 58.

53. Ibid., 62.

54. HIM, "Statement #2: Clarification: Human Kingdom—Visible and Invisible," 1975, American Religions Collection, ARC Mss 1, Department of Special Collections, University Libraries, University of California, Santa Barbara.

55. HIM, "Prospective Candidate Letter."

56. Robert W. Balch, "'When the Light Goes out, Darkness Comes': A Study of Defection from a Totalistic Cult," in *Religious Movements: Genesis, Exodus, and Numbers*, ed. Rodney Stark (New York: Paragon House Publishers, 1985), 21.

57. Balch, "Waiting for the Ships," 154.

58. Balch, "A Study of Defection," 21–23.

59. After their interviews with Steiger and Phelan, the next primary sources available for scholars are a set of behavioral guidelines called "The Seventeen Steps," written in 1976, a collection of aphorisms, "Ruffles," composed in 1979, and a short booklet, *Preparing for Service*, prepared in 1985 before the death of Bonnie Lu Nettles. Here I focus on a section of the last of these materials, the *Preparing for Service* booklet. Heaven's Gate, *Preparing for Service*, (1985). Heaven's Gate, "Ruffles: Snacks for Thinkers," (1979) and Heaven's Gate, "The Seventeen Steps," in HGA, sec. 2, 8 (originally produced 1976). The latter two sources were available from Rkkody, "Other Heaven's Gate Materials," http://www.rkkody.com/rkk/rkkomat.htm (accessed 13 November, 1997 [Defunct]).

60. The former member used the later names of the Two, Ti (Nettles) and Do (Applewhite), which I have replaced with Bo and Peep. Heaven's Gate, *Preparing for Service*.

61. Ibid.

62. The movement would briefly operate under the "Anonymous Sexaholics Celibate Church" in 1987, and a year later in 1988 use the name "Total Overcomers Anonymous." They did not use the name "Heaven's Gate" until the final years of the movement's history.

63. Heaven's Gate, *Preparing for Service*.

64. One might compare the Heaven's Gate members' desire to control their body's chemistry to the practice of alchemy, especially as developed in Christian, Daoist, and Hindu (Tantric) circles.

65. Heaven's Gate, *Preparing for Service.*

66. Stmody (see chap. 6) wrote that "[t]o the best of my knowledge, using 'sex magic,' 'black magic,' Tantric or Daoist techniques to 'raise the kundalini,' to 'raise consciousness,' 'open chakras,' or to awaken the 'spiritual eye' are backward distortions." Stmody, "Evolutionary 'Rights' for 'Victims,'" in HGA, sec. A, 71–79 (originally produced 1996). Applewhite, then writing under the name Do, rejected a similar concept, the Tantric view of the kundalini energy. For his view on kundalini, see Heaven's Gate, *"Beyond Human—the Last Call,* sess, 6," in HGA, sec. 4, 62–73 (originally produced 1992), 69; Heaven's Gate, *"Beyond Human—the Last Call,* sess. 7," in HGA, sec. 4, 74–84 (originally produced 1992), 80.

67. Heaven's Gate, *Preparing for Service.*

NOTES TO CHAPTER 6

1. Thirty-nine members of Heaven's Gate died in the Rancho Santa Fe mansion. Two members of the group were not present and subsequently ritually ended their lives: Wayne Cooke (b. 1943) died 6 May 1997; Chuck Humphrey (b. 1943) died 17 February 1998.

2. During the early 1990s, Heaven's Gate spelled Nettles's religious name "Te," but switched to "Ti" before the suicides.

3. Heaven's Gate, "Introduction to *'88 Update,*" in HGA, sec. 3, 1. The group included the text of the booklet in their anthology, *How and When "Heaven's Gate" May Be Entered.* All citations refer to the reproduction of the source in that anthology. For more on the *'88 Update,* see Heaven's Gate, *"Beyond Human—the Last Call,* sess. 1," in HGA, sec. 4, 5–15 (originally produced 1992), 15.

4. Heaven's Gate, *'88 Update,* in HGA, 17.

5. The footnote referred to the movement's view of scripture and its relation to the next level, and read, "If any true religious scholars sincerely try to digest any of this strange puzzle, they may understand more of the 'real' meaning of their studies." Ibid. in HGA, 11.

6. Ibid. in HGA, 17–19.

7. Ibid. in HGA, 4.

8. For more on docetism and adoptionism, see Walter Bauer, *Orthodoxy and Heresy in Earliest Christianity,* trans. Robert Kraft (Philadelphia: Fortress, 1971), Bart D. Ehrman, *The Orthodox Corruption of Scripture: The Effect of Early Christological Controversies on the Text of the New Testament* (New York: Oxford University Press, 1993).

9. See, for example, the third statement's position that the next level is the "kingdom of God" to which followers of the HIM system could graduate, or the Two's exhortation at the Waldport meeting that they taught a system for how to join "a level that you refer to as the Kingdom of God," which periodically accepts new members from Earth. HIM, "Statement #3: The Only Significant Resurrection," 1975, American Religions Collection, ARC Mss 1, Department of Special Collections, University Libraries, University of California, Santa Barbara, 1; Muss, "'Grave Not Path to Heaven,' Disciples Told."

10. Heaven's Gate, "'88 Update," in HGA, 10.

11. The classic account of direct encounter between a human being and extraterrestrial is Whitley Strieber's *Communion,* but see also Richard Hall, *Uninvited Guests: A Documentary History of UFO Sightings, Alien Encounters, and Coverups* (Santa Fe, NM: Aurora Press, 1988); and Whitney Strieber, *Communion: A True Story* (New York: Beach Tree Books,

1987). Many ufologists who discuss crashed alien bodies combine this view with "exposés" of alleged government coverups. For a good example of this, see Lawrence Fawcett and Barry J. Greenwood, *Clear Intent: The Government Coverup of the UFO Experience* (Englewood Cliffs, NJ: Prentice-Hall, 1984).

12. Heaven's Gate, "*'88 Update*," in HGA, 15.

13. Ibid., 12.

14. Ibid., 8.

15. Leon Festinger, Henry W. Riecken, and Stanley Schachter, *When Prophecy Fails* (Minneapolis: University of Minnesota Press, 1956), 27.

16. Ibid. For an examination of Festinger's main points as well as an analysis of his study, see the chapters by Stone, Zygmunt, and Melton in Jon R. Stone, ed., *Expecting Armageddon: Essential Readings in Failed Prophecy* (New York: Routledge, 2000).

17. Heaven's Gate, "*'88 Update*," in HGA, 9–10.

18. Ibid., 10.

19. See especially the 1992 video series, *Beyond Human*, sess. 4.

20. Heaven's Gate, "*'88 Update*," in HGA, 12.

21. Heaven's Gate provided a precise chronology of this period in their anthology, including newspapers and dates of their republication of the *USA Today* advertisement (21 July–25 September 1993) as well as locations and dates of their meetings (November 1993–19 August 1994). Heaven's Gate, "List of Meetings by Date," in HGA, sec. 6, 2; Heaven's Gate, "Publications Where '93 Statement Appeared," in HGA, sec. 5, 7.

22. Heaven's Gate created a transcript of the *Beyond Human* broadcasts, which I have relied upon for all quotations and citations that I offer here. Though the actual videos are no longer available, several university libraries own digital copies of the series as distributed by the former Heaven's Gate member named Rkkody. I have viewed the twelve sessions in their entirety and concluded that the transcription process was quite accurate. The transcripts omit Do's interjections, occasional repetitions, and of course his vocal mannerisms but otherwise capture his words entirely accurately.

23. Emphasis in the original. Heaven's Gate, "*Beyond Human* Video Tape Jacket," in HGA, sec. 4, 2 (originally produced 1992).

24. Emphasis in the original. Heaven's Gate, "*Beyond Human—the Last Call*, sess. 1," in HGA, 1.

25. Heaven's Gate, "*Beyond Human—the Last Call*, sess. 3," in HGA, sec. 4, 27–38 (originally produced 1992), 32.

26. Heaven's Gate used this poster to advertise their final meeting on 19 August 1994. The mention to the nonreptilian nature of next-level aliens no doubt referred to one of the popular images of extraterrestrials as monstrous reptilian creatures. Several times in other sources, Do repeats the claim that next-level creatures are neither reptilian nor mammalian. Heaven's Gate, "The Shedding of Our Borrowed Human Bodies May Be Required [Poster]," in HGA, sec. 6, 11 (originally produced 1994).

27. Heaven's Gate, "*Beyond Human—the Last Call*, sess. 12," in HGA, 141.

28. Heaven's Gate, "He's Back, We're Back, Where Will You Stand? [poster]," in HGA, sec. 6, 9 (originally produced 1994). Christian theology calls this position adoptionism, a view that the orthodox church rejected. See Ehrman, *Orthodox Corruption of Scripture*.

29. Heaven's Gate, "*Beyond Human—the Last Call*, sess. 5," in HGA, sec. 4, 50–61 (originally produced 1992), 55.

30. Compare also to Do's statement during the fifth session that Christ's resurrection had almost no importance, what was a direct contradiction of the earliest statements that he and Ti (then Bo and Peep) made: "that illustration had relatively very little significance to His purpose here. His purpose was, as He told His disciples, 'Go teach about the Truth, give out the good news about the Kingdom of Heaven. It's at hand!'" Ibid. in HGA.

31. Heaven's Gate, "*Beyond Human—the Last Call*, sess 7," in HGA, 77–78.

32. Ibid., sess. 8," in HGA, 78.

33. Here Do repeats a classic proof for the existence of God, the teleological argument made famous by Paley's watchmaker analogy and repeated by Satsvarupa Damodara Dasa in *The Scientific Basis of Krsna Consciousness*, produced by ISKCON two years after Applewhite met Nettles. Heaven's Gate, "*Beyond Human—the Last Call*, sess. 7," in HGA, 78–79.

34. Tom Sorell, *Scientism: Philosophy and the Infatuation with Science* (London: Routledge, 1991), 1.

35. Heaven's Gate, "*Beyond Human—the Last Call*, sess, 1," in HGA, 8; Heaven's Gate, "*Beyond Human—the Last Call*, sess. 11," in HGA, 129. For more on the mind as computer, see Heaven's Gate, "*Beyond Human—the Last Call*, sess. 12," in HGA, 156–57.

36. Heaven's Gate, "*Beyond Human—the Last Call*, sess. 4," in HGA, sec. 4, 39–49 (originally Produced 1992), 48.

37. See Heaven's Gate, "*Beyond Human—the Last Call*, sess. 9," in HGA, 100; Heaven's Gate, "*Beyond Human—the Last Call*, sess. 12," in HGA, 141.

38. Heaven's Gate, "*Beyond Human—the Last Call*, sess. 12," in HGA, 141.

39. Heaven's Gate, "'UFO Cult' Resurfaces with Final Offer [*USA Today* Advertisement]," in HGA.

40. For example, consider the statement on one poster, "[y]ou cannot *preserve* the Truth in your religions. It is present only as long as a *Truth bearer* (Older Member from the *true* Kingdom of God) is present." Heaven's Gate, "Crew from the Evolutionary Level above Human Offers—Last Chance to Advance *Beyond Human* [extended poster]," in HGA.

41. Heaven's Gate, "*Beyond Human—the Last Call*, sess. 12," in HGA, 158.

42. Jnnody, "Incarnating and Discarnating," in HGA, sec. A, 89–97 (originally produced 1996), 89.

43. Smmody, "T.E.L.A.H.—the Evolutionary Level above Human," in HGA, sec. A, 22–23 (originally produced 1996), 22.

44. For example, see Chkody's contribution to the volume, wherein she declared of the "'Space Aliens' or 'Luciferians'[:] Yes, they are real, and yes, they use what is termed as 'UFOs.'" Chkody, "The Hidden Facts of Ti and Do," in HGA, sec. A, 32–37 (originally produced 1996), 3. Jwnody provides a representative view of the next-level aliens, whom she refers to as "the most *advanced* species in the literal heavens, the Evolutionary Level Above Human[;] we represent the true, real, factual Kingdom of God. Jwnody, "Religions Are Humans' #1 Killers of Souls," in HGA, sec. A, 65–70 (originally produced 1996), 65.

45. Chkody, "The Hidden Facts of Ti and Do," in HGA, 36.

46. Heaven's Gate, "Planet About to Be Recycled—Your Only Chance to Survive— Leave with Us [edited transcript]."

47. Chkody, "The Hidden Facts of Ti and Do," in HGA, 32–33.

48. Ibid. in HGA, 33.

49. Jwnody, "Religions Are Humans' #1 Killers of Souls," in HGA, 65.

50. Ibid., 66.

51. Jnnody, "Incarnating and Discarnating," in HGA, 96.

52. Anlody, "Investments," in HGA, sec. A, 98–100 (originally produced 1997), 98.

53. Ibid.

54. Ibid.

55. Frank Edwards as quoted in Denzler, *Lure of the Edge*, 127.

56. Qstody, "My Ode to Ti and Do! What This Class Has Meant to Me," in HGA, sec. A, 30–31 (oiginally oroduced 1996), 30, Yrsody, "The Way Things Are," in HGA, sec. A, 24–26 (originally produced 1996), 24. See also Lggody's diatribe, which targeted Christianity explicitly, but religion more broadly. Lggody, "The World's Most Successful Con Game," in HGA, sec. A, 85–88 (originally produced 1996).

57. Lvvody, "Ingredients of a Deposit—Becoming a New Creature," in HGA, sec. A, 8–14 (originally produced 1996), 9.

58. Drrody, "A Farewell Message to Those Who Remain Behind," in HGA, sec. A, 27–29 (originally produced 1996), 27.

59. Jwnody, "'Away Team' from Deep Space Surfaces before Departure," in HGA, sec. A, 38–45 (originally produced 1996), 39.

60. Ibid.

61. Lvvody, "Ingredients of a Deposit—Becoming a New Creature," in HGA, 10.

62. Wknody, "A Matter of Life or Death? You Decide," in HGA, sec. A, 18–21 (originally produced 1996), 18.

63. Heaven's Gate, "Exit Press Release: Heaven's Gate 'Away Team' Returns to Level above Human in Distant Space," http://www.heavensgate.com/pressrel.htm (accessed 13 November 1997 [Defunct]).

64. Heaven's Gate, "Heaven's Gate—How and When It May Be Entered," http://www.heavensgate.com (accessed 13 November 1997 [Defunct]).

NOTES TO CONCLUSION

1. Susan Jean Palmer, *Moon Sisters, Krishna Mothers, Rajneesh Lovers: Women's Roles in New Religions* (Syracuse, NY: Syracuse University Press, 1994), 1.

2. Thomas A. Tweed, *The American Encounter with Buddhism, 1844–1912: Victorian Culture and the Limits of Dissent* (Bloomington: Indiana University Press, 1992).

3. Charles Taliaferro, "Dualism," in *Encyclopedia of Science and Religion*, vol. 1, ed. J. Wentzel Vrede van Huyssteen (New York: Macmillan Reference USA, 2003), 230. Emphasis mine.

4. For details on the nature of dualism, materialism, idealism, and Cartesian dualism, see Stephen P. Stich and Ted A. Warfield, eds., *The Blackwell Guide to Philosophy of Mind* (Malden, MA: Blackwell Publishing, 2003).

5. Sydney E. Ahlstrom, *A Religious History of the American People* (New Haven: Yale University Press, 1972), Catherine L. Albanese, *American Religious History: A Bibliographic Essay* (Washington, DC: United States Department of State, Bureau of Education and Cultural Affairs, 2002), 6.

Works Cited

SECONDARY SOURCES

"Cults: Out of This World." *TIME*, 20 October 1975, 25–26.

"20 Missing in Oregon after Talking of a Higher Life." *New York Times*, 7 October 1975, 71.

"Boisean Remembers Knowing Bonnie Lu, 'UFO Recruiter.'" *Idaho Statesman*, 2 November 1975, 12D.

"Flying Saucery in the Wilderness." *TIME*, 27 August 1979, 58.

Ahlstrom, Sydney E. *A Religious History of the American People*. New Haven, CT: Yale University Press, 1972.

Albanese, Catherine L. *American Religious History: A Bibliographic Essay*. Washington, DC: United States Department of State Bureau of Educational and Cultural Affairs, 2002.

Aviezer, Nathan. *In the Beginning: Biblical Creation and Science*. Hoboken, NJ: KTAV Publishing House, 1990.

Bainbridge, William Sims. *The Endtime Family: Children of God*. Albany: State University of New York Press, 2002.

Balch, Robert W. "Looking Behind the Scenes in a Religious Cult: Implications for the Study of Conversion." *Sociological Analysis* 41, no. 2 (1980): 137–43.

———. "Bo and Peep: A Case Study of the Origins of Messianic Leadership." In *Millennialism and Charisma*, edited by Roy Wallis. Belfast: The Queen's University, 1982.

———. "'When the Light Goes out, Darkness Comes': A Study of Defection from a Totalistic Cult." In *Religious Movements: Genesis, Exodus, and Numbers*, edited by Rodney Stark. New York: Paragon House Publishers, 1985.

———. "Waiting for the Ships: Disillusionment and the Revitalization of Faith in Bo and Peep's UFO Cult." In *The Gods Have Landed: New Religions from Other Worlds*, edited by James R. Lewis, 137–66. Albany: State University of New York Press, 1995.

———. "The Evolution of a New Age Cult: From Total Overcomers Anonymous to Death at Heaven's Gate." In *Sects, Cults, and Spiritual Communities: A Sociological Analysis*, edited by William W. Zellner and Marc Petrowsky. Westport, CT: Praeger Publishers, 1998.

Balch, Robert W., and David Taylor. "Salvation in a UFO." *Psychology Today* 10, no. 5 (1976): 58ff.

———. "Seekers and Saucers: The Role of the Cultic Milieu in Joining a UFO Cult." *American Behavioral Scientist* 20, no. 6 (1977): 839–60.

———. "Making Sense of the Heaven's Gate Suicides." In *Cults, Religion, and Violence*, edited by David G. Bromley and J. Gordon Melton, 209–228. Cambridge: Cambridge University Press, 2002.

Barker, Eileen. "Who'd Be a Moonie? A Comparative Study of Those Who Join the Unification Church in Britain." In *The Social Impact of New Religious Movements*, edited by Bryan Wilson. New York: Rose of Sharon Press, 1981.

———. *The Making of a Moonie: Choice or Brainwashing?* Oxford: Basil Blackwell Publishing Ltd, 1984.

———. "The Cage of Freedom and the Freedom of the Cage." In *On Freedom: A Centenary Anthology*, edited by Eileen Barker. London: The London School of Economics and Political Science, 1997.

Basu, Shamita. *Religious Revivalism as Nationalist Discourse: Swami Vivekananda and New Hinduism in Nineteenth Century Bengal*. New York: Oxford University Press, 2002.

Bauer, Walter. *Orthodoxy and Heresy in Earliest Christianity*. Translated by Robert Kraft. Philadelphia: Fortress, 1971.

Bednarowski, Mary Farrell. *New Religions and the Theological Imagination in America*. Bloomington: Indiana University Press, 1989.

Bellah, Robert, Richard Madsen, William M. Sullivan, Ann Swidler, and Steven M. Tipton, eds. *Habits of the Heart: Individualism and Commitment in American Life*. Berkeley: University of California Press, 1985.

Berry, Thomas, C.P. *The New Story*. Chambersburg, PA: Ameican Teilhard Association for the Future of Man, 1978.

———. *Management: The Managerial Ethos and the Future of Planet Earth*. Chambersburg, PA: American Teilhard Association for the Future of Man, 1980.

———. "Ecology and the Future of Catholicism: A Statement of the Problem." 1982.

———. *The Dream of Earth*. San Francisco: Sierra Club Books, 1988.

Biermans, John T. *The Odyssey of New Religions Today: A Case Study of the Unification Church*. Lewiston, NY: E. Mellen Press, 1988.

Bocking, Stephen. *Ecologists and Environmental Politics: A History of Contemporary Ecology*. New Haven: Yale University Press, 1997.

Bostock, Cliff. "Heaven's Gate: Some Brief Questions and Observations from a Depth-Psychological Perspective." http://www.soulworks.net/writings/essays/site_008.html. (Accessed 2 February 2007).

Boyer, Paul S. *When Time Shall Be No More: Prophecy Belief in Modern American Culture*. Cambridge: Belknap Press of Harvard University Press, 1992.

———. *By the Bomb's Early Light: American Thought at the Dawn of the Atomic Age*. Chapel Hill: University of North Carolina Press, 1994.

Bramwell, Anna. *Ecology in the 20th Century: A History*. New Haven: Yale University Press, 1989.

Breen, Michael. *Sun Myung Moon: The Early Years, 1920–53*. Hurstpierpoint, West Sussex: Refuge Books, 1997.

Bromley, David G. "Financing the Millennium: The Economic Structure of the Unificationist Movement." *Journal for the Scientific Study of Religion* 24, no. 3 (1985): 253–74.

Bromley, David G., and J. Gordon Melton. *Cults, Religion, and Violence*. Cambridge: Cambridge University Press, 2002.

Bromley, David G., and Larry D. Shinn, eds. *Krishna Consciousness in the West*. Lewisburg: Bucknell University Press, 1989.

Bromley, David G., and Anson D. Shupe, Jr. *Moonies in America: Cult, Church, and Crusade*. Beverly Hills: Sage Publications, 1979.

———. "'Just a Few Years Seem Like a Lifetime': A Role Theory Approach to Participation in Religious Movements." In *Research in Social Movements, Conflicts, and Change*, edited by Louis Kriesberg, 159–85. Greenwich, CT: Jai Press, 1979.

Bromley, David G., Anson D. Shupe, Jr., and Donna L. Oliver. "Perfect Families: Visions of the Future in a New Religious Movement." In *Cults and the Family*, edited by Florence Kaslow and Marvin B. Sussman, 119–29. New York: Haworth Press, 1982.

Brown, Michael F. *The Channeling Zone: American Spirituality in an Anxious Age*. Cambridge, MA: Harvard University Press, 1997.

Brubacher, John S., and Willis Rudy. *Higher Education in Transition: A History of American Colleges and Universities*. New Brunswick, NJ: Transaction Publishers, 1997.

Bruce, Robert V. *The Launching of American Science, 1846–1876*. New York: Alfred A. Knopf, 1987.

Bryant, Edwin, and Maria Ekstrand, eds. *The Hare Krishna Movement: The Postcharismatic Fate of a Religious Transplant*. New York: Columbia University Press, 2004.

Brzezinski, Jan. "Charismatic Renewal and Institutionalization in the History of Gaudiya Vaishnavism and the Gaudiya Math." In *The Hare Krishna Movement: The Postcharismatic Fate of a Religious Transplant*, edited by Edwin Bryant and Maria Ekstrand, 73–96. New York: Columbia University Press, 2004.

Buderi, Robert. *The Invention That Changed the World: How a Small Group of Radar Pioneers Won the Second World War and Launched a Technological Revolution*. New York: Simon and Schuster, 1996.

Burke, Peter. *What is Cultural History?* Cambridge: Polity, 2004.

Burr, Angela, and International Society for Krishna Consciousness. *I Am Not My Body: A Study of the International Hare Krishna Sect*. New Delhi: Vikas, 1984.

Buzo, Adrian. *The Making of Modern Korea*. London: Routledge, 2002.

Capra, Fritjof. *The Tao of Physics: An Exploration of the Parallels between Modern Physics and Eastern Mysticism*. Berkeley: Shambhala, 1975.

Carey, Séan. "The Indianization of the Hare Krishna Movement in Great Britain." In *Hinduism in Great Britain*, edited by Richard Burghart. London: Tavistock, 1987.

Carmell, Aryeh, and Cyril Domb, eds. *Challenge: Torah Views on Science and Its Problems*. London: Association of Orthodox Jewish Scientists, 1976.

Cha, K. Y., D. P. Wirth, and R. A. Lobo. "Does Prayer Influence the Success of in Vitro Fertilization-Embryo Transfer?" *Journal of Reproductive Medicine* 46 (2001): 781–87.

Chidester, David. *Salvation and Suicide: An Interpretation of Jim Jones, the Peoples Temple, and Jonestown*. Bloomington: Indiana University Press, 1988.

Chryssides, George D. *The Advent of Sun Myung Moon: The Origins, Beliefs, and Practices of the Unification Church*. New York: St. Martin's Press, 1991.

Comte, Auguste. *The Catechism of Positive Religions*. Translated by Richard Congreve. 1st English ed. London: Kegan Paul, Trench, Trübner, & Co. Ltd, 1891.

Constantine, Peggy. "No Mother Superior in His Religion." *Chicago Sun Times*, 10 July 1975.

Cumings, Bruce. "The Origins and Development of the Northeastern Asian Political Economy: Industrial Sectors, Product Cycles, and Political Consequences." *International Organization* (Winter 1984): 1–40.

———. *Korea's Place in the Sun: A Modern History*. New York: W. W. Norton, 1997.

Dalton, Anne Marie. *A Theology for the Earth: The Contributions of Thomas Berry and Bernard Lonergan.* Ottawa: University of Ottawa Press, 1999.

Daner, Francine Jeanne. *The American Children of Krsna: A Study of the Hare Krsna Movement.* New York: Holt, Rinehart and Winston, 1976.

Daniel, David. "The Beginning of the Journey." *Newsweek,* 13 April 1997.

Denzler, Brenda. *The Lure of the Edge: Scientific Passions, Religious Beliefs, and the Pursuit of UFOs.* Berkeley: University of California Press, 2001.

Dimock, Edward C., and Tony Kevin Stewart. *Caitanya Caritamrta of Krsnadasa Kaviraja: A Translation and Commentary by Edward C. Dimock, Jr.* Cambridge, MA: Harvard University Press, 1999.

Ditmer, Joanne. "Durango Businessman Reported with UFO Group." *Denver Post,* 23 October 1975, 33.

Draper, John William. *History of the Conflict between Religion and Science.* New York: D. Appleton & Company, 1874.

Ehrman, Bart D. *The Orthodox Corruption of Scripture: The Effect of Early Christological Controversies on the Text of the New Testament.* New York: Oxford University Press, 1993.

Ellul, Jacques. *The Technological Society.* 1st American ed. New York: Knopf, 1964.

Ellwood, Robert S., Jr. *Religious and Spiritual Groups in Modern America.* Englewood Cliffs, NJ: Prentice-Hall, Inc., 1973.

———. *Alternative Alters: Unconventional and Eastern Spirituality in America.* Chicago: University of Chicago Press, 1979.

Fawcett, Lawrence, and Barry J. Greenwood. *Clear Intent: The Government Coverup of the UFO Experience.* Englewood Cliffs, NJ: Prentice-Hall, 1984.

Festinger, Leon, Henry W. Riecken, and Stanley Schachter. *When Prophecy Fails.* Minneapolis: University of Minnesota Press, 1956.

Foerstel, Herbert N. *Secret Science: Federal Control of American Science and Technology.* Westport, CT: Praeger, 1993.

Forsthoefel, Thomas A., and Cynthia Ann Humes, eds. *Gurus in America.* Albany: State University of New York Press, 2005.

Fowler, Robert Booth. *The Greening of Protestant Thought.* Chapel Hill: University of North Carolina Press, 1995.

Furniss, Norman F. *The Fundamentalist Controversy, 1918–1931.* Archon Books, 1963.

Gaines, James R. "Cults: Bo-Peep's Flock." *Newsweek,* 20 October 1975, 32.

Gallup Organization. "America's Mood in the Mid-Sixties." February 1965. Retrieved 10 August 2006 from Lexus Nexus Academic Database.

Gallup Organization Institute for International Social Research. "Hopes and Fears." 1 October 1964. Retrieved 10 August, 2006 from Lexus Nexus Academic Database.

Gauchet, Marcel. *The Disenchantment of the World: A Political History of Religion.* Translated by Oscar Burge. Princeton: Princeton University Press, 1997.

Gelberg, Steven J., ed. *Hare Krishna, Hare Krishna: Five Distinguished Scholars on the Krishna Movement in the West.* New York: Grove Press, 1983.

———. "The Call of the Lotus-Eyed Lord: The Fate of Krishna Consciousness in the West." In Miller, *When Prophets Die: The Postcharismatic Fate of New Religious Movements,* 149–64. Albany: State University of New York Press, 1991.

Gilbert, James. *Redeeming Culture: American Religion in an Age of Science.* Chicago, University of Chicago Press, 1997.

Glock, Charles Y., and Robert N. Bellah, eds. *The New Religious Consciousness*. Berkeley: University of California Press, 1976.

Gottlieb, Roger S. *A Greener Faith: Religious Environmentalism and Our Planet's Future*. New York: Oxford University Press, 2006.

Gould, Stephen Jay. *Rock of Ages: Science and Religion in the Fullness of Life*. New York: Ballantine Books, 1999.

Guerlac, Henry. *Radar in World War II*. New York: American Institute of Physics, 1987.

Haber, Heinz. *The Walt Disney Story of Our Friend the Atom*. New York: Dell Publishing Group, 1956.

Hall, Richard. *Uninvited Guests: A Documentary History of UFO Sightings, Alien Encounters, & Coverups*. Santa Fe, NM: Aurora Press, 1988.

Haskell, Edward, ed. *Full Circle: The Moral Force of Unified Science*. New York: Gordon and Breach, 1972.

Hoddeson, Lillian. *Critical Assembly: A Technical History of Los Alamos During the Oppenheimer Years, 1943–1945*. Cambridge: Cambridge University Press, 1993.

Hodgetts, Victoria. "UFO Cult Mystery Turns Evil." *Village Voice*, 1 December 1975, 12–13.

Hofstadter, Richard. *Anti-Intellectualism in American Life*. New York: Knopf, 1963.

Hopkins, Thomas J. "The Social and Religious Background for Transmission of Gaudiya Vaisnavism to the West." In *Krishna Consciousness in the West*, edited by David G. Bromley and Larry D. Shinn, 35–54. Lewisburg: Bucknell University Press, 1989.

Horowitz, Irving Louis. *Science, Sin, and Scholarship*. Cambridge, MA: MIT Press, 1978.

Hughes, Jeff. *The Manhattan Project: Big Science and the Atom Bomb*. New York: Columbia University Press, 2002.

Introvigne, Massimo. *The Unification Church*. Salt Lake City: Signature Books, 2000.

Jackson, Carl T. *Vedanta for the West: The Ramakrishna Movement in the United States*. Bloomington: Indiana University Press, 1994.

Johnson, Douglas W., Paul R. Picard, and Bernard Quinn. *Churches and Church Membership in the United States: An Enumeration by Region, State, and County*. Washington, DC: Glenmary Research Center, 1974.

Jones, Greta. *Science, Politics and the Cold War*. New York: Routledge, 1988.

Judah, J. Stillson. *Hare Krishna and the Counterculture*. New York: Wiley, 1974.

Kevles, Daniel J. *The Physicists: The History of a Scientific Community in Modern America*. Cambridge, MA: Harvard University Press, 1995.

Kneeland, Douglas E. "500 Wait in Vain on Coast for 'the Two,' U.F.O. Cult Leaders." *New York Times*, 10 October 1975, 16.

Knott, Kim. *My Sweet Lord: The Hare Krishna Movement, New Religious Movements Series*. Wellingborough, U.K.: Aquarian, 1986.

———. "Healing the Heart of ISKCON: The Place of Women." In *The Hare Krishna Movement: The Postcharismatic Fate of a Religious Transplant*, edited by Edwin Bryant and Maria Ekstrand, 291–311. New York: Columbia University Press, 2004.

Kolker, Robert, ed. *Stanley Kubrick's 2001: A Space Odyssey: New Essays*. New York: Oxford University Press, 2006.

Kopf, David. *The Brahmo Samaj and the Shaping of the Modern Indian Mind*. Princeton: Princeton University Press, 1979.

Kotnala, M.C. *Raja Ram Mohun Roy and Indian Awakening*. New Delhi: Gitanjali Prakashan, 1975.

Kubrick, Stanley, and Arthur Charles Clarke. *2001: A Space Odyssey*: Metro-Goldwyn-Mayer, 1968.

LaChance, Albert J., and John E. Carroll, eds. *Embracing Earth: Catholic Approaches to Ecology*. Maryknoll, NY: Orbis Books, 1994.

Lapp, Ralph Eugene. *The New Priesthood: The Scientific Elite and the Uses of Power*. 1st ed. New York: Harper & Row, 1965.

Larson, Edward J. *Trial and Error: The American Controversy over Creation and Evolution*. New York: Oxford University Press, 1985.

Lenzer, Gertrud, ed. *Auguste Comte and Positivism*. New Brunswick, NJ: Transaction Publishers, 1998.

Leslie, Stuart W. *The Cold War and American Science: The Military-Industrial-Academic Complex at MIT and Stanford*. New York: Columbia University Press, 1993.

Lewis, James R., ed. *The Unification Church: Outreach*. Edited by J. Gordon Melton. 3 vols. Vol. 3, *Cults and New Religions*. New York: Garland, 1990.

———, ed. *The Gods Have Landed: New Religions from Other Worlds*. Albany: State University of New York Press, 1995.

———. *Legitimating New Religions*. New Brunswick: Rutgers University Press, 2003.

Lewis, James R. and Gordon Melton, eds. *Perspectives on the New Age*. Albany: State University of New York Press, 1992.

Lindberg, David C., and Ronald L. Numbers. *When Science and Christianity Meet*. Chicago: University of Chicago Press, 2003.

Livingstone, David N. "Situating Evangelical Responses to Evolution." In *Evangelicals and Science in Historical Perspective*, edited by David N. Livingstone, D. G. Hart and Mark A. Noll, 193–219. New York: Oxford University Press, 1999.

Livingstone, David N., D. G. Hart, and Mark A. Noll, eds. *Evangelicals and Science in Historical Perspective*. New York: Oxford University Press, 1999.

Lofland, John, and Rodney Stark. "Becoming a World-Saver: A Theory of Conversion to a Deviant Perspective." *American Sociological Review* 30, no. 6 (1965): 862–75.

Lorenz, Ekkehard. "The Guru, Mayavadins, and Women: Tracing the Origins of Selected Polemical Statements in the Works of A. C. Bhaktivedanta Swami." In *The Hare Krishna Movement: The Postcharismatic Fate of a Religious Transplant*, edited by Edwin Bryant and Maria Ekstrand, 112–28. New York: Columbia University Press, 2004.

———. "Race, Monarchy, and Gender: Bhaktivedanta Swami's Social Experiment." In *The Hare Krishna Movement: The Postcharismatic Fate of a Religious Transplant*, edited by Edwin Bryant and Maria Ekstrand, 347–90. New York: Columbia University Press, 2004.

Louis Harris and Associates. "Harris Survey." 8 October–16 October 1977. Retrieved 10 August 2006 from Lexus Nexus Academic Database.

———. "Harris Survey." January 1971. Retrieved 10 August 2006 from Lexus Nexus Academic Database.

Lowen, Rebecca S. *Creating the Cold War University: The Transformation of Stanford*. Berkeley: University of California Press, 1997.

Majumdar, Asoke Kumar. *Caitanya, His Life and Doctrine: A Study in Vaisnavism*. Mumbai: Bharatiya Vidya Bhavan, 1969.

Markovits, Claude. *A History of Modern India, 1480–1950*. Translated by Nisha George and Maggy Hendry. London: Anthem, 2002.

Martin, William. "Waiting for the End: The Growing Interest in Apocalyptic Prophecy." *Atlantic Monthly*, June 1982, 31–37.

Matczak, Sebastian A. *Unificationism : A New Philosophy and Worldview*, Philosophical Questions Series 11. Jamaica, NY: Learned Publications, 1982.

McCloud, Sean. *Making the American Religious Fringe: Exotics, Subversives, and Journalists, 1955–1993*. Chapel Hill: University of North Carolina Press, 2004.

McDonagh, Sean, S.S.C. *The Greening of the Church*. Maryknoll, NY: Orbis Books, 1990.

McGrath, Paul. "UFO 'Lost Sheep' Tell Cult Secrets." *Chicago Sun-Times*, October 16 1975, 1ff.

Means, John O. *The Prayer-Gauge Debate*. Boston: Congregational Publishing Society, 1876.

Mickler, Michael L. *The Unification Church in America: A Bibliography and Research Guide*. New York: Garland, 1987.

———, ed. *The Unification Church: Views from the Outside*. Edited by J. Gordon Melton. 3 vols. Vol. 1, *Cults and New Religions*. New York: Garland, 1990.

———, ed. *The Unification Church: Inner Life*. Edited by J. Gordon Melton. 3 vols. Vol. 2, *Cults and New Religions*. New York: Garland, 1990.

———. *40 Years in America: An Intimate History of the Unification Movement, 1959–1999*. New York: HSA Publications, 2000.

Mickler, Michael L., and James R. Lewis. *The Unification Church*. New York: Garland, 1990.

Miller, Timothy, ed. *When Prophets Die: The Postcharismatic Fate of New Religious Movements*. Albany: State University of New York Press, 1991.

Moore, R. Laurence. *Selling God: American Religion in the Marketplace of Culture*. New York: Oxford University Press, 1994.

Mullin, Robert Bruce. *Miracles and the Modern Religious Imagination*. New Haven: Yale University Press, 1996.

———. "Science, Miracles, and the Prayer-Gauge Debate." In *When Science and Christianity Meet*, edited by David C. Lindberg and Ronald L. Numbers, 203–24. Chicago: University of Chicago Press, 2003.

Murphy, Charles M. *At Home on Earth: Foundations for a Catholic Ethic of the Environment*. New York: Crossroad, 1989.

Muss, Eve. "'Grave Not Path to Heaven,' Disciples Told." *Oregon Journal*, 10 October 1975.

———. "No Disease Promised." *Oregon Journal*, 9 October 1975.

Muster, Nori J. *Betrayal of the Spirit: My Life Behind the Headlines of the Hare Krishna Movement*. Urbana: University of Illinois Press, 1997.

———. "Life as a Woman on Watseka Avenue: Personal Story I." In *The Hare Krishna Movement: The Postcharismatic Fate of a Religious Transplant*, edited by Edwin Bryant and Maria Ekstrand, 312–20. New York: Columbia University Press, 2004.

Nanda, Meera. *Prophets Facing Backwards: Postmodern Critiques of Science and Hindu Nationalism in India*. New Brunswick, NJ: Rutgers University Press, 2003.

National Cancer Institute. *Division of Cancer Control and Population Sciences: 2005 Overview and Highlights*. Washington, DC: U.S. Department of Health and Human Services, 2005.

National Opinion Research Center. "SRS Amalgam Survey." April 1968. Retrieved 10 August 2006 from Lexus Nexus Academic Database.

Nelkin, Dorothy. *The Creation Controversy: Science or Scripture in the Schools.* New York: W. W. Norton, 1982.

Numbers, Ronald L. *Darwinism Comes to America.* Cambridge, MA: Harvard University Press, 1998.

———. *The Creationists: From Scientific Creationists to Intelligent Design.* Expanded Edition. Cambridge, MA: Harvard University Press, 2006.

Opinion Research Corporation. "Attitudes toward Science and Technology, 1972." 13 May–28 May 1972. Retrieved 10 August 2006 from Lexus Nexus Academic Database.

———. "Attitudes toward Science and Technology, 1974." 19 July–10 August 1974. Retrieved 10 August 2006 from Lexus Nexus Academic Database.

———. "Attitudes toward Science and Technology, 1976." 13 September–30 September 1976. Retrieved 10 August 2006 from Lexus Nexus Academic Database.

Paley, William. *Natural Theology; or Evidences of the Existence and Attributes of the Deity, Collected from the Appearances of Nature.* Trenton, NJ: Daniel Fenton, 1824.

Palmer, Susan J. "Women's 'Cocoon Work' in New Religious Movements: Sexual Experimentation and Feminine Rites of Passage." *Journal for the Scientific Study of Religion* 32, no. 4 (1993): 343–55.

———. *Moon Sisters, Krishna Mothers, Rajneesh Lovers: Women's Roles on New Religions.* Syracuse: Syracuse University Press, 1994.

———. *Aliens Adored: Raël's UFO Religion.* New Brunswick, NJ: Rutgers University Press, 2004.

Partridge, Christopher H. *UFO Religions.* London: Routledge, 2003.

Phelan, James S. "Looking For: The Next World." *New York Times,* 29 February 1976, 12ff.

Planck, Max. *Where Is Science Going?* Translated by James Murphey. English ed. London: George Allen & Unwin Ltd., 1933.

Pope John Paul II. *Redemptor Hominis.* Vatican City: 1979.

Ramakanta, Chakravarti. *Vaisnavism in Bengal, 1486–1900.* Calcutta: Sanskrit Pustak Bhandar, 1985.

Rauschenbusch, Walter. *Christianity and the Social Crisis.* New York: Hodder, 1907.

Reed, Pat. "Two Women UFO Disciples Reveal Identity; Say They Are Not Cult." *Houston Chronicle,* 26 November 1975, 9.

Rhodes, Richard. *The Making of the Atomic Bomb.* New York: Simon and Schuster, 1986.

Ritchie, Dennis M. "The Development of the C Language." In *History of Programming Languages,* edited by Thomas J. Bergin, Jr. and Richard G. Gibson, Jr. New York: ACM Press, 1996.

Robbins, Thomas, Dick Anthony, and Thomas Curtis. "Youth Culture Religious Movements: Evaluating the Integrative Hypothesis." *Sociological Quarterly* 16, no. 1 (1975): 48–64.

Robbins, Thomas, Dick Anthony, Madeline Doucas, and Thomas Curtis. "The Last Civil Religion: Reverend Moon and the Unification Church." *Sociological Analysis* 37, no. 2 (1976): 111–25.

Robinet, Isabelle. *Taoism: Growth of a Religion.* Translated by Phyllis Brooks. Stanford, CA: Stanford University Press, 1997.

Rochford, E. Burke, Jr. *Hare Krishna in America.* New Brunswick, NJ: Rutgers University Press, 1985.

———. "Hare Krishna in America: Growth, Decline, and Accommodation." In *America's Alternative Religions*, edited by Timothy Miller. Albany: State University of New York Press, 1995.

———. "Reactions of Hare Krishna Devotees to Scandals of Leaders' Misconduct." In *Wolves within the Fold: Religious Leadership and Abuses of Power*, edited by Anson D. Shupe Jr. New Brunswick: Rutgers University Press, 1998.

———. "Education and Collective Identity: Public Schooling of Hare Krishna Youths." In *Children in New Religions*, edited by Susan J. Palmer and Charlotte E. Hardman. New Brunswick: Rutgers University Press, 1999.

Roper Organization. "Public Opinion Poll." June 1958. Retrieved 10 August 2006 from Lexus Nexus Academic Database.

Rosner, Fred. "The Efficacy of Prayer: Scientific vs. Religious Evidence." *Journal of Religion & Health* 14, no. 4 (1975).

Rothstein, Mikael, and International Society for Krishna Consciousness. *Belief Transformations: Some Aspects of the Relation between Science and Religion in Transcendental Meditation (TM) and the International Society for Krishna Consciousness (ISKCON)*. Aarhus, Denmark: Aarhus University Press, 1996.

Saliba, John A. "Religious Dimensions of UFO Phenomena." In *The Gods Have Landed: New Religions from Other Worlds*, edited by James R. Lewis, 15–64. Albany: State University of New York Press, 1995.

Schroeder, Gerald L. *Genesis and the Big Bang: The Discovery of Harmony between Modern Science and the Bible*. New York: Bantam Books, 1990.

Schroeder, Susan Diane. "The Unification Theological Seminary: An Historical Study." EdD diss., Columbia University, 1993.

Schumacher, E. F. *Small Is Beautiful: A Study of Economics as If People Mattered*. London: Blond and Briggs, 1973.

Schweig, Graham M. "Krishna, the Intimate Deity." In *The Hare Krishna Movement: The Postcharismatic Fate of a Religious Transplant*, edited by Edwin Bryant and Maria Ekstrand, 13–30. New York: Columbia University Press, 2004.

Scott, Austin. "Music Teacher, Nurse Led Search for 'Higher Life.'" *Washington Post*, 18 October 1975, A7.

Sen, Amiya P. *Hindu Revivalism in Bengal, 1872–1905: Some Essays in Interpretation*. Delhi: Oxford University Press, 1993.

———. *Swami Vivekananda*. New York: Oxford University Press, 2000.

Sherbow, Paul H. "Bhaktivedanta Swami's Preaching in the Context of Gaudiya Vaishnavism." In *The Hare Krishna Movement: The Postcharismatic Fate of a Religious Transplant*, edited by Edwin Bryant and Maria Ekstrand, 129–46. New York: Columbia University Press, 2004.

Shin, Gi-Wook, and Michael Robinson, eds. *Colonial Modernity in Korea*. Cambridge, MA: Harvard University Asia Center, 1999.

Shinn, Larry D. *The Dark Lord: Cult Images and the Hare Krishnas in America*. Philadelphia: Westminster Press, 1987.

Shupe, Anson D., Jr., ed. "Vicissitudes of Public Legitimacy for Religious Groups: A Comparison of the Unification and Roman Catholic Churches." *Review of Religious Research* 39, no. 2 (1997): 172–83.

———. *Wolves within the Fold: Religious Leadership and Abuses of Power*. New Brunswick, NJ: Rutgers University Press, 1998.

———. "Frame Alignment and Strategic Evolution in Social Movements: The Case of Sun Myung Moon's Unification Church." In *Religion, Mobilization, and Social Action*, edited by Anson D. Shupe, Jr. and Misztal Bronislaw. Westport, CT: Praeger Publishers, 1998.

Shupe, Anson D., Jr., and David G. Bromley. "The Moonies and the Anti-Cultists: Movement and Countermovements in Conflict." *Sociological Analysis* 40, no. 4 (1979): 325–34.

Sil, Narasingha P. *Ramakrishna Revisted: A New Biography*. Lanham, MD: University Press of America, 1998.

Simpos. "Heaven's Gate Mass Suicide." http://www.stelling.nl/simpos/heavgate.htm. (accessed 2 February 2007).

Simross, Lynn. "Invitation to an Unearthly Kingdom." *Los Angeles Times*, 31 October 1975, Giff.

Smith, John E., Harry S. Stout, and Kenneth P. Minkema, eds. *A Jonathan Edwards Reader*. New Haven: Yale University Press, 1995.

Soll, Rick. "Hare Krishna Followers Bow to a 64-Ounce Brain." *Chicago Tribune*, 10 July 1975.

Song Hang-Nyong. "A Short History of Taoism in Korea." *Korea Journal* 26, no. 5 (1986): 13–18.

Sontag, Frederick. *Sun Myung Moon and the Unification Church*. Nashville: Abingdon Press, 1977.

Sorell, Tom. *Scientism: Philosophy and the Infatuation with Science*. London: Routledge, 1991.

Squarcini, Federico, and Eugenio Fizzotti. *Hare Krishna*. Edited by Massimo Introvigne, *Studies in Contemporary Religion*. Salt Lake City: Signature Books, 2004.

Stenmark, Mikael. *Scientism: Science, Ethics and Religion*. Aldershot, U.K.: Ashgate, 2001.

Stich, Stephen P., and Ted A. Warfield, eds. *The Blackwell Guide to Philosophy of Mind*. Malden, MA: Blackwell Publishing, 2003.

Stoicheff, Boris P. "Gerhard Herzberg and 'the Temple of Science.'" Paper presented at American Physical Society, Palais des Congres de Montreal, Montreal, Quebec, Canada, 22–26 March 2004.

Stone, Jon R., ed. *Expecting Armageddon: Essential Readings in Failed Prophecy*. New York: Routledge, 2000.

Strieber, Whitney. *Communion: A True Story*. New York: Beach Tree Books, 1987.

Suh, Sang-Chul. *Growth and Structural Changes in the Korean Economy, 1910–1940*. Cambridge, MA: Council on East Asian Studies of Harvard University, 1978.

Thomas, Evan. "Web of Death." *Newsweek*, 7 April 1997.

Tumminia, Diana, and R. George Kirkpatrick. "Unarius: Emergent Aspects of an American Flying Saucer Group." In *The Gods Have Landed: New Religions from Other Worlds*, edited by James R. Lewis, 85–104. Albany: State University of New York Press, 1995.

Tweed, Thomas A. *The American Encounter with Buddhism, 1844–1912: Victorian Culture and the Limits of Dissent*. Bloomington: Indiana University Press, 1992.

U.S. Catholic Bishops. *Global Climate Change: A Plea for Dialogue, Prudence and the Common Good*. Washington, DC: United States Conference of Catholic Bishops, 2001.

Van Huyssteen, J. Wentzel Vrede. *Encyclopedia of Science and Religion*. New York: Macmillan Reference USA, 2003.

Vonnegut, Kurt, Jr. *Cat's Cradle*. New York: Holt, Rinehart and Winston, 1963.

Wallis, Roy. *The Road to Total Freedom: A Sociological Analysis of Scientology*. New York: Columbia University Press, 1977.

———. *The Elementary Forms of the New Religious Life*. London: Routledge and Kegan Paul, 1984.

Weber, Max. *The Protestant Ethic and the Spirit of Capitalism*. Translated by Talcott Parsons. New York: Scribner, 1958.

Weiss, Arnold S., and Richard H. Mendoza. "Effects of Acculturation into the Hare Krishna Movement on Mental Health and Personality." *Journal for the Scientific Study of Religion* 29, no. 2 (1990): 173–84.

Wessinger, Catherine Lowman. *How the Millennium Comes Violently: From Jonestown to Heaven's Gate*. New York: Seven Bridges Press, 2000.

Westfall, Catherine Lee. "The First 'Truly National Laboratory': The Birth of Fermilab." PhD diss., Michigan State University, 1988.

Whitcomb, John Clement, and Henry Madison Morris. *The Genesis Flood: The Biblical Record and Its Scientific Implications*. Philadelphia: Presbyterian and Reformed Pub. Co., 1961.

White, Andrew Dickson. *A History of the Warfare of Science with Theology in Christendom*. New York: D. Appleton & Company, 1896.

White, Edward A. *Science and Religion in American Thought*. Stanford: Stanford University Press, 1952.

Williamson, George. "'It Was a Sham': Why One Convert Left the UFO Cult." *San Francisco Chronicle*, 13 October 1975, 2.

Wilson, Bryan, ed. *The Social Impact of New Religious Movements*. New York: Rose of Sharon Press, Inc., 1981.

Wolpert, Stanley A. *A New History of India*. New York: Oxford University Press, 2004.

Wright, Susan. "Recombinant DNA Technology and Its Social Transformation, 1972–1982." *Osiris* 2 (1986): 303–60.

Wuthnow, Robert. *The Consciousness Reformation*. Berkeley: University of California Press, 1976.

Zablocki, Benjamin, and Thomas Robbins, eds. *Misunderstanding Cults: Searching for Objectivity in a Controversial Field*. Toronto: University of Toronto Press, 2001.

Zeller, Benjamin E. "Scaling Heaven's Gate: Individualism and Salvation in a New Religious Movement." *Nova Religio: The Journal of Alternative and Emergent Religions* 10, no. 2 (2006): 75–102.

PRIMARY SOURCES ON THE UNIFICATION CHURCH

"Moon's Credibility Game." *Christian Century*, 24 September 1975, 812–13.

Sun Myung Moon. New York: Unification Church of America, 1977.

"Professors Praise Science Meeting Sponsored by Unification Church." *New York Times*, 28 November 1977, 10.

"Rev. Moon's Boycotters Are Jealous or Ignorant, Savants Attending Say." *Sacramento Bee*, 26 November 1977, B1.

"Towards a Global Congress of World Religions." *Cornerstone* 2, no. 11 (1978): 1ff.

Explaining Unification Thought. New York: Unification Thought Institute, 1981.

The Freedom Leadership Foundation, (pamphlet). ca. 1976. New Religious Movements Organizations: Vertical Files Collection, GTU 99-8-1, The Graduate Theological Union Archives, Berkeley, CA.

Adler, Cy A. "A Moon Shines on Science." *New Engineer*, March 1976, 39–41.

Agres, Ted. "*Industrial Research*: Science & Values: Turning Point?," (reprinted article). 1976. Warder [Michael] Collection, ARC Mss 31, Department of Special Collections, University Libraries, University of California, Santa Barbara.

———. "Science & Values: Turning Point?" *Industrial Research* 18, no. 1 (1976): 22ff.

Berg, Sraffan. "Big Bang Theory Makes a Commotion." *World Student Times*, 12 December 1978, 6.

Bevilacqua, Richard, and Earl Marchand. "Moon Eludes Pickets at Boston Conference." *Boston Herald American*, 25 November 1978, 1ff.

Blake, Andrew F. "'Messiah' Sponsors World Science Meet." *Boston Sunday Globe*, 17 November 1974, 62.

C. H. "Science and Value Discussed at Moon-Sponsored Parley." *Science* 190, no. 4219 (1975): 1073.

———. "Moon's Annual Science Meeting Is Becoming a Tradition." *Science* 194, no. 4271 (1976): 1254.

Carr, Howie. "Anti-Moonies to Picket His Science Conclave." *Boston Herald American*, 23 November 1978, 23.

Choi, Sang Ik. *Principles of Education: Purpose of Mankind*. San Francisco: Re-Education Center, 1969.

———. *Principles of Education: Theory of the Ideal Man*. San Francisco: Re-Education Center, 1969.

———. *Principles of Education: Theory of Universal Value*. San Francisco: Re-Education Center, 1969.

———. *Principles of Education: Theory of the Origin of Crimes*. San Francisco: Re-Education Center, 1969.

———. *Principles of Education: Theory of Happiness*. San Francisco: Re-Education Center, 1970.

Cooke, Robert. "Moon Conference: Demonstration That Jargon Is Universal." *Boston Sunday Globe*, 26 November 1978, 32.

———. "Foes Ask a Boycott on Moon Meeting." *Boston Globe*, 23 November 1978, 3.

———. "Scientists Defend Role at Moon Parley." *Boston Globe*, 25 November 1978, 3.

Durst, Mose. *To Bigotry, No Sanction : Reverend Sun Myung Moon and the Unification Church*. Chicago: Regnery Gateway, 1984.

Eccles, Sir John. "Letter to Participants, October 15, 1976," (personal correspondence). 1976. Warder [Michael] Collection, ARC Mss 31, Department of Special Collections, University Libraries, University of California, Santa Barbara.

General Board of the National Council of Churches of Christ in the United States of America. "Christian Concern and Responsibility for Economic Life in a Rapidly Changing Technological Society." 24 February 1966.

Gruber, Brian. "World Scientists Launch Assault on Global Problems." *World Student Times*, 12 December 1978, 1ff.

Gullery, Jonathan, ed. *The Path of a Pioneer: The Early Days of Reverend Sun Myung Moon and the Unification Church*. New York: HSA Publications, 1986.

International Conference on the Unity of the Sciences. *Modern Science and Moral Values: Proceedings of the Second International Conference on the Unity of the Sciences, Tokyo, November 18–21, 1973.* Tokyo: International Cultural Foundation, 1973.

————. *Science and Absolute Values: Proceedings of the Third International Conference on the Unity of the Sciences, November 21–24, 1974, London, United Kingdom.* 2 vols. Tarrytown, NY: International Cultural Foundation, 1974.

————. *The Centrality of Science and Absolute Values: Proceedings of the Fourth International Conference on the Unity of the Sciences, November 27–30, 1975, New York.* 2 vols. Tarrytown, NY: International Cultural Foundation, 1975.

————. *The Search for Absolute Values: Harmony among the Sciences: Proceedings of the Fifth International Conference on the Unity of the Sciences, November 26–28, 1976, Washington, D.C.* 2 vols. New York: International Cultural Foundation Press, 1977.

————. *The Search for Absolute Values in a Changing World: Proceedings of the Sixth International Conference on the Unity of the Sciences, November 25–27, 1977, San Francisco.* New York: International Cultural Foundation Press, 1978.

————. *The Re-Evaluation of Existing Values and the Search for Absolute Values: Proceedings of the Seventh International Conference on the Unity of the Sciences, November 24–26, 1978, Boston, Massachusetts.* 2 vols. New York: International Cultural Foundation Press, 1979.

————. *The Responsibility of the Academic Community in the Search for Absolute Values: Proceedings of the Eighth International Conference on the Unity of the Sciences, November 22–25, Los Angeles, California.* 2 vols. New York: International Cultural Foundation Press, 1980.

————. *Absolute Values and the Search for the Peace of Mankind: Proceedings of the Ninth International Conference on the Unity of the Sciences, November 22–30, 1980, Miami Beach, Florida.* 2 vols. New York: International Cultural Foundation Press, 1981.

————. *The Search for Absolute Values and the Creation of the New World: Proceedings of the Tenth International Conference on the Unity of the Sciences, November 9–13, 1981, Seoul, Korea.* 2 vols. New York: International Cultural Foundation Press, 1982.

————. *Absolute Values and the Creation of the New World: Proceedings of the Eleventh International Conference on the Unity of the Sciences, November 25–28, 1982.* 2 vols. New York: International Cultural Foundation Press, 1983.

————. *Absolute Values and the New Cultural Revolution: Commemorative Volume of the Twelfth International Conference on the Unity of the Sciences, Chicago, Illinois, 1983.* New York: ICUS Books, 1984.

————. *ICUS XIII Commemorative Volume, 1984.* New York: International Cultural Foundation, 1985.

————. *ICUS XIV Commemorative Volume, 1985.* New York: International Cultural Foundation Press, 1986.

————. *ICUS XV Commemorative Volume, 1986* New York: International Cultural Foundation, 1987.

————. *ICUS XVI Commemorative Volume, 1987.* New York: International Cultural Foundation Press, 1988.

————. *Absolute Values and the Reassessment of the Contemporary World: Proceedings of the Seventeenth International Conference on the Unity of the Sciences, Los Angeles, 1988.* New York: International Conference on the Unity of the Sciences, 1991.

———. *ICUS XVIII Commemorative Volume, 1991.* New York: International Conference on the Unity of the Sciences, 1992.

———. *ICUS XIX Commemorative Volume, 1992.* Lexington, KY: International Conference on the Unity of the Sciences, 1995.

———. *Absolute Values and the Unity of the Sciences: The Origin and Human Responsibility : Commemorative Volume of the Twentieth International Conference on the Unity of the Sciences, 1995.* Lexington, KY: International Conference on the Unity of the Sciences, 1997.

———. *Searching for Absolute Values and Unity in the Sciences: Science for the Benefit of Humanity (Proceedings of the Twenty-First ICUS).* Lexington, KY: International Conference on the Unity of the Sciences, 1999.

International Cultural Foundation. *What ICUS Is,* (booklet). 1978. New Religious Movements Organizations: Vertical Files Collection, GTU 99-8-1, The Graduate Theological Union Archives, Berkeley, CA.

———. "Statement of Purpose of ICUS XVI," (leaflet). 1987. American Religions Collection, Vertical Files Collection, Department of Special Collections, University Libraries, University of California, Santa Barbara.

Johnson, Kurt. "The Scientific Basis of Divine Principle: Religion and Society 590," (coursepack). 1981. Unification Theological Seminary Special Access Collection.

———. "The Unification Principle and Science; Promise, Paradox, and Predicament." In *Unity in Diversity: Essays in Religion by Members of the Faculty of the Unification Theological Seminary,* edited by Henry O. Thompson. Barrytown (NY): Unification Theological Seminary, 1984.

Jones, W. Farley, ed. *A Prophet Speaks Today: The Words of Sun Myung Moon.* New York: HSA-UWC Publications, 1975.

Kaplan, Morton A. "Letter to Dr. J. Gordon Melton, December 15, 1982," (personal correspondence). 1982. American Religions Collection, Vertical Files Collection, Department of Special Collections, University Libraries, University of California, Santa Barbara.

Kim, David Sang Chul. *Individual Preparation for His Coming Kingdom.* Portland, OR: United Chapel of Portland, 1968.

Kim, Won Pil. *Father's Course and Our Life of Faith: 21 Lectures.* London: HSA-UWC Publications, 1982.

Kim, Young Oon. "The Divine Principles, by Young Oon Kim [1st ed., 1960]." http://www.tparents.org/Library/Unification/Books/DP60/ (accessed 13 July 2006).

———. *The Divine Principles.* San Francisco: HSA, 1963.

Kwak, Chung Hwan, ed. *Christian Tradition and Unification Theology: Questions and Answers, Q&A Series.* New York: HSA, 1985.

Lerner, Daniel. "Letter to Dr. Morris Zelditch, January 13, 1977," (personal correspondence). 1977. Warder [Michael] Collection, ARC Mss 31, Department of Special Collections, University Libraries, University of California, Santa Barbara.

Loyd, Linda. "Rev. Moon Addresses Conference's 1st Session." *Philadelphia Inquirer,* 27 November 1982, B1.

———. "Science Meeting Told of Religion, Moon Style." *Philadelphia Inquirer,* 29 November 1982, B1.

MacRobert, Alan. "Moon Science Conference: Walking into 1984." *Real Paper,* 9 December 1978, 1-2.

McCarthy, Kevin, and Sun Myung Moon. *Unificationism Perspectives on Christian Faith.* [Barrytown, NY?]: Unification Church, 1984. Videorecording (vid); Videocassette (vca); VHS tape (vhs).

Mellanby, Kenneth. "Attending a Moon Conference." *Nature* 258, no. 5536 (1975): 560.

Miller, Richard. "Scientists Exchange Ideas, Hear Rev. Moon's Critics." *Daily Californian* 1977, 1ff.

Moon, Sun Myung. *The Master Speaks.* 1960.

———. *The Master Speaks: [Second Series].* Washington: Unified Family, 1967.

———. *Master Speaks.* Los Angeles, 1971.

———. *Rev. Sun Myung Moon: Public Talks.* London: U.F.E. Publications, 1972.

———. *New Hope; Twelve Talks.* Washington, DC: HSA, 1973.

———. *Unification Thought.* New York: Unification Thought Institute, 1973.

———. *Divine Principle.* New York: The HSA, 1973.

———. *Christianity in Crisis: New Hope.* Washington: HSA-UWC, 1974.

———. *The New Future of Christianity.* Washington: Unification Church International, 1974.

———. *An Interview with Rev. Sun Myung Moon.* New York: Newsweek International, 1976.

———. *God's Hope for America.* New York: Bicentennial God Bless America Committee, 1976.

———. *America in God's Providence : Two Speeches.* New York: Bicentennial God Bless America Committee, 1976.

———. *The Kingdom of God on Earth and the Ideal Family.* New York: HSA, 1977.

———. *Divine Principle : Four Hour Lecture.* Washington, DC: HSA, 1977.

———. *America and God's Will.* [Long Island City, NY: Unification Church, 1978.

———. "Our Position," (sermon, 2 January 1979, trans. Bo Hi Pak). 1979. Unification Church order# 79-01-02.

———. *The Way of Tradition.* New York: HSA Publications, 1980.

———. *Proposal for International Highway,* (pamphlet). 1981. American Religions Collection, Vertical Files Collection, Department of Special Collections, University Libraries, University of California, Santa Barbara.

———. *Science & Absolute Values: 10 Addresses.* New York: ICF Press, 1982.

———. *Home Church: The Words of Reverend Sun Myung Moon.* 1st ed. New York: HSA, 1983.

———. *The Unification Principles an in-Depth Presentation of the Theology of the Unification Church.* New York: HSA Communications, 1984.

———. *God's Warning to the World : Reverend Moon's Message from Prison.* New York: HSA-UWC, 1985.

———. *God's Will and the World.* New York: The HSA, 1985.

———. *Christianity in Crisis : New Hope.* New York: HSA, 1986.

———. *Exposition of the Divine Principle.* New York: The HSA, 1996.

———. *Science and Absolute Values: Twenty Addresses.* Lexington, KY: International Conference on the Unity of the Sciences, 1997.

Neighbors, Linda. "'The Moonies Are Coming, the Moonies Are Coming!'" 1977(?). Center for the Study of New Religious Movements Collection, GTU 91-9-03, The Graduate Theological Union Archives, Berkeley, CA.

Nixon, Alan C. "Unpublished Letter to Editor of *Science*, January 4, 1977," (personal correspondence). 1977. Warder [Michael] Collection, ARC Mss 31, Department of Special Collections, University Libraries, University of California, Santa Barbara.

Society for Common Insights. "Journal of the Society for Common Insights." Brooklyn: National Council for the Church and Social Action, 1976.

Unification Theological Seminary. "UTS Course Catalog," 1977/1978. American Religions Manuscript Collection, ARC Mss 1, Department of Special Collections, University Libraries, University of California, Santa Barbara.

———. "UTS Course Catalog," 1979/1980. American Religions Manuscript Collection, ARC Mss 1, Department of Special Collections, University Libraries, University of California, Santa Barbara.

Windman, Nate. "An Introduction to the Divine Principle: What the Moonies Believe." *World Student Times*, October 1980, 11.

Wood, Allen Tate. "Statement by Mr. Allen Tate Wood, Former Member and Official of the Moon Organization, 22 November 1978," (typewritten note). 1978. Cult Awareness Network (CAN) Collection, ARC Mss 19, Department of Special Collections, University Libraries, University of California, Santa Barbara.

PRIMARY SOURCES ON ISKCON

"Editorial." *Back to Godhead* 1, no. 2 (1966): 1–2.

"Advertisement: Two Essays." *Back to Godhead* 1, no. 17 (1968): 1.

Bali Mardan Dasa. "Darwin's Mistake." *Back to Godhead* 10, no. 10 (1975): 10–14.

Bhaktivedanta Swami, A.C. "Godhead and Potentialities." *Back to Godhead*, February 1944, 4–9.

———. "Theosophy Ends in Vaishnavism." *Back to Godhead*, February 1944, 9–17.

———. "The Science of Congregational Chanting of the Name of the Lord." *Back to Godhead*, February 1944, 17–27.

———. "Advertisement: Geetopanishad, by Abhay Charan De." *Back to Godhead*, February 1944, 36.

———. "Who Is a Sadhu?" *Back to Godhead*, March 1956, 1–2.

———. "The S.R.C. Catastrophe." *Back to Godhead*, March 1956, 1–2.

———. "Submissions Policy." *Back to Godhead*, March 1956, 4.

———. "All Compact in Thought." *Back to Godhead*, April 1956, 3–4.

———. "Lord Shri Chaitanya, His Welfare Activities (and His Teachings)." *Back to Godhead*, April 1956, 3–4.

———. "Lord Buddha." *Back to Godhead*, May 1956, 3–4.

———. "Religion Pretentious and Religion Real (Religiosity Real and Apparent)." *Back to Godhead*, June 1956, 1–3.

———. "Shri Chaitanya Mahaprabhu (Lord Chaitanya & His Teachings)." *Back to Godhead*, June 1956, 3–4.

———. "Sufferings on Humanity." *Back to Godhead*, May 1956, 1–2.

———. "Back to Godhead." *Back to Godhead*, June 1956, 4.

———. "Progressive Ambition (and Unsatiated Lust)." *Back to Godhead*, October 1956, 2–3.

———. "Definition of Vice & Its Scope." *Back to Godhead*, November 1956, 1–3.

———. "As Essential Service." *Back to Godhead*, November 1956, 1–3ff.

———. "Standard Morality." *Back to Godhead*, November 1958, 2–3.

———. "Variety of Planetary Systems." *Back to Godhead*, April 1960, 1–2.

———. "Sri Ishopanishad." *Back to Godhead*, April 1960, 1–4.

———. *Easy Journey to Other Planets*. Delhi: League of Devotees, 1960.

———. "From the Lectures of Swami A. C. Bhaktivedanta." *Back to Godhead* 1, no. 2 (1966): 3–7.

———. "From the Lectures of Swami A. C. Bhaktivedanta." *Back to Godhead* 1, no. 14 (1967): 5–7.

———. "From the Lectures of Swami A. C. Bhaktivedanta." *Back to Godhead* 1, no. 15 (1967): 5–11.

———. "Questions and Answers from Congregants to Prabhupada, 9–12/1966." *Back to Godhead* 1, no. 15 (1967): 1–5.

———. "A Study in Mysticism." *Back to Godhead* 1, no. 25 (1969): 10–21.

———. "Sri Ishopanisad." *Back to Godhead* 1, no. 22 (1969): 16–28.

———. "Life Comes from Life." *Back to Godhead* 10, no. 12 (1975): 4–9.

———. *Life Comes from Life: Morning Walks with His Divine Grace A. C. Bhaktivedanta Prabhupada*. Los Angeles: Bhaktivedanta Book Trust, 1979.

———. *Consciousness: The Missing Link: Scientists of the Bhaktivedanta Institute Examine Key Underlying Concepts of the Modern Life Sciences in Light of India's Age-Old Vedic Knowledge* Los Angeles: Bhaktivedanta Book Trust, 1980.

———. "Letter to Jawaharial Nehru, 20 January, 1952." In *The Bhaktivedanta Vedabase (Version 2003.1)*. Sandy Ridge, NC: The Bhaktivedanta Archives, 2003.

———. "Letter to Raja Mohendra Pratap, 13 July, 1947." In *The Bhaktivedanta Vedabase (Version 2003.1)*. Sandy Ridge, NC: The Bhaktivedanta Archives, 2003.

———. "Letter to Sardar Patel, 28 February, 1949." In *The Bhaktivedanta Vedabase (Version 2003.1)*. Sandy Ridge, NC: The Bhaktivedanta Archives, 2003.

———. "Letter to Mahatma Gandhi, 12 July 1947." In *The Bhaktivedanta Vedabase (Version 2003.1)*. Sandy Ridge, NC: The Bhaktivedanta Archives, 2003.

———. "Morning Walk—April 19, 1973, Los Angeles (730419mw.La)." In *The Bhaktivedanta Vedabase (Version 2003.1)*. Sandy Ridge, NC: The Bhaktivedanta Archives, 2003.

———. "Morning Walk—April 28, 1973, Los Angeles (730428mw.La)." In *The Bhaktivedanta Vedabase (Version 2003.1)*. Sandy Ridge, NC: The Bhaktivedanta Archives, 2003.

———. "Morning Walk—May 3, 1973, Los Angeles (730503mw.La)." In *The Bhaktivedanta Vedabase (Version 2003.1)*. Sandy Ridge, NC: The Bhaktivedanta Archives, 2003.

———. "Morning Walk—April 29, 1973, Los Angeles (730429mw.La)." In *The Bhaktivedanta Vedabase (Version 2003.1)*. Sandy Ridge, NC: The Bhaktivedanta Archives, 2003.

———. "Morning Walk at Cheviot Hills Golf Course—May 13, 1973, Los Angeles (730513mw.La)." In *The Bhaktivedanta Vedabase (Version 2003.1)*. Sandy Ridge, NC: The Bhaktivedanta Archives, 2003.

———. "Morning Walk—May 14, 1973, Los Angeles (730514mw.La)." In *The Bhaktivedanta Vedabase (Version 2003.1)*. Sandy Ridge, NC: The Bhaktivedanta Archives, 2003.

———. "Morning Walk at Cheviot Hills Golf Course—May 15, 1973, Los Angeles (730515mw.La)." In *The Bhaktivedanta Vedabase (Version 2003.1)*. Sandy Ridge, NC: The Bhaktivedanta Archives, 2003.

———. "Morning Walk—December 2, 1973, Los Angeles (731202mw.La)." In *The Bhaktivedanta Vedabase (Version 2003.1)*. Sandy Ridge, NC: The Bhaktivedanta Archives, 2003.

———. "Morning Walk—December 3, 1973, Los Angeles (731203mw.La)." In *The Bhaktivedanta Vedabase (Version 2003.1)*. Sandy Ridge, NC: The Bhaktivedanta Archives, 2003.

———. "Morning Walk—December 7, 1973, Los Angeles (731207mw.La)." In *The Bhaktivedanta Vedabase (Version 2003.1)*. Sandy Ridge, NC: The Bhaktivedanta Archives, 2003.

———. "Morning Walk—December 10, 1973, Los Angeles (731210mw.La)." In *The Bhaktivedanta Vedabase (Version 2003.1)*. Sandy Ridge, NC: The Bhaktivedanta Archives, 2003.

Dharmadhyaksa Dasa, Jayadvaita Dasa, Bahulasva Dasa, and Nara-narayana Dasa. *Spiritual Revolution*, (pamphlet). 1975. New Religious Movements Organizations: Vertical Files Collection, GTU 99-8-1, The Graduate Theological Union Archives, Berkeley, CA.

Erber, Jerry. "New Indian Religion Sends You Higher Than LSD!: Secrets of Krishna Consciousness." *National Insider*, 23 April 1967, 10–11.

Hayagriva Das Brahmachary. "Krishna: The End of Knowledge." *Back to Godhead* 1, no. 5 (1967): 8–20.

———. "Doubt, Thy Name Is Bondage." *Back to Godhead* 1, no. 7 (1967): 10–22.

———. "Krishna Consciousness in American Poetry." *Back to Godhead* 1, no. 12 (1967): 15–28.

———. "Krishna Consciousness and American Poetry, Part IV." *Back to Godhead* 1, no. 13 (1967): 19–35.

———. "The Hare Krishna Explosion: The Birth of Krishna Consciousness in America, 1966–1969." In *The Bhaktivedanta Vedabase (Version 2003.1)*. Sandy Ridge, NC: The Bhaktivedanta Archives, 2003.

Hayagriva Das Brahmachary, and Rayarama Das Brahmachary. "Back to Godhead." *Back to Godhead* 1, no. 1 (1966): 2–4.

International Society for Krishna Consciousness. "The Bhaktivedanta Institute," (brochure). 1974(?). American Religions Collection, ARC Mss 1, Department of Special Collections, University Libraries, University of California, Santa Barbara.

———. "Life Comes from Life," (manuscript). ca. 1977. Muster Betrayal of the Spirit Collection, ARC Mss 28, Department of Special Collections, University Libraries, University of California, Santa Barbara.

Kenney, J. Frank, and Pancaratna Das. "An Experimental Course in Krishna Consciousness." *Council on the Study of Religion Bulletin* 5, no. 5 (1974): 3–5.

Nayana Bhiran Das Brahmachary. "Parts and Parcels." *Back to Godhead* 1, no. 20 (1968): 5.

Pancaratna Das. Telephone call to author, 27 December 2006.

Rayarama Das Brahmachary. "The Unconditioned State." *Back to Godhead* 1, no. 3 (1966): 10–21.

———. "The Transmigration of the Soul." *Back to Godhead* 1, no. 8 (1967): 10–20.

Satsvarupa Dasa Goswami. "Man on the Moon: A Case of Mass Brainwashing." *Back to Godhead* 12, no. 5 (1977): 10–14.

———. *A Lifetime in Preparation, India 1986–1965*. Vol. 1, *Srila Prabhupada-Lilamrta: A Biography of His Divine Grace A. C. Bhaktivedanta Swami Prabhupada*. Los Angeles: Bhaktivedanta Book Trust, 1980.

———. *Planting the Seed, New York City 1965–1966*. Vol. 2, *Srila Prabhupada-Lilamrta: A Biography of His Divine Grace A. C. Bhaktivedanta Swami Prabhupada*. Los Angeles: Bhaktivedanta Book Trust, 1980.

Sikes, James R. "Swami's Flock Chants in Park to Find Ecstasy." *New York Times*, 9 October 1966, 24.

Singh, T. D., Ravi V. Gomatam, and World Congress for the Synthesis of Science and Religion. *Synthesis of Science and Religion : Critical Essays and Dialogues.* 1st ed. San Francisco: Bhaktivedanta Institute, 1987.

Stapp, Henry P. *A Report on the Gaudiya Vaishnava Vedanta Form of Vedic Ontology.* Mumbai: The Bhaktivedanta Institute, 1994.

Svarupa Damodara Dasa. *The Scientific Basis of Krsna Consciousness.* New York: Bhaktivedanta Book Trust, 1974.

The Bhaktivedanta Archives, ed. *The Bhaktivedanta Vedabase (Version 2003.1).* Sandy Ridge, NC: The Bhaktivedanta Archives, 2003.

Wolf-Rottkay, Dr. W. H. . "Dr. W. H. Wolf-Rottkay to Srila Prabhupada, 10/1975," (letter). 1975. J. Stillson Judah: New Religious Movements Collection, GTU 95-6-01, The Graduate Theological Union Archives, Berkeley, CA.

World Congress for the Synthesis of Science and Religion. *Interviews with Nobel Laureates and Other Eminent Scholars.* Mumbai: Published by the Bhaktivedanta Institute, 1986.

Yogesvara Dasa. "Primal Origins." *Back to Godhead* 1, no. 67 (1974): 23–26.

———. "Here Comes the Sun: The Author." http://www.herecomesthesunbook.com/press.author.html. (accessed 7 February, 2007).

PRIMARY SOURCES ON HEAVEN'S GATE

"Bo and Peep, Interview with Hayden Hewes and Dan Garcia, July 13, 1974." In *UFO Missionaries Extraordinary*, edited by Hayden Hewes and Brad Steiger. New York: Pocket Books, 1976.

"Bo and Peep, Interview with Brad Steiger, 7 January 1976." In *UFO Missionaries Extraordinary*, edited by Hayden Hewes and Brad Steiger. New York: Pocket Books, 1976.

"A Statement Prepared by the Two." In *UFO Missionaries Extraordinary*, edited by Hayden Hewes and Brad Steiger. New York: Pocket Books, 1976.

Anlody. "Investments." In *HGA*, sec. A, 98–100. Originally Produced 1997.

Brnody. "Up the Chain." In *HGA*, sec. A, 60–64. Originally Produced 1996.

Chkody. "The Hidden Facts of Ti and Do." In *HGA*, sec. A, 32–37. Originally produced 1996.

Drrody. "A Farewell Message to Those Who Remain Behind." In *HGA*, sec. A, 27–29. Originally produced 1996.

Glnody. "Earth Exit Statement: Why We Must Leave at This Time." http://www.heavens-gate.com/exitgln.htm. (accessed 13 November, 1997 [Defunct]).

Glondy. "Warning: For Those Who Are Prone to Hasty Judgments." In *HGA*, sec. A, 4–7. Originally Produced 1996.

Heaven's Gate. "Introduction to '88 Update." In *HGA*, sec. 3, 1.

———. "Publications Where '93 Statement Appeared." In *HGA*, sec. 5, 7.

———. "List of Meetings by Date." In *HGA*, sec. 6, 2.

———. "First Statement of Ti and Do." In *HGA*, sec. 2, 3–4. Originally produced 1975.

———. "The 17 Steps." In *HGA*, sec. 2, 8. Originally produced 1976.

———. "Ruffles: Snacks for Thinkers," 1979.

———. *Preparing for Service.* 1985.

———. "'88 Update." In *HGA*, sec. 3, 2–19. Originally produced 1988.

———. "*Beyond Human*—the Last Call, sess. 1." In *HGA*, sec. 4, 5–15. Originally produced 1992.

———. "*Beyond Human*—the Last Call, sess. 2." In *HGA*, sec. 4, 16–26. Originally produced 1992.

———. "*Beyond Human*—the Last Call, sess. 3." In *HGA*, sec. 4, 27–38. Originally produced 1992.

———. "*Beyond Human*—the Last Call, sess. 4." In *HGA*, sec. 4, 39–49. Originally produced 1992.

———. "*Beyond Human*—the Last Call, sess. 5." In *HGA*, sec. 4, 50–61. Originally produced 1992.

———. "*Beyond Human*—the Last Call, sess. 6." In *HGA*, sec. 4, 62–73. Originally produced 1992.

———. "*Beyond Human*—the Last Call, sess. 7." In *HGA*, sec. 4, 74–84. Originally produced 1992.

———. "*Beyond Human*—the Last Call, sess. 8." In *HGA*, sec. 4, 85–96. Originally produced 1992.

———. "*Beyond Human*—the Last Call, sess. 9." In *HGA*, sec. 4, 97–108. Originally produced 1992.

———. "*Beyond Human*—the Last Call, sess. 10." In *HGA*, sec. 4, 109–20. Originally produced 1992.

———. "*Beyond Human*—the Last Call, sess. 11." In *HGA*, sec. 4, 121–40. Originally produced 1992.

———. "*Beyond Human*—the Last Call, sess. 12." In *HGA*, sec. 4, 141–62. Originally produced 1992.

———. "*Beyond Human* Video Tape Jacket." In *HGA*, sec. 4, 2. Originally produced 1992.

———. "'UFO Cult' Resurfaces with Final Offer [*USA Today* advertisement]." In *HGA*, sec. 5, 3. Originally produced 1993.

———. "Extraterrestrials Return with Final Offer." In *HGA*, sec. 5, 4–6. Originally produced 1993.

———. "Total Overcomers Anonymous Admissions Requirements." In *HGA*, sec. 5, 8–12. Originally produced 1993.

———. "Organizer Religion (Especially Christian) Has Become the Primary Pulpit for Misinformation and the "Great Cover-up" [poster]." In *HGA*, sec. 6, 6. Originally produced 1994.

———. ""UFO Cult" Resurfaces with a Final Offer [Poster]." In *HGA*, sec. 6, 7. Originally produced 1994.

———. "He's Back, We're Back, Where Will You Stand? [poster]." In *HGA*, sec. 6, 9. Originally produced 1994.

———. "The Shedding of Our Borrowed Human Bodies May Be Required [poster]." In *HGA*, sec. 6, 11. Originally produced 1994.

———. "Planet About to Be Recycled—Your Only Chance to Survive—Leave with Us [edited transcript]." http://www.heavensgate.com/misc/vt100596.htm. (accessed 13 November, 1997 [Defunct]).

———. "Last Chance to Evacuate Earth before It's Recycled [transcript of videotape]." http://www.heavensgate.com/vt092996.htm. (accessed 13 November, 1997 [Defunct]).

———. "Heaven's Gate—How and When It May Be Entered." http://www.heavensgate. com. (accessed 13 November, 1997 [Defunct]).

———. "Our Position against Suicide." http://www.heavensgate.com/letter.htm. (accessed 13 November, 1997 [Defunct]).

———. "How a Member of the Kingdom of Heaven Might Appear." http://www.heavens-gate.com/member.htm. (accessed 13 November, 1997 [Defunct]).

———. "Exit Press Release: Heaven's Gate 'Away Team' Returns to Level above Human in Distant Space." http://www.heavensgate.com/pressrel.htm. (accessed 13 November, 1997 [Defunct]).

———. How and When "Heaven's Gate" (the Door to the Physical Kingdom Level above Human) May Be Entered. Mill Springs, NC: Wild Flower Press, 1997.

Hewes, Hayden, and Brad Steiger. UFO Missionaries Extraordinary. New York: Pocket Books, 1976.

Human Individual Metamorphosis. "Statement #1: Human Individual Metamorphosis," 1975. American Religions Collection, ARC Mss 1, Department of Special Collections, University Libraries, University of California, Santa Barbara.

———. "Statement #2: Clarification: Human Kingdom - Visible and Invisible," 1975. American Religions Collection, ARC Mss 1, Department of Special Collections, University Libraries, University of California, Santa Barbara.

———. "Statement #3: The Only Significant Resurrection," 1975. American Religions Collection, ARC Mss 1, Department of Special Collections, University Libraries, University of California, Santa Barbara.

———. "What's Up?," 1975. American Religions Collection, ARC Mss 1, Department of Special Collections, University Libraries, University of California, Santa Barbara.

———. "Prospective Candidate Letter." http://www.rkkody.com/rkk/rkkomat.htm. (accessed 13 November, 1997 [Defunct]).

Jmmody. "Be Fruitful and Multiply." In HGA, sec. A, 56–59. Originally produced 1996.

Jnnody. "Incarnating and Discarnating." In HGA, sec. A, 89–97. Originally produced 1996.

Jwnody. "Overview of the Present Mission." In HGA, sec. o, vii–ix.

———. "Ti and Do as "Smelling Salts"." In HGA, sec. A, 2–3. Originally produced 1996.

———. "'Away Team' from Deep Space Surfaces before Departure.'" In HGA, sec. A, 38–45. Originally produced 1996.

———. "Religions Are Humans' #1 Killers of Souls." In HGA, sec. A, 65–70. Originally produced 1996.

Lggody. "The World's Most Successful Con Game." In HGA, sec. A, 85–88. Originally produced 1996.

Lvvody. "Ingredients of a Deposit—Becoming a New Creature." In HGA, sec. A, 8–14. Originally produced 1996.

Nrrody. "The Truth Is . . . " In HGA, sec. A, 15–17. Originally produced 1996.

Qstody. "My Ode to Ti and Do! What This Class Has Meant to Me." In HGA, sec. A, 30–31. Originally produced 1996.

Rkkody. "Other Heaven's Gate Materials." http://www.rkkody.com/rkk/rkkomat.htm [Defunct]. (accessed 13 November, 1997 [Defunct]).

Scofield, C. I., ed. The Scofield Reference Bible. New York: Oxford University Press, 1901.

Slvody. "Older Member—Younger Member—Their Relationship." In HGA, sec. A, 48–52. Originally produced 1996.

Smmody. "T.E.L.A.H.—the Evolutionary Level above Human." In *HGA*, sec. A, 22–23. Originally produced 1996.

Srrody. "A Testament." In *HGA*, sec. A, 46–47. Originally produced 1996.

———. "Earth Exit Statement: Why We Must Leave at This Time." http://www.heavens-gate.com/exitsrr.htm. (accessed 13 November, 1997 [Defunct]).

Stmody. "Evolutionary 'Rights' for 'Victims.'" In *HGA*, sec. A, 71–79. Originally produced 1996.

Tddody. "Statement of a Crewmembe." In *HGA*, sec. A, 53–55. Originally produced 1996.

Wknody. "A Matter of Life or Death? You Decide." In *HGA*, sec. A, 18–21. Originally produced 1996.

Yrsody. "The Way Things Are." In *HGA*, sec. A, 24–26. Originally produced 1996.

Index

Comte, Augustus, 41
Conflict thesis. *See* Science and religion, relationship between
Conversion of Doctor Mud, The, 108–109
Cosmology, 100
Council for Unified Research and Education (CURE), 53–54
Counterculture, 6–7, 88, 91, 92, 108, 163; and critique of science, 7, 88–89, 94; and new religious movements, 11
Cournand, André, 62
Creation Research Society, 99
Cross-cultural flows, 26
Cultural history, 17
Cumings, Bruce, 25

Daoism, 12, 36–37, 60
Darwinian evolution. *See* Evolution
Death of God theology, 9, 49
Demonstration, the, 127, 135, 146, 148
Denzler, Brenda, 118, 159
Dimock, Edward C., Jr., 78
Dispensationalism, 126. *See also* Millennialism
Divine Principle, 35–45, 48
Docetism, 144
Drrody, 160–161
Dualism: mind-body, 39, 166–167; physical-spiritual, 42

Easy Journey to Other Planets, 1, 85
Eccles, Sir John, 21, 22–23
Eddington, Arthur Stanley, 111, 189n57
Eden, Garden of. *See* Fall of humanity
Einstein, Albert, 111
Electrons, 36, 106, 110
Ellul, Jacques, 88, 95
Empiricism: as basis of science, 4; as basis of UFO subculture, 118; as contrasted with textual evidence, 98, 101, 106; doubts about, 153; as invalid, 83, 84, 97; positive value of, 135, 155–156
Enlightenment, 41, 43
Environment, 109; and pollution, 60–61; and religion, 9

Evolution: and Heaven's Gate, as a description of heaven, 144, 157; and ISKCON, 82, 96, 98, 102, 107, 113; and Unificationism, 24, 52, 58

Faith, 133, 135–136, 153, 154
Fall of humanity, 40, 41
Fermi National Laboratory, 1
Festinger, Leon, 147
Focusing (meditation exercise), 138–141
Fordham University, 102–103
Foucault, Michel, 3
Fowler, Robert Booth, 60
Freedom Leadership Foundation (FLF), 49

Gandhi, Mahatma, 76, 87
Gaudiya Vaishnavism: history of, 78–79; reform of, 79–80; as a science, 83–84, 87, 111; theology of 77–78
Ginsberg, Alan, 71
Gland, role of in salvation, 138–139, 140
Gould, Stephen Jay, 42, 58

Haber, Heinz, 6, 39
Haldane, J. B. S., 111, 189n57
Hare Krishna movement. *See* International Society for Krishna Consciousness
Haskell, Edward, 54
Hayagriva Das, 93–94
Heaven, as a physical place, 131, 143, 145, 150, 156
Heaven's Gate: and the absorption of science, 3, 8; and American social norms, 12; and catastrophic millennialism, 168; end of, 142; formation of, 129–130; growing acceptance of religion in, 133–134; and lack of colonial background, 166; and philosophical dualism, 167; and rejection of Christianity, 124
Higher education, and ISKCON's rejection of, 89, 91, 94
Hippies, 88, 90, 92
Holy Spirit Association for the Unification of World Christianity (HAS-UWS): as Christian, 175n12; and colonial experi-

ence, 166; founding of, 27; the guiding of science, 3, 5, 7, 23, 58–59, 65; messianic role of, in relation to science, 31, 33; as offering scientifically-grounded religion, 43; philosophical dualism in, 167–168; progressive millennialism in, 168; support for scientific establishments, 23

Hopkins, Thomas J., 79

Hrdayananda Dasa Goswami, 97

Human Individual Metamorphosis (HIM), 124, 134, 141. *See also* Heaven's Gate

"Human Individual Metamorphosis," 123–124, 134

Idealism as a philosophical tenet, 167

Ignorance: science as dispelling, 40–41; science as representative of, 81

India, modernization of, 75–76, 78–79

Individualism, 137

Institute on Religion in an Age of Science (IRAS), 53

Intellectual history, 16–17

Intelligent Design (ID), 9, 99, 105–106

International Conference on the Unity of the Sciences (ICUS), 1, 22–23; first, 53–54; second, 54, 60, 62; third, 54–55, 56, 61; fourth, 59, 61, 62, 63; seventh, 21, 58; eighth, 58, 59; tenth, 56–57; eleventh, 59, 63; criticism of, 22, 55, 63, 64–65; millennialism, 64, 168; the replacing of science, 3, 7–8, 71–72

International Cultural Foundation (ICF), 21–22, 57; and millennialism, 57

International Society for Krishna Consciousness (ISKCON): colonial experience, 166; as in consensus with Western science, 101–102; as differing from science, 97; incorporation of, 92; Indian cultural elements in, 90–91; nature of, 73; as offering scientific knowledge of God, 70; as the only real science, 105, 108; philosophical dualism, 167; as a science, 90, 97, 103, 108

Jammer, Max, 22

Jeans, Sir James, 111

Jesus Christ, 33, 40, 126, 131, 143, 151, 159; crucifixion of, 126; as an extraterrestrial, 119, 158; as an extraterrestrial-human hybrid, 144; Resurrection of, 127, 133, 152; second coming of, 123; Transfiguration of, 152

Jnnody, 157, 158–159

Johnson, Kurt, 51–53

Jones, R. V., 21, 55

Jwnody, 158–159, 161

Kaplan, Morton, 63

Kapoor, O. B. L., 111

Karandhara Dasa, 97

Kim, David, 33–34

Kim, Oon Kim, 33–34

Know Place, 123

Korea: Christianity in, 26; cultural transformation, 25–26

Korean War, 27

Kuhn, Thomas, 3, 10, 52

Lapp, Ralph E., 93, 101

Latour, Bruno, 3, 173n6

Legitimating strategy/ies: ICUS as part of, 63–65; religion as a, 30, 31; science as a, 23, 39, 41, 85–86, 163, 166

Lerner, Daniel, 21

Lewis, James R., 39, 86, 218

Life Comes From Life, 96–99, 187n12

Lindberg, David C., 174n21

Lvvody, 160–161

Mantra, Hare Krishna, 70–71

Markovitz, Claude, 75

Materialism, 125–126, 132, 134, 141, 151, 153, 162; as basis of UFO subculture, 118; Christ in relation to, 144, 151; defined, 119; in relation to heaven, 150; ISKCON's opposition to, 90, 93, 97

Mellanby, Kenneth, 21, 55

Melton, J. Gordon, 128

Metamorphosis, in Heaven's Gate, 125, 140, 141, 146, 148

Metaphoric use of science. *See* Science, rhetorical use of

Millennialism, 28, 30–31, 32, 52–53, 60, 126, 159, 168; and ICUS, 53, 56–57; and Unificationist view of coming era, 29, 46–47

Miracles, 43

Modernity, science as representative of, 82, 95, 164, 166

Moon, Sun Myung: birth and early life, 25–27; founder's addresses at ICUS, 58–62; scientific training of, 26; sermons of, 27–33

Mulliken, Robert, 62

Nanda, Meera, 87

National Council of Churches, 29

Naturalism, 125–126, 130, 133, 148–149, 149, 153, 159, 162; defined, 119

Nehru, Jawaharlal, 87

Nettles, Bonnie Lu: death of, 142 148, 160; early life, 121; meeting Applewhite, 1, 122; religious names of, 192n13; religious upbringing of, 190–191n1

New Age, 12, 118, 122, 125, 128, 131, 157, 192n18

New religious movements, 11–12; as indicators of religious change, 2, 164; as indicators of social changes, 9, 171; as offering a typology of the responses to science, 8–9; as offering visions of complete transformation, 11, 164; as radical but representative, 29, 49, 53, 65, 94–95, 99, 128, 159, 163

New Testament, 127, 132, 133, 146, 162

Non-overlapping magisteria, 42

Nuclear energy, 6, 28

Nuclear waste, 60

Nuclear weapons, 28, 107

Numbers, Ronald L., 174n21

Only Significant Resurrection, The, 34

Ozone hole, 61

Pak, Colonel Bo Hi, 33

Palmer, Susan, 164

Pancaratna Dasa, 102–103

Partridge, Christopher, 118, 119

Patel, Sardal, 86

Peale, Norman Vincent, 49

Pentecostalism, 26

Phelan, James, 131, 136

Physicalism, as a philosophical tenet, 167

Physics, 36, 37, 48, 52, 85, 110

Popper, Karl, 52

Positivism. *See* Comte, Augustus

Post-millennialism, 24, 31

Prabhupada. *See* Bhaktivedanta, A. C., Swami Prabhupada

Pratap, Raja Mohendra, 86

Pre-millennialism, 31. *See also* Millennialism

Progressive millennialism, 32–33; and science, 59, 168–169

Protons, 36

Puranas, 107; *Bhagavatam*, 69–70

Qstody, 159

Radical but representative. See New religious movements, as radical but representative

Raelian Church, 118, 119

Ramakrishna, 79

Rapture, the, 126, 135, 137. *See also* Dispensationalism

Rauschenbusch, Walter, 31

Rayarama Das, 93

Religion: criticism of, 157; emulation of, 136; as inherently inferior to science, 154–155; rejection of the nature of, 129, 132, 154; as a twin of science, 40–42

Religion and science. *See* Science and religion, relationship between

Religion as legitimating strategy. *See* Legitimating strategies

Religions, critiques of: as corrupt, 154; as unscientific, 48, 150; as untruthful, 155

Religions, new. *See* New religious movements

Religions, perceived decline of, 43

Representative but radical. *See* New religious movements, as radical but representative

Resurrection of Christ. *See* Jesus Christ

UFO religions, 118; as materialistic, 119
UFO subculture, 144, 145
"UFO Two," 143
Ufology. *See* UFO subculture
UFOs, 123, 125, 143, 161; and Jesus Christ, 126; as part of the Rapture, 126
Unification Church. *See* Holy Spirit Association for the Unification of World Christianity
Unification Theological Seminary, 50–51
Upanishads, 91

Vaishnavism. *See* Gaudiya Vaishnavism
Vedas, 89, 90, 97, 107, 110
Vehicle, human body as, 141, 147, 151
Vivekananda, Swami, 79, 183n1

Warder, Michael, 21, 23
Warfare thesis. *See* Science and religion, relationship between
Weber, Max, 178n61
Weinberg, Alvin, 63
Wessinger, Catherine, 32, 168
What's Up?, 128
Wigner, Eugene, 21
Wolli Hesul, 27–28
Wolli Kangron, 28, 35
World Student Times, 47

Yoga, 140
Yogananda, Paramahansa, 183n1
Yogesvara Dasa, 100–101
Yrsody, 159

About the Author

Benjamin E. Zeller is an assistant professor of religious studies at Brevard College in Brevard, North Carolina.